IMAGES
of America

OVERBROOK FARMS

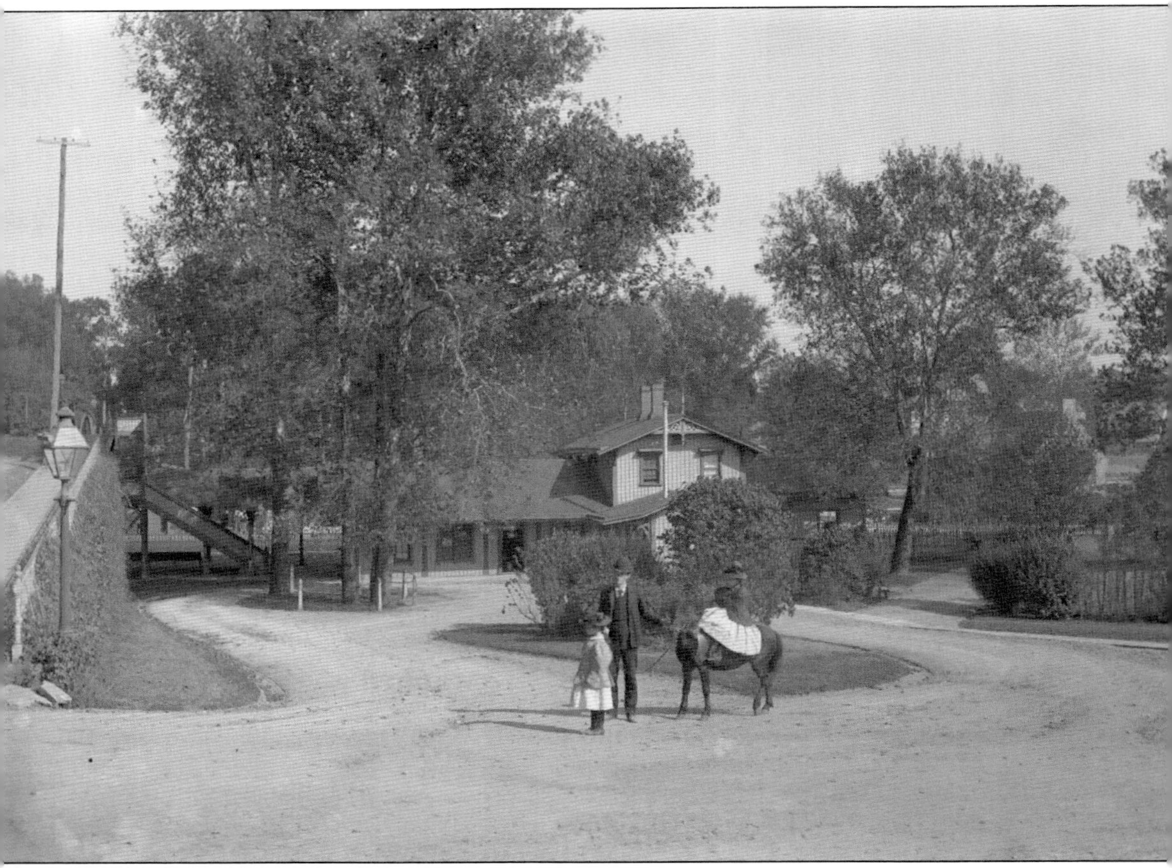

ON THE COVER: Built in 1858, the Overbrook railroad station was a major catalyst for the development of Overbrook Farms. It is the oldest surviving station on the main line between Philadelphia and Pittsburgh. (Courtesy of Radnor Historical Society.)

IMAGES
of America

OVERBROOK FARMS

The Overbrook Farms Club

ARCADIA
PUBLISHING

ISBN 978-1-4671-2159-0

Published by Arcadia Publishing
Charleston, South Carolina

Printed in the United States of America

Library of Congress Control Number: 2013950888

For all general information, please contact Arcadia Publishing:
Telephone 843-853-2070
Fax 843-853-0044
E-mail sales@arcadiapublishing.com
For customer service and orders:
Toll-Free 1-888-313-2665

Visit us on the Internet at www.arcadiapublishing.com

Dedicated to the men and women who envisioned, developed, cultivated, and lovingly tend this "Suburb Deluxe" known as Overbrook Farms.

Contents

ACKNOWLEDGMENTS

Special recognition goes to the women who spent countless hours gathering photographs, researching the history of Overbrook Farms, interviewing long-term residents, writing, coordinating schedules, and other untold tasks. Without their talents and dedication this book would never have reached the publisher. Thank-you Victoria Wilson, Vernyce Dannells, Melanie Ellison-Roach, and Nancy Callan!

If the axiom that declares many hands make light work applies here, Overbrook Farms is indebted to a score of proud, generous, connected history lovers. Assembling, interpreting, and enriching the materials gathered were contributing authors Victoria Wilson, Vernyce Dannells, Nancy Callan, and Melanie Ellison-Roach. Were it not for the Radnor Historical Society and the Athenaeum of Philadelphia, many of the captivating images herein would not be available for this publication. We obtained funding and collateral materials from Community Design Collaborative and Preservation Alliance for Greater Philadelphia, legal assistance from Margaret Rover, Esq., rare archival postcards from Ted Greenberg, and historical background or materials from Edith Willoughby and Anne Willoughby McMillan, Jane Rozmiarek, Dorothy Riday, Michael Brody, Corrado Minimo, Larry and Jean Andreozzi, Tom Stafford, Jean Tracy, and Mark Wallacavage. Photographic talent included Adjoa Love-Dorsey, Rick Pullin, Kip Krieger, and Jabar Singh Wilson.

Throughout this book, the Overbrook Farms Club will be referred to as OFC.

INTRODUCTION

Work on Overbrook Farms began in 1892, a mere decade after the city's 1882 headline-grabbing bicentennial. The fete was closely followed by an 1887 constitutional centennial that brought Grover Cleveland and his entourage to Philadelphia for three memorable days. And all of this attention to the city had been preceded by the inimitable 1876 centennial, its 227 buildings sprawled over 284 acres of the city. Remnants of the centennial reverberate in the city more than 100 years later. Back then, more than a staggering 10 million visitors were attracted to marvel and wonder over the national and international exhibits and inventions displayed and at the splendid city that hosted their numbers with aplomb and grace.

Philadelphia had taken firm root, bolstered in part by its strategic geographical location, its lengthy waterways—home to manufacturing, shipping, banking, medicine, and textiles—and by a swelling influx of immigrants who fled beleaguered homelands to seek more promising possibilities.

It was a city that had become tightly clustered and congested, with all the accompanying challenges—erosion of privacy and safety, pollution, and decay. The relocation of its municipal center, migration to farther-flung grandly designed and built homes commissioned by the city's trendsetting wealthy, and added acreage dedicated to Fairmount Park contributed to loosening the grip many felt to remain in its crowded core.

Especially critical in the city's outward growth was expansion by the Columbia Railroad. It seems the dictum "go west, young man" was still in operation when the Columbia Railroad laid westward tracks from the city in 1832. Overbrook Station became a flag stop for the gentleman farmers and estate owners whose land circled the city boundary.

Trains from the city became more frequent as early as the late 1890s, and the deep-pocketed railroad owners and investors began to envision the rail commuter system as a way to dramatically grow their capital. Despite the reluctance of many dwellers to relocate, the most progressive, well-heeled, influential citizens started their exodus from the tight knot of the city. They began by building lavish summer retreats that benefited from the railroad's westward expansion. Venture capitalists recognized that these communities, built along the line, meant that commuters would use the trains to travel back and forth to the city.

Armed with their economic analysis and firm in their vision that commuters would indeed fuel the railroad's growth, the partners in the investment bank of Drexel & Co. saw an opportunity to boost the success of their investment when a parcel of land owned by the John M. George estate became available. Anthony J. Drexel—senior partner of Drexel & Co., then one of the most powerful investment banks in the world—completed the negotiations for the purchase in October 1892. The parcel contained approximately 170 acres of mostly open land bisected by the main line tracks, Lancaster Pike, and Merion Road and was obtained for the tidy sum of $425,000. The land where verdant farmland once stood would soon hold a lavish suburb.

The George estate, like much of the land that marked Philadelphia's western border, was largely arboreal farmland splashed by small streams and ponds. Prior to deliberate development, a few colonial inns had sprung up in the area to accommodate coach travelers who trekked 12 hours to cover the 65 miles from Lancaster to Philadelphia and such "regulars" in need of off-site accommodation as students of the diocesan seminary of Saint Charles Borromeo, opened in June 1832. When the George farmland was bought to develop into Overbrook Farms, there were few roads other than the main highways of City Line, Merion and Darby Roads, Lancaster Pike, Old Lancaster Road, and Haverford Road. The histories of all these roads are closely connected with the growth of the community.

The rail lines began offering more than six trains per day, and many who might not have considered living year-round away from the city's center began to rethink their reluctance. They were also helped along in this movement by popular press articles touting the healthful benefits of suburban living and national interest in movement away from city centers. Visionary industrialists, bankers, and professionals—such as doctors, professors, lawyers, and merchants—led the charge to relocate to outlying areas where more spacious, safe surroundings still permitted their participation in otherwise situated enterprise.

Once the notion of suburban living took root, Overbrook Farms became a nearly obvious choice. Its established connection to the main line, paired with the lure of well-situated, built, and marketed housing options, made the area as sure a sell as any possibilities that sought to rival the area for residents. Moreover, Overbrook Farms would eventually be known for its several closely clustered and distinctive churches. Overbrook Farms already boasted an iconic church before development or residences sprang up in the area. Quaker Wistar Morris owned the adjacent estate of Greenhill Farm and supported the founding of a nearby Presbyterian congregation. He purchased a tract of land in 1888 from the John M. George estate. Located at City and Lancaster Avenues, a cornerstone was laid in October 1889. Addison Hutton designed the building, dedicated in February 1890. The congregation grew as quickly as Overbrook Farms, and the size of the church doubled in 1905, featuring the notable addition of a tower facing City Avenue. From the beginning, Overbrook Presbyterian assumed an active role in the community. Today, it is host to the Overbrook Farms Club, Overbrook Preschool, Narberth Community Theater, a weekly farmers' market, and numerous other organizations large and small.

The overall plan of Overbrook Farms is a rectangle that follows the railroad, incorporating approximately 170 acres at the city's western edge. The former Pennsylvania Railroad, now used by Amtrak and SEPTA's Regional Rail Division, bisects the community. Lancaster Avenue, formerly a turnpike road until 1917, both bisects the community and remains a major thoroughfare. City Avenue (US Route 1) forms the northwestern boundary of the district as well as the Philadelphia city boundary. Morris Park, part of the Fairmount Park system, bounds the district to the southwest adjacent to Sixty-sixth Street. Row homes and the grounds of the Overbrook School for the Blind mark the southeastern boundary of the community along Woodbine Avenue. The northeastern boundary is Fifty-eighth Street and the property of the Sisters of the Visitation of Holy Mary in the 2400 block of North Fifty-eighth Street at City Avenue. The two railroad crossings that transect Overbrook Farms are the Art Deco concrete bridge that carries City Avenue over the railroad tracks and the stone bridge over Woodbine Avenue running under the railroad tracks.

Suburban development stretched outward to West Philadelphia as early as the 1850s, then linked to the city center by a growing streetcar system. Prior undertakings had created a narrow necklace of homes built by individual speculator developers. Now fueled by the Drexel Syndicate's access to enormous amounts of capital, the already high-profile developers Herman Wendell and Walter Bassett Smith were commissioned to create Overbrook Farms. They proceeded at an unprecedented pace, building and promoting quality homes and anticipating and providing essential services. Their foresight would establish a unique suburban community that maintains its stability, beauty, and significance more than a century later.

Marketing materials assured buyers that their finished homes would still offer painstaking details and distinctive finishes, at the same time saving their owners the expenses that might arise with customization. Details boasted of a unique water filtration system that protected the earliest Overbrook residents from the city's deadly 1898 typhoid fever outbreak. Overbrook Farms "is from 200 to 250 feet above the level of the city, insuring good drainage, coolness in summer, pure air, and as a result of all three, good health to its people." A dedicated steam heat plant meant easily managed house temperatures. Electric lighting was a cherished feature in all homes. Commuters were assured that 64 trains stopped at Overbrook Station at half-hour intervals "all day, and late into the night." And further, "[T]he plotting of the Farms is arranged according to the most advanced ideas of modern landscape gardening, and the old trees are preserved wherever possible. This takes away from the homes that aggressive air of newness that exists in so many new suburbs."

The homes at Overbrook Farms were aimed toward the upper middle class and the wealthy. Following the movement of the city's trendsetters from the celebrated but crowded city to spacious homes built on lands that once held sizeable country estates, there were restrictions in the deeds for typical Overbrook Farms lots. Each required the construction of houses valued typically at no less than $7,000 and sometimes more. In the mid-1890s, twin homes in Overbrook Farms sold for about $8,000, with the larger twins, such as 5950 Overbrook Avenue, selling for $11,500 in 1894. Single homes sold for $11,000 and upwards, depending on amenities and alterations, to $18,000, $20,000, and even $30,000—some 10 times the average $3,000 selling price for a house and lot in Philadelphia.

And just who among Philadelphia's most notable residents came to Overbrook Farms homes? William F. Harrity was not only wealthy, but one of Philadelphia and the country's most powerful men in the 1890s. He was an attorney and an avid Democrat in an age dominated by Republicans. Harrity supported Grover Cleveland for president of the United States in 1884 and served as Philadelphia's postmaster general during Cleveland's first term. As campaign manager and leader of the state Democratic Party, he twice helped elect his friend Robert E. Pattison, a fellow Democrat and Overbrook neighbor, to Pennsylvania's governorship (1883–1887 and 1891–1895). Harrity eventually concentrated his attention upon business interests.

Gov. Edwin Stuart (1907–1911) was 38 years of age when he served as Philadelphia's youngest mayor of record (1891–1895). Stuart lived at 5841 Drexel Road in a house built in 1897 that is attributed to David Knickerbocker Boyd. Stuart would later become the first former Philadelphia mayor to serve as governor.

John Weaver, a reform-minded mayor of Philadelphia (1903–1907) later lived in the house built by Governor Pattison.

City select council member Frank Caven, who served in the early 1900s, became the director of public works for the city in the 1920s. Caven lived at 5914 Overbrook Avenue.

Clarence H. Geist owned the Atlantic City Gas Company and made his fortune in the utilities industry. He had the house at 6399 Drexel Road (now known as St. Katharine's Hall) built in 1909. By 1930, he was the largest holder of utility stocks in the country. He owned other properties near Philadelphia, including the 50-acre property in Radnor where the Academy of Notre Dame now stands. The Seaview Marriott Resort in Atlantic City was once known as the Seaview Country Club, founded by Geist and known to serve as his personal golf retreat.

Albert M. Greenfield was referred to as "Mr. Philadelphia" in the national media. Greenfield bought 6399 Drexel Road around 1935. Born in Ukraine in 1887, Greenfield moved to Philadelphia in 1896. He attended Philadelphia public schools and founded his own real estate firm at the age of 17. He was a civic leader, philanthropist, and political powerbroker.

Following the aesthetic admired in the era, many architectural styles that were popular in the late 19th and early 20th centuries are represented in the district. Nearly 20 such styles or combinations are on view in Overbrook Farms. The majority of houses are Colonial or Tudor Revivals. Other styles visible from the late 19th and early 20th centuries include Arts and Crafts, Art Deco, Dutch Colonial Revival, Gothic Revival, Queen Anne, Prairie, Romanesque, and Shingle. Two-and-a-half- to three-story buildings are most common, wrought from stone (largely Wissahickon schist harvested from several on-site quarries), brick, and stucco. Nearly universal features are large front porches (many of them covered), ornate chimneys, classical columns, projecting bays, stained or leaded glass, dormers, and decorative masonry features, such as cartouches, quoins, and gargoyles.

Scattered among single-family detached and semi-detached homes are a few strategically placed grand apartment buildings and religious institutions, often located at the corners of several of the blocks in both sections of the district. More recently, several Jewish organizations were established on the east side of the district.

Along with these places of worship, commercial and educational buildings comprise nonresidential uses. Two-story commercial buildings are located on Sixty-third Street between the railroad and Lancaster Avenue. Historically, these commercial buildings, specifically those located along the east side of Sixty-third Street, included uses as a general store, pharmacy, doctor's office, and a livery. Currently, these buildings contain restaurants, medical and dental offices, day care centers, delicatessens, dry cleaners, and other small retail and service providers.

Perhaps one of the strongest factors in the neighborhood's vitality, success, and stability is the Overbrook Farms Club. The club naturally evolved as a result of the careful planning and promotion that drew the city's progressives to the area. Arguably the oldest continually operating civic association in the country, the Overbrook Farms Club was formed as early as 1896. It remains a significant presence in the community and the city of Philadelphia. Initially named the Overbrook Club, an amendment to the charter in 1931 changed its name to designate the area over which it had jurisdiction.

The focus of the Overbrook Farms Club has always been on preserving and protecting the historic character of the community while maintaining the quality of life for its residents.

An awareness of the power of collective interest and a history of activism has marked this dynamic association of neighborhood homeowners. From athletics and aesthetics to zoning issues, this group has consistently nurtured a sense of community among neighborhood residents. Constantly on the alert to the affect of zoning irregularities on its stability, a signature effort is its continual work with city officials to maintain the single-family dwellings deemed critical to the quality of the neighborhood. But the accomplishments of the club extend to far broader concerns.

Communication has ever been important. The club was instrumental in obtaining a telegraph operator at the Overbrook Station in 1898 and telephone service a year later. It regulated the running of the telephone wires and published a directory of numbers. Through the years, a diligent effort was made to keep a post office box, and this effort proved successful until the 1970s. Presently, the club periodically publishes a newsletter that is mailed to all residents and facilitates a community listserv and biannual community meetings.

Since the community was developed around the Overbrook train stop, efforts by the club were instrumental in securing funds to renovate and restore the historic Overbrook Station to its period of significance at the turn of the 19th century. Overbrook Farms was listed in the National Register of Historic Places in 1985. This accomplishment was due to the efforts of the club, under whose supervision the application and accompanying documentation were facilitated and prepared. Application to the Philadelphia Historical Commission for historic designation is currently pending, an effort again directly facilitated by the club. The Overbrook Farms Club operates with a board of directors and bylaws. Directors serve without remuneration, and many of the early members served many years. The present directors are prevented by the bylaws from serving more than eight consecutive years.

One

First Suburb

Like the strivers who initially found their way to the neighborhood, developers Wendell and Smith often harnessed the skills of young architects who had yet to achieve the prominence that they would enjoy later in their careers. An 1898 promotional brochure, *A Little Talk With the Home Seeker*, promised that prospective owners could "build a home according to your own ideas, or, if you don't care to wait, or don't feel like grappling with the numerous perplexities and annoyances that arise when you look after the building of a house yourself, we will sell you a lot and finished house at a definite price."

Wendell and Smith's realized vision was to attract achievers to a location characterized in prominent publications as "probably the most luxurious suburb in America." When the two set about their task, they capitalized on prior successes and economies of scale. They turned a keen eye toward the trends and aspirations of prospective buyers. The pair assembled stellar architectural talent to build the homes, which their marketing materials promised would universally feature affordable electric light and aerated pure water extracted from proprietary underground springs completely independent of the city's municipal water system. The homes received steam heat from a dedicated, locally situated plant. Indeed, long-term residents recall that during the period when the steam plants functioned, no snow settled onto the wide Overbrook Farms roads because the underground pipes kept the neighborhood's roads so warm that flakes could not accumulate. The team also provided a drainage system that disposed of sewage and storm water. In short, all utilities were provided directly by the developers, not the government, which many considered crass and graft-ridden. A frisson of unanticipated delight arose when telephones were introduced in 1899, with the exchange located in a house on Sixty-third Street, between Woodbine and Lancaster Avenues.

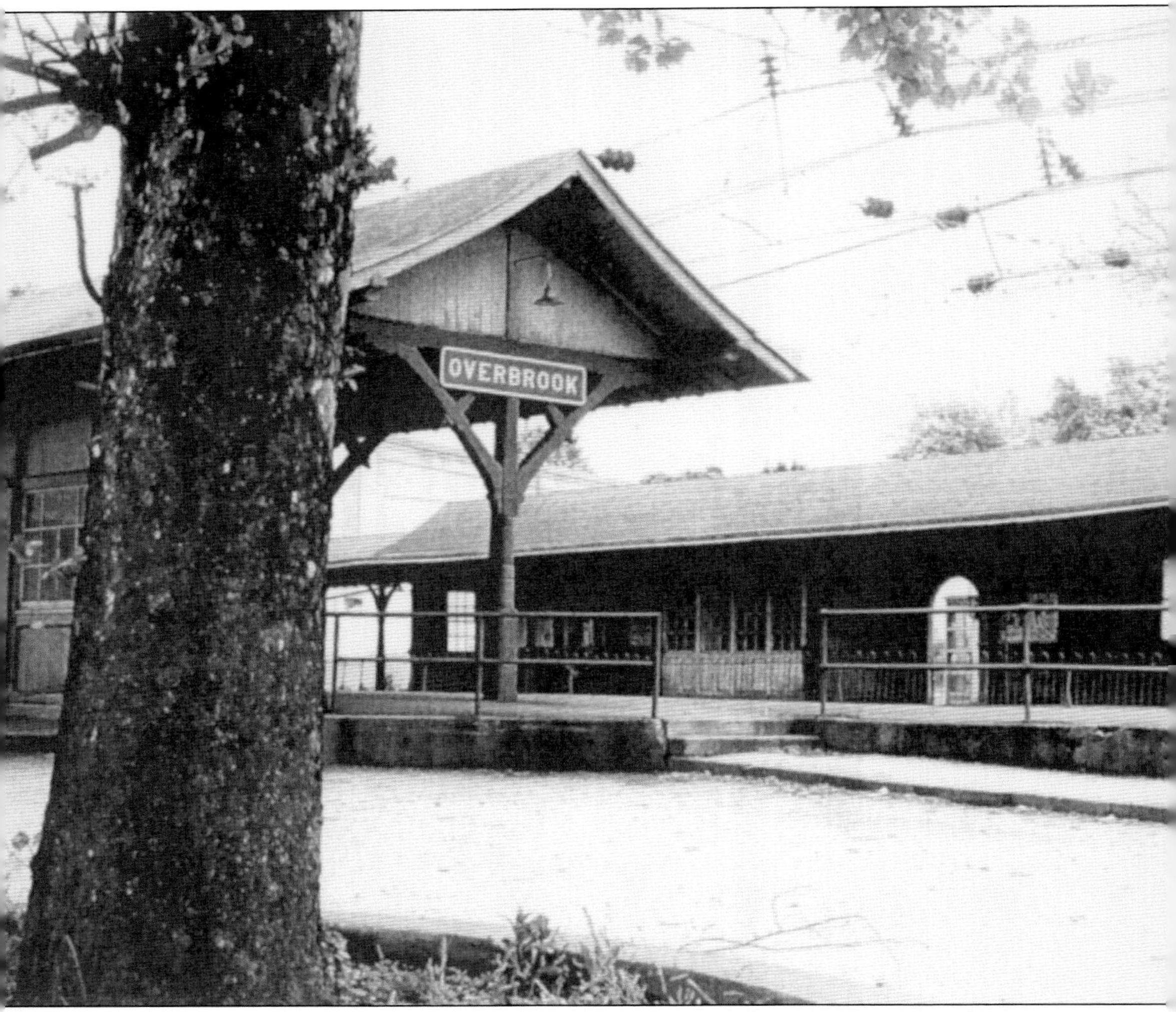

In the 1890s, the Overbrook railroad station underwent the most extensive alterations in its history, including the extension of the platforms on the inbound side and the construction of Queen Anne–style platform shelters on both sides. A passenger tunnel was built under the tracks between 1893 and 1894. Buildings for baggage and a post office were also built during this period but were demolished during the 20th century. (Courtesy of Ted Greenberg.)

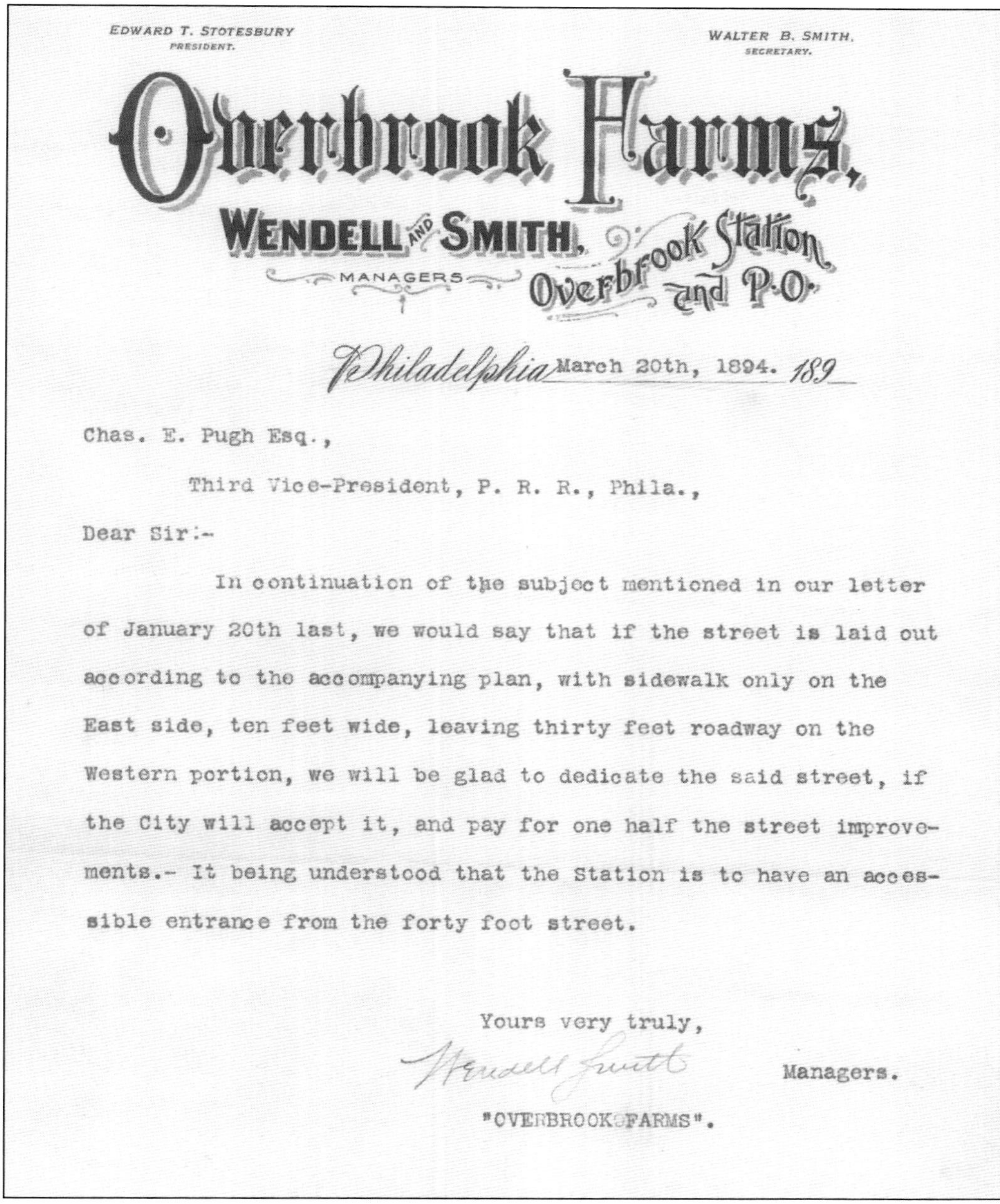

EDWARD T. STOTESBURY
PRESIDENT.

WALTER B. SMITH.
SECRETARY.

Overbrook Farms,

WENDELL AND SMITH,
MANAGERS

Overbrook Station and P.O.

Philadelphia March 20th, 1894. 189

Chas. E. Pugh Esq.,

Third Vice-President, P. R. R., Phila.,

Dear Sir:-

In continuation of the subject mentioned in our letter of January 20th last, we would say that if the street is laid out according to the accompanying plan, with sidewalk only on the East side, ten feet wide, leaving thirty feet roadway on the Western portion, we will be glad to dedicate the said street, if the City will accept it, and pay for one half the street improvements.- It being understood that the Station is to have an accessible entrance from the forty foot street.

Yours very truly,

Wendell Smith

Managers.

"OVERBROOK FARMS".

Developers Wendell and Smith invested significantly in the infrastructure of the community. This is an example of the many letters sent that requested assistance from the City of Philadelphia and other authorities in order to develop a first-class community with all of the modern amenities available at the time, which included water, sewage, electricity, and steam heat. (Courtesy of Frank Weer.)

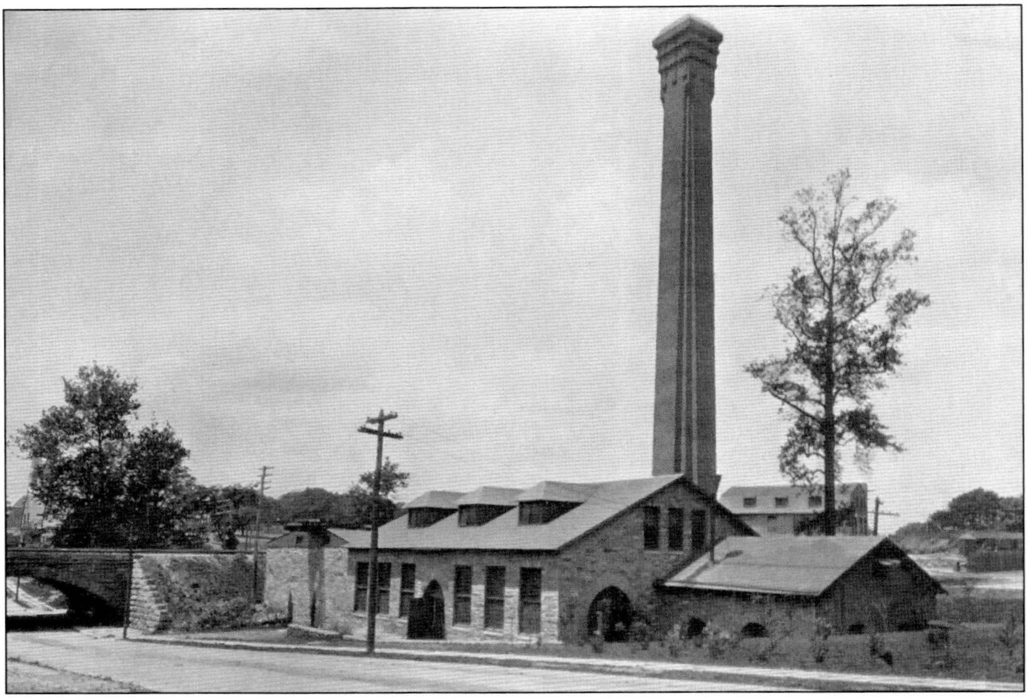

The Overbrook Steam Heat Company was built in 1893 and generated steam that was distributed to each home's cellar by protected pipes. This eliminated polluting high-maintenance coal-fired furnaces in homes and reduced the number of servants necessary to assist the household. (Courtesy of Radnor Historical Society.)

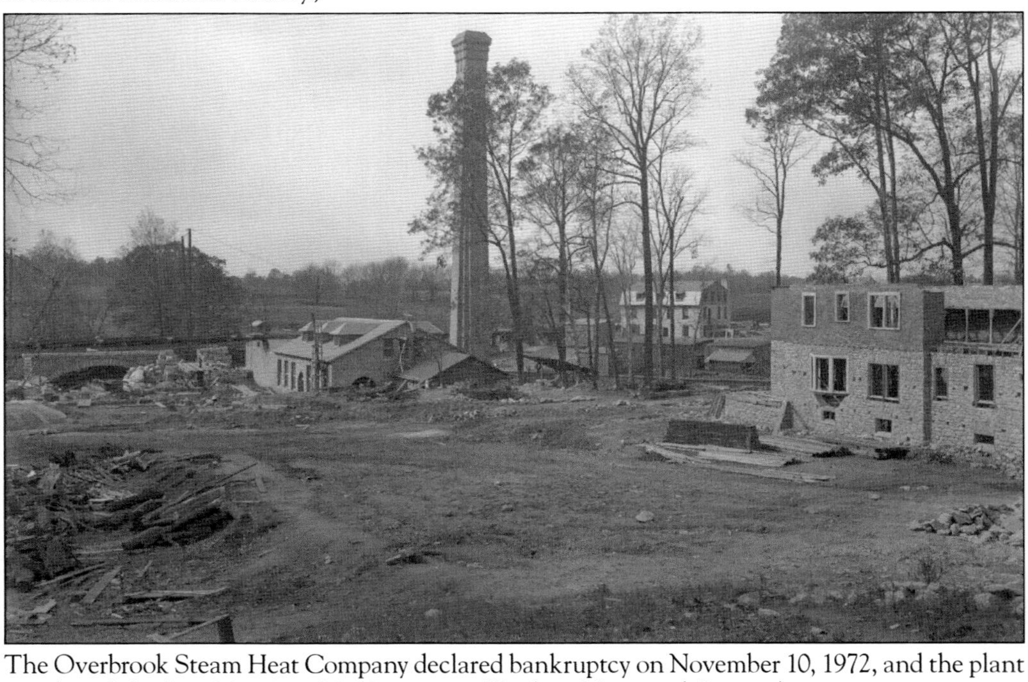

The Overbrook Steam Heat Company declared bankruptcy on November 10, 1972, and the plant was demolished on May 8, 1976. (Courtesy of Radnor Historical Society.)

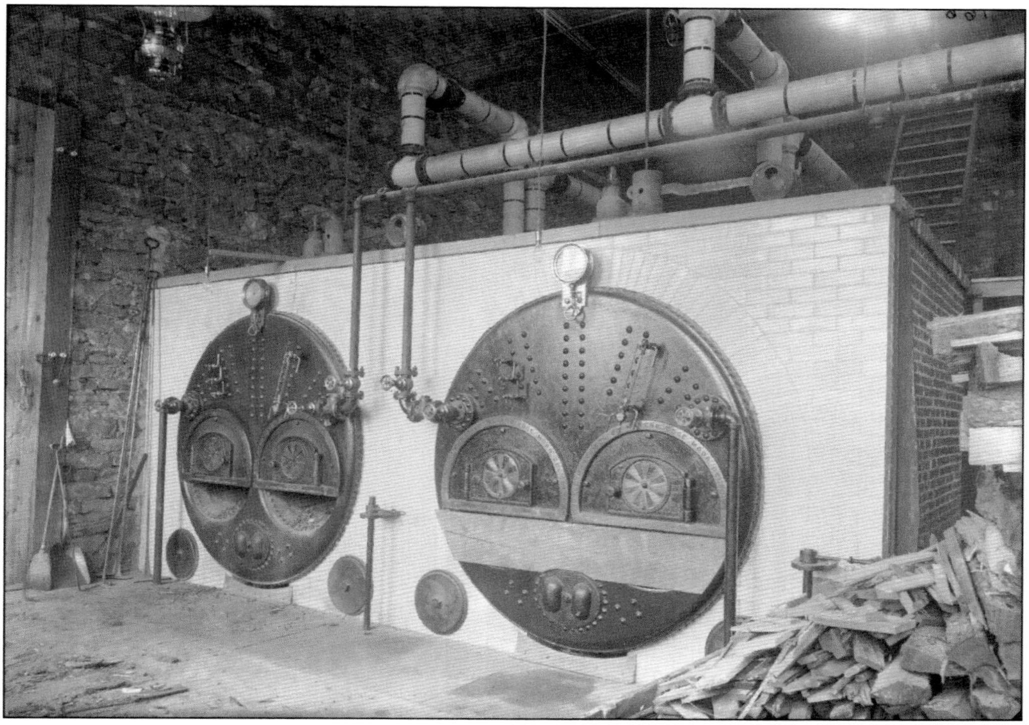

Steam boilers at the Overbrook Steam Heat Company are pictured here. (Courtesy of Radnor Historical Society.)

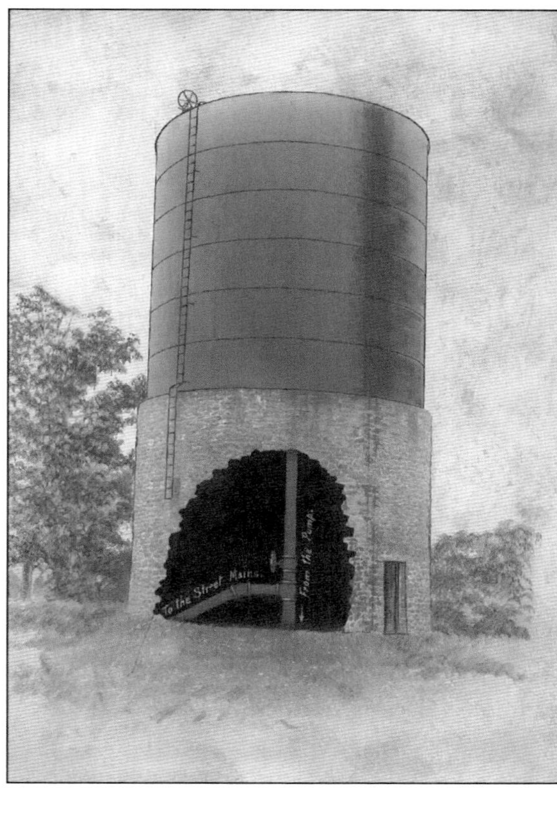

Renowned engineer Henry Birkenbine developed a water distribution system independent of the city's water system. His design required wells that tunneled 200 feet deep. Once these were drilled, the compressed air forced the water up to the mains and reservoirs. Wendell and Smith advertised the purity of Overbrook Farms' water, which was reputed to effervesce because of the forced-air method. The tower for well water was located on Woodbine Avenue. (Courtesy of the OFC.)

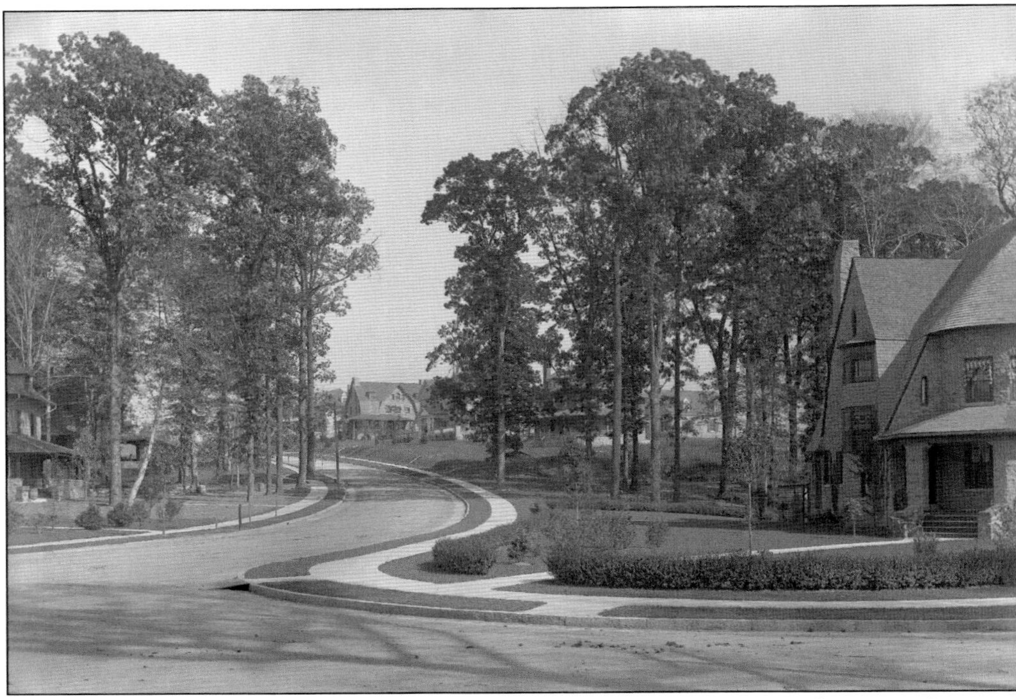

At the time the Drexel Syndicate purchased the Overbrook Farms tract, only two roads crossed it, Lancaster Pike and Merion Road. Wendell and Smith's engineers designed the visionary street system, considered a significant accomplishment for the times. The new sidewalks and roadways, which were described in marketing materials as "generous and grand," are shown here at the intersection of Drexel Road and Upland Way in 1894. (Courtesy of Radnor Historical Society.)

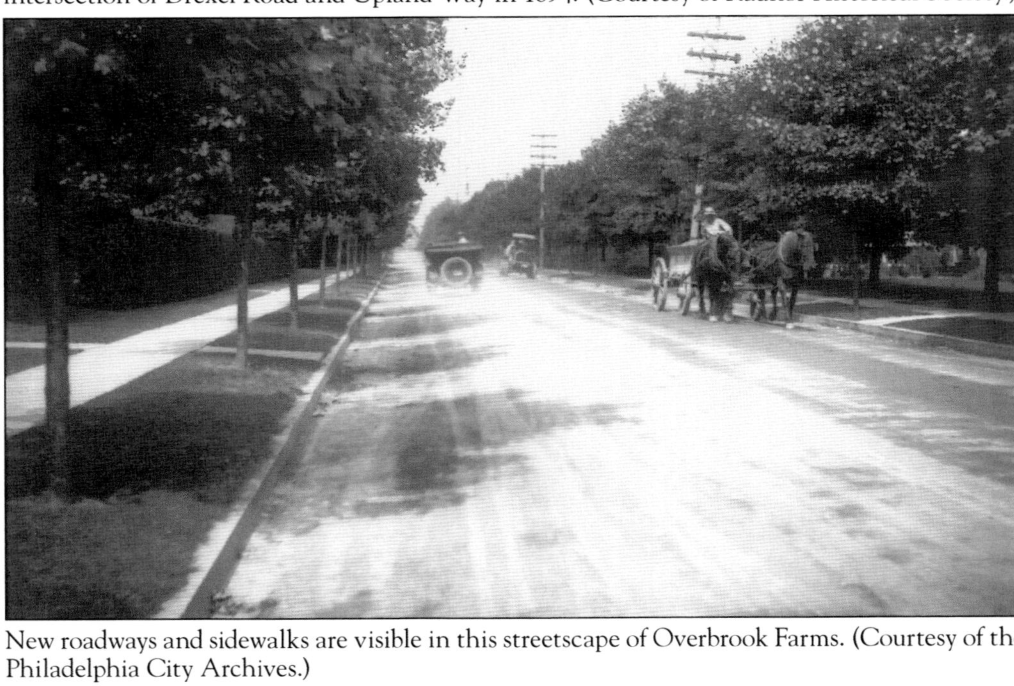

New roadways and sidewalks are visible in this streetscape of Overbrook Farms. (Courtesy of the Philadelphia City Archives.)

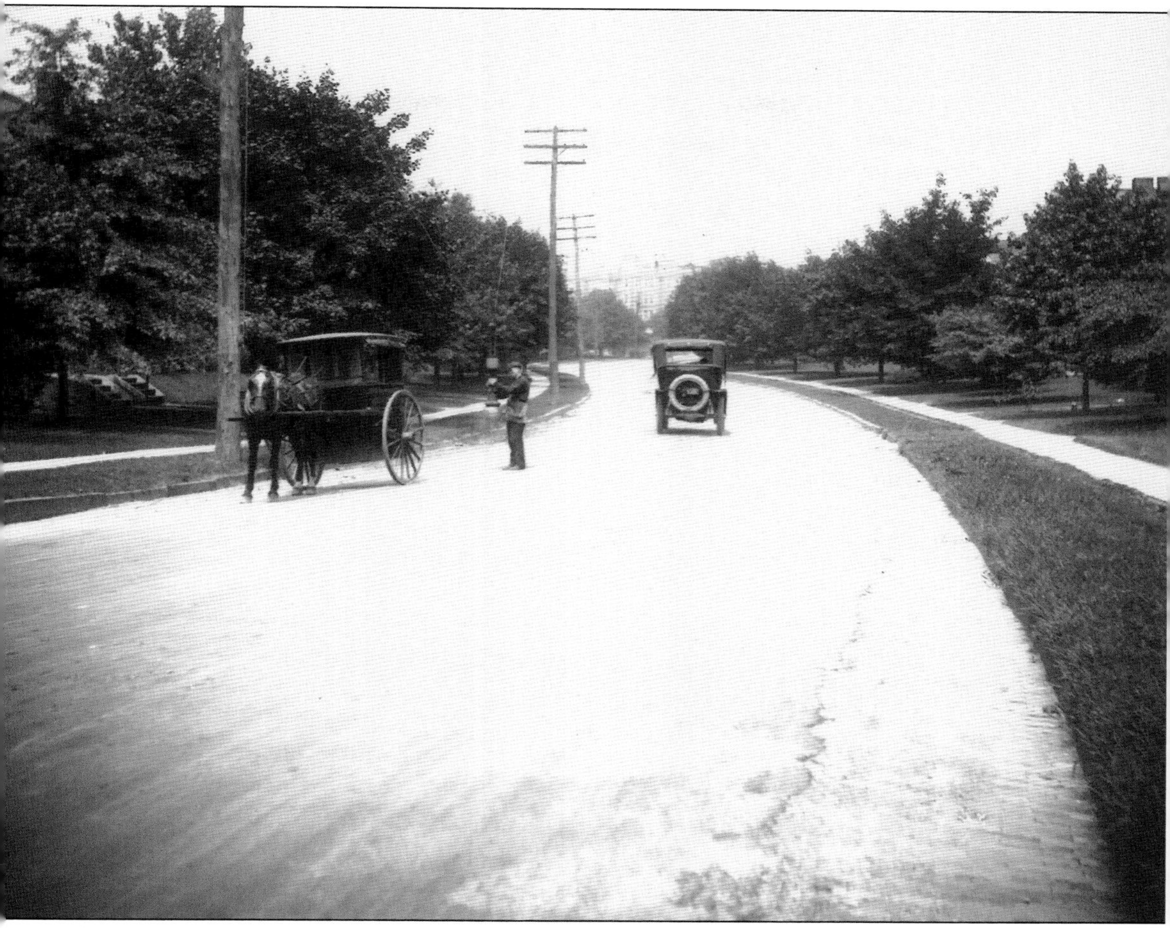

A Philadelphia Electric Company worker services a streetlight on Sixty-third Street in 1913. (Courtesy of Philadelphia City Archives.)

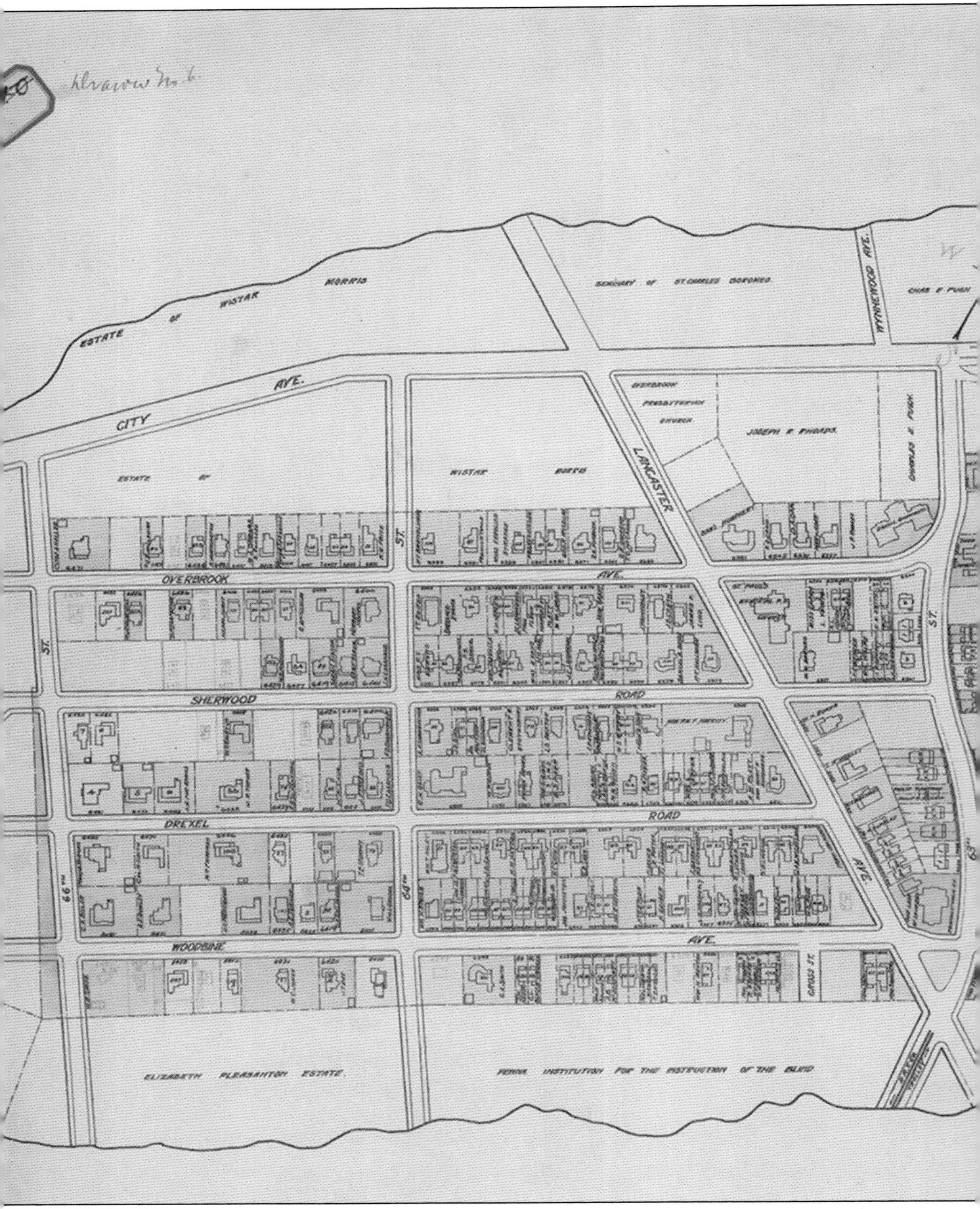

In 1912, Wendell and Smith produced this map, which displays each parcel along with its street address and, where possible, the name of its owner. (Courtesy of Radnor Historical Society, on

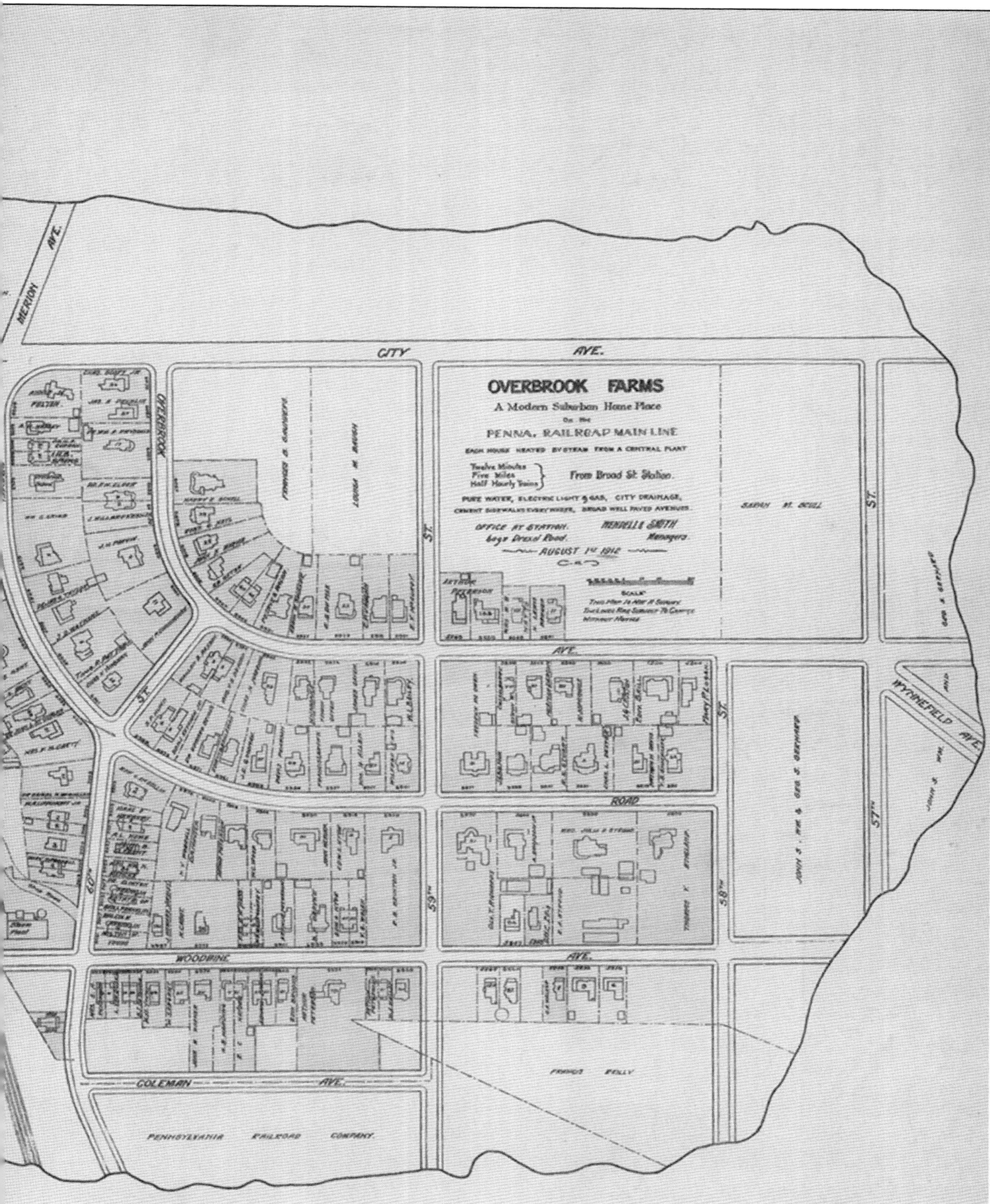

long-term loan to the Athenaeum of Philadelphia.)

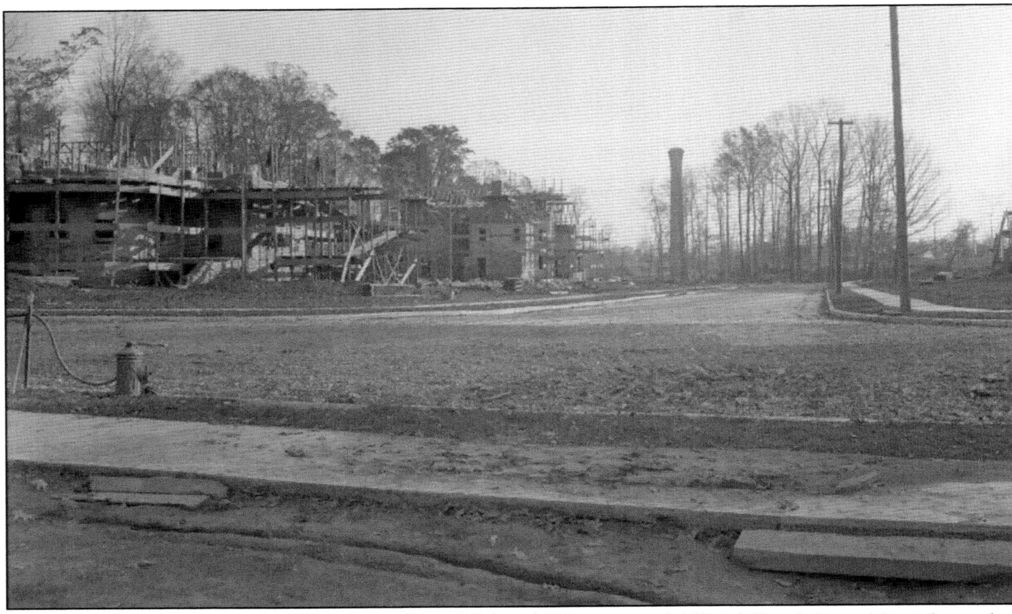

This home construction was under way on Upland Way around 1894. Wendell and Smith worked almost exclusively with one builder, Milton Walter Young, who served as general contractor. Young also did masonry, carpentry, roofing, and cabinetry work. At least one Overbrook Farms resident reports drawers bearing Young's signature on their undersides in the butler's pantry. (Courtesy of Radnor Historical Society.)

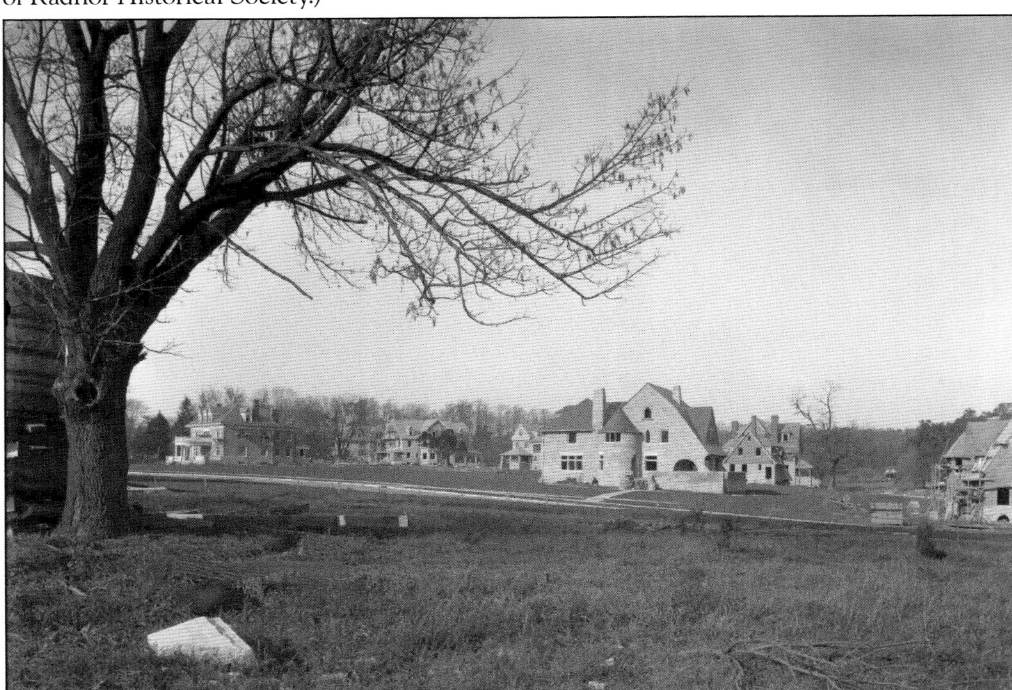

The 6000 block of Drexel Road is pictured here around 1894. (Courtesy of Radnor Historical Society.)

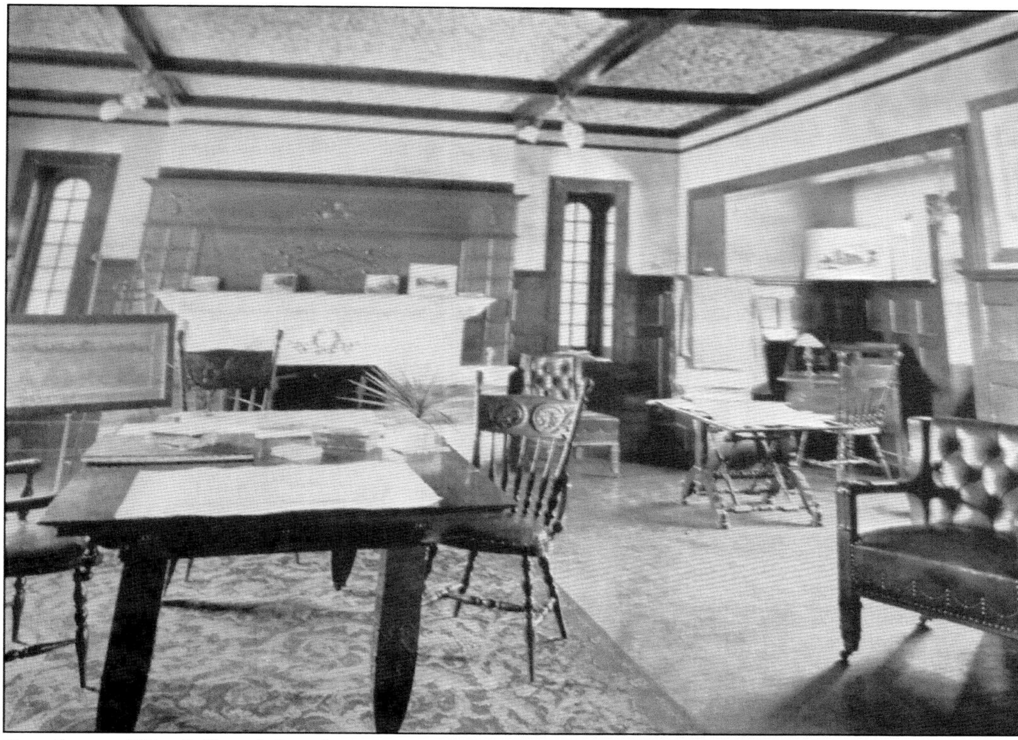

Developers Wendell and Smith constructed a handsome two-story building with a circular tower and neo-Romanesque arch over the main entrance to house their strategically designed and located sales office at 6092 Drexel Road. Prospective buyers could review samples and home features available in the reception hall of the sales office. (Courtesy of the OFC.)

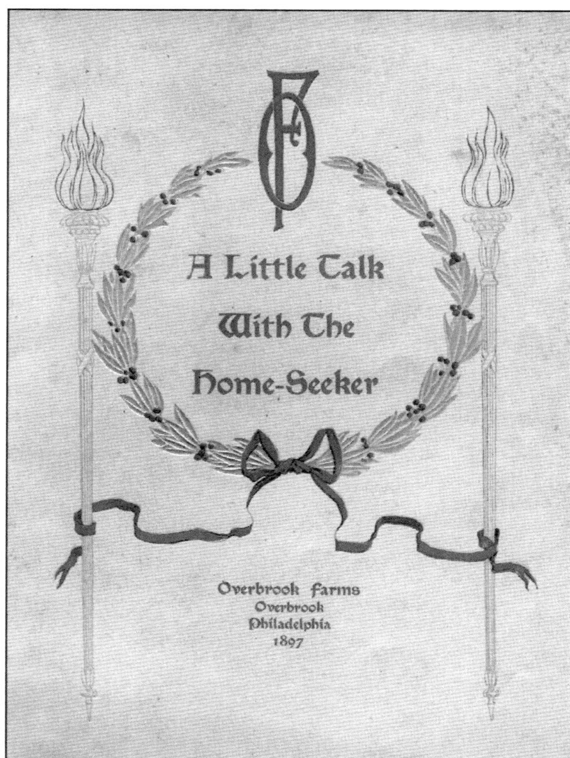

Assuring its success, Overbrook Farms was inventively and aggressively marketed by developers Wendell and Smith. The two received glowing reviews for their advertising campaign in newspapers, magazines, pamphlets, booklets, and other promotional materials, including a 16-page booklet entitled *A Little Talk with the Home Seeker*. (Courtesy of Radnor Historical Society.)

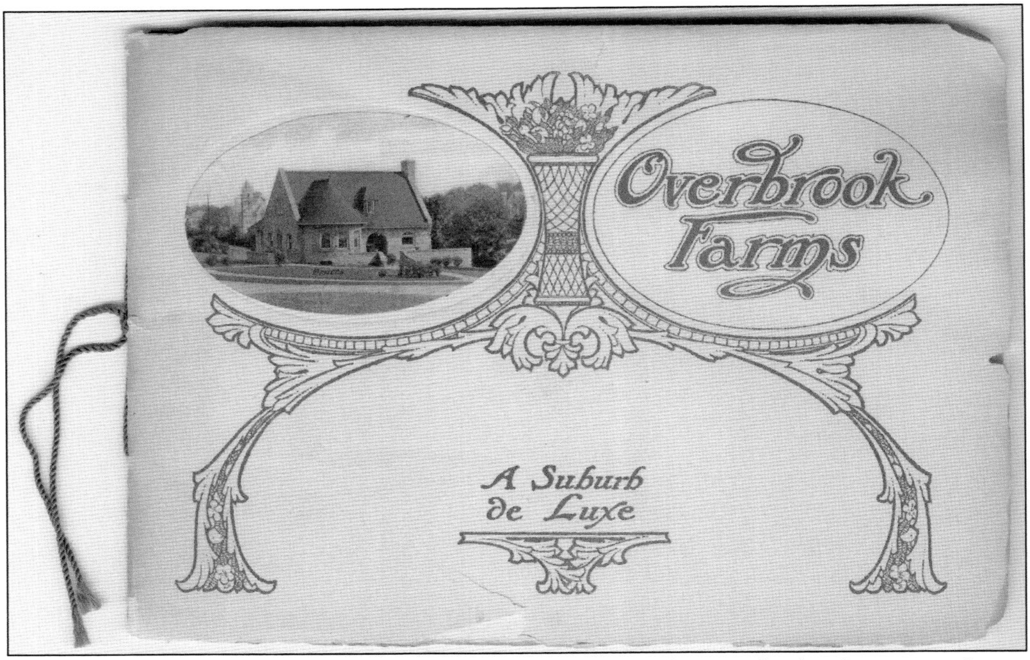

A *Suburb Deluxe* brochure created by Wendell and Smith to advertise the development is shown here. (Courtesy of Radnor Historical Society.)

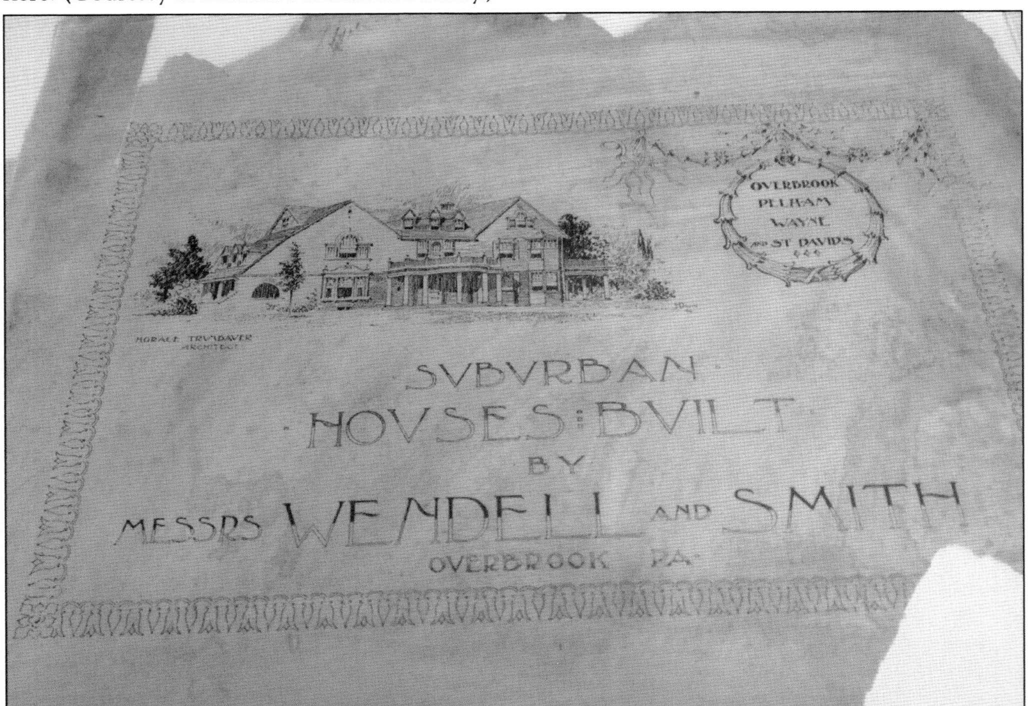

Pictured is the cover of Wendell and Smith's marketing booklet *Suburban Houses Built by Messrs. Wendell and Smith.* (Courtesy of the Athenaeum of Philadelphia.)

Two

Astral Architects and Their Clients

It took a constellation of stars to create the universe of Overbrook Farms. The assembled architects, more than 50 in all, were inevitably attracted to designing homes and grand apartments on sizable tracts of arboreal land. From 1893 until 1912, they collaborated to complete all but a small area of the approximately 170 acres that made up the development. By 1934, all of the 413 properties that originally populated the Overbrook Farms boundaries were complete.

Among the most recognizable individuals drawn to design for the neighborhood were Charles Barton Keen, best known for his notion of the Colonial Revival country house, and T.P. Lonsdale, creator of the Pennsylvania Building for the World's Columbian Exposition (Chicago, 1893). Scholar, watercolorist, and photographer Walter F. Price joined his two brothers, Frank L. and William L. Price, in their firm. These three distinguished themselves in designing for Overbrook Farms. Another standout, despite his short lifespan, was Clarence E. Schermerhorn, an aggressive self-promoter and prolific home and institutional designer and architect.

No self-respecting developers would overlook the work of Horace Trumbauer, whose modest academic preparation and shy demeanor did not stop his work from rising to wide recognition. Trumbauer cut his teeth creating homes for Wendell and Smith, in evidence in such widely distant locales as Overbrook Farms, Germantown, Pelham, St. Davids, and Wayne. Throughout his career, Trumbauer successfully sought wealthy clients from around the country. His initial work was often residential but broadened into designing for his client's cherished philanthropic endeavors.

Many of the architects who left their indelible signature on the neighborhood brought to their work an awareness of historical, classical, and contemporary aesthetics. They wrought the homes from Wissahickon schist, Pompeian brick, and stucco over brick. Their designs combined the broad range of styles informed by Europe, Asia, and Colonial-era revivals. These designs remain as timeless and alluring today as when they first opened their doors more than 100 years ago.

The immense wealth accumulated by principals in the industries of steel, utilities, coal, and gas became those who were occasional renters and, more often, residents of homes in the Overbrook Farms community.

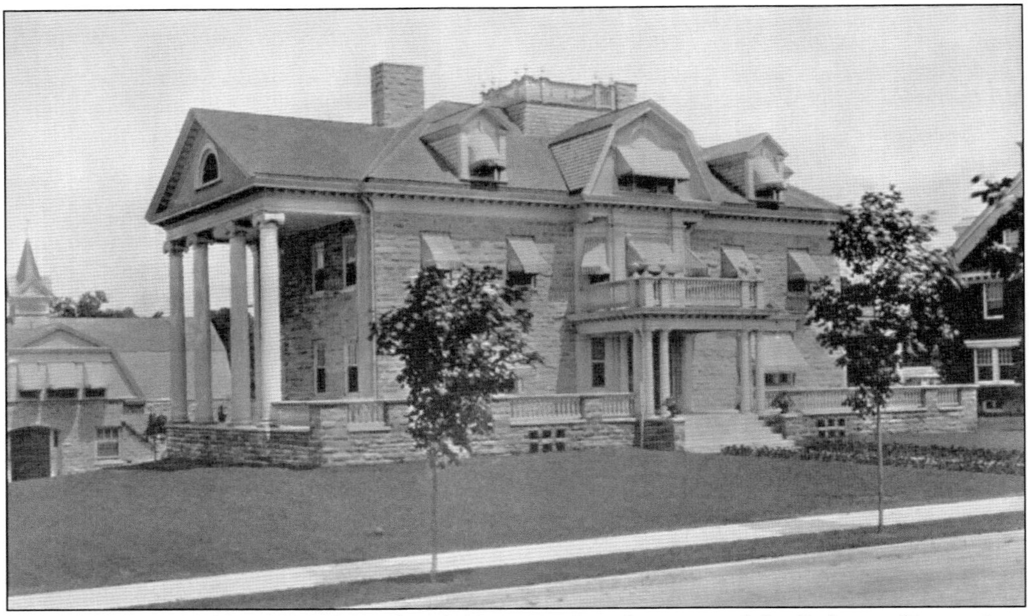

Standing at the highest part of Overbrook Farms, with a clear view of the Delaware River when first built, is the grand Colonial residence of Frederick McOwen. He served as treasurer of Berwind-White Coal Mining Co. and as director of Merchants National Bank, City Trust Co. Located at 5871 Drexel Road, it was designed by Thomas P. Lonsdale. Today, it is the home of Congregation Beth Tovim. (Courtesy of Radnor Historical Society.)

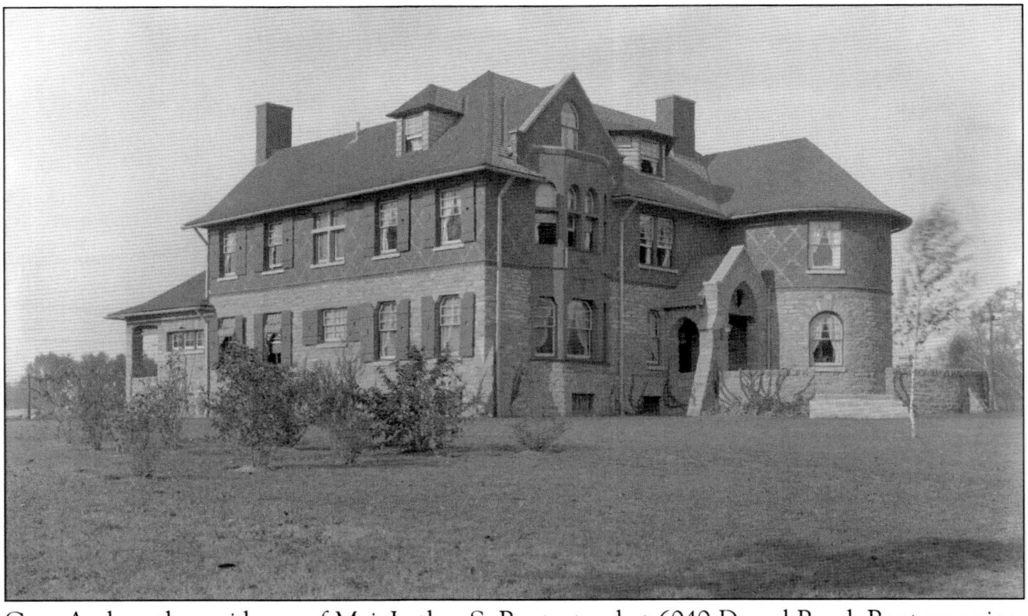

Gray Arches, the residence of Maj. Luther S. Bent, stood at 6040 Drexel Road. Bent was vice-president of Pennsylvania Steel. Designed by Boyd & Boyd, it was the first home constructed in the area. Gray Arches first consumed two lots and eventually added four others, assembling one of the largest parcels in Overbrook Farms. Bent was a prominent industrialist and civil engineer. Gray Arches was demolished in February 1989. (Courtesy of Radnor Historical Society.)

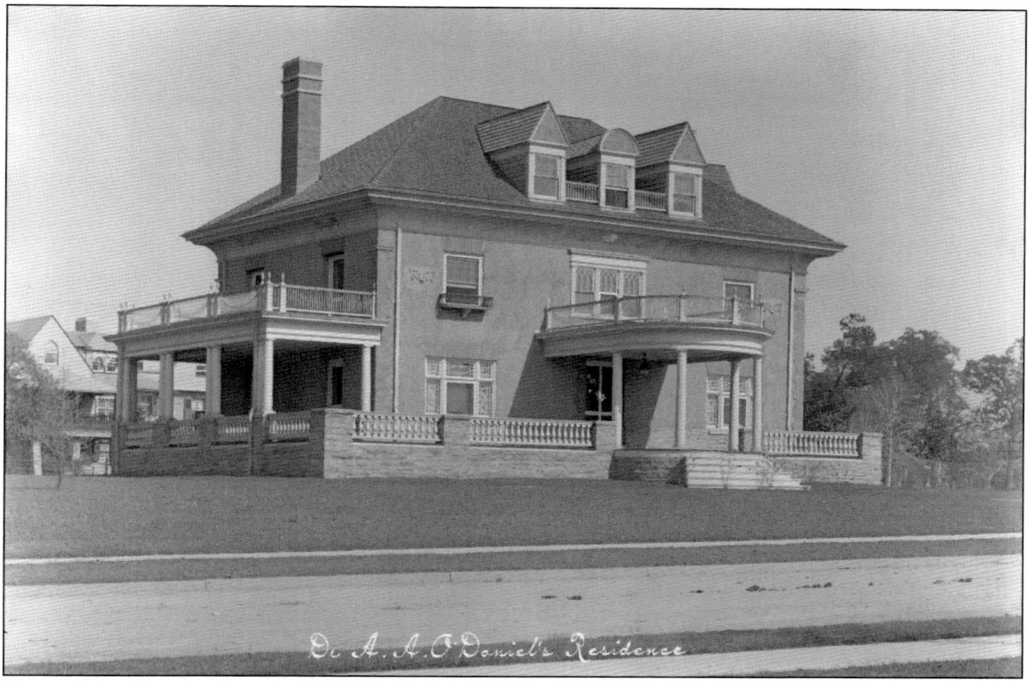

Horace Trumbauer designed this home at 6055 Drexel Road for Dr. A. Allison O'Daniel. Despite a nondescript exterior, the interior boasts a semicircular entry porch, an oval dining room, and a round den under the staircase. It was featured in the September 1896 issue of *Scientific American*'s Building Edition. The above photograph shows the original home, and the photograph below is a later view of the house. (Both, courtesy of Radnor Historical Society.)

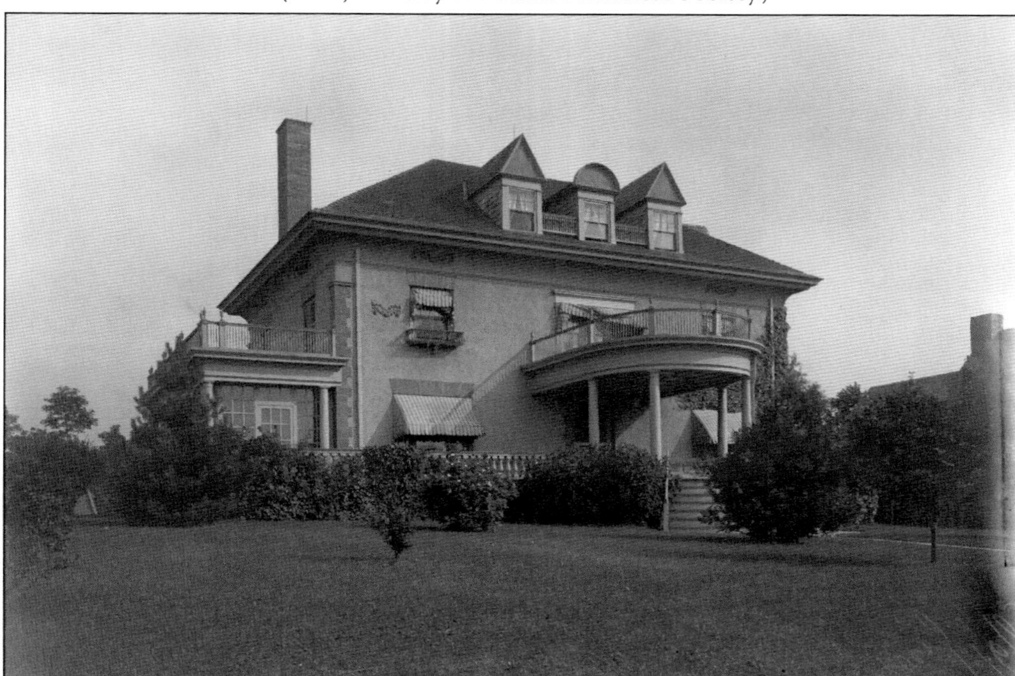

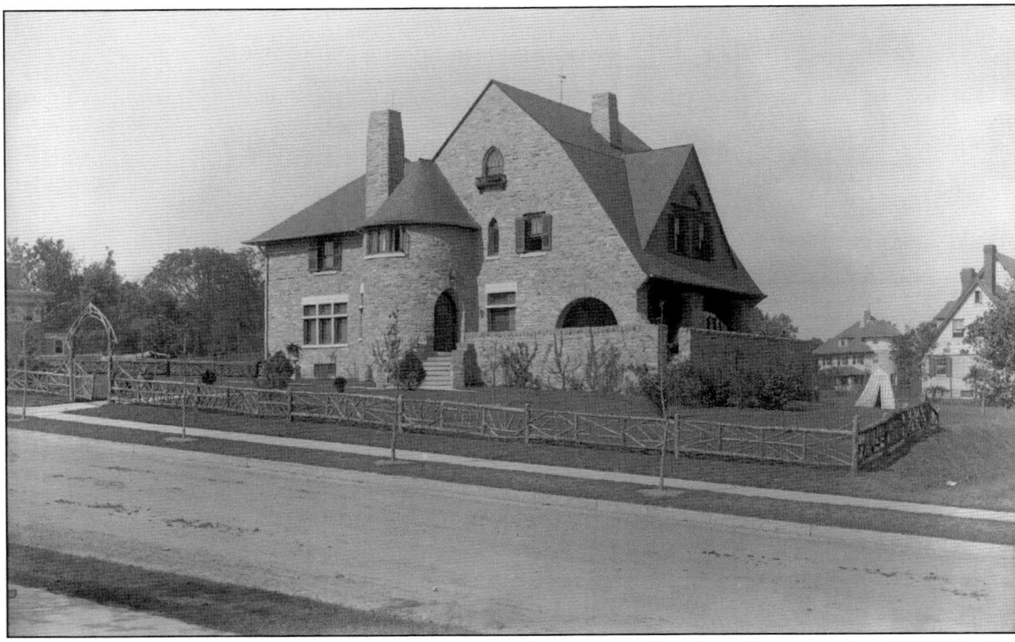

Named Redruth Manse, borrowed from an English mansion, this large home in the 6000 block of Drexel Road was designed by Horace Trumbauer for U.S. Grant Megargee and his wife, Elizabeth. Like many of Trumbauer's houses, the design emerged from a steep gambrel and cylindrical tower. (Courtesy of Radnor Historical Society.)

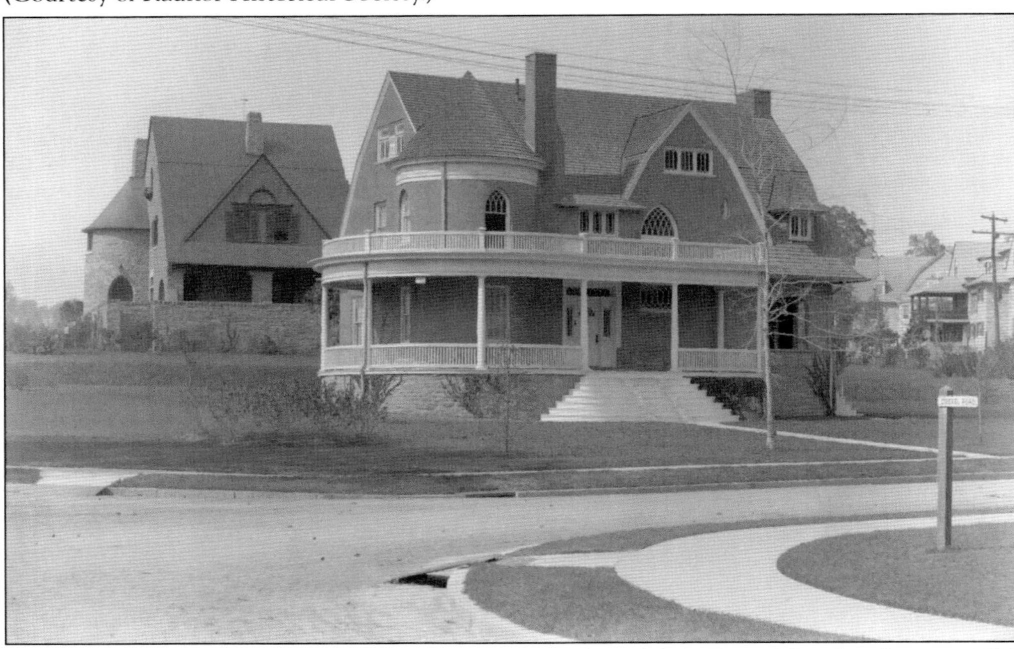

Wilfred Lewis and his wife, Emily Sargent Lewis, purchased 5901 Drexel Road in January 1895. Their house was designed by architects Yarnall & Goforth. Lewis, an engineer, made his own fortune and was president of the Tabor Manufacturing Company. His wife, Emily Sargent Lewis, was a poet. (Courtesy of Radnor Historical Society.)

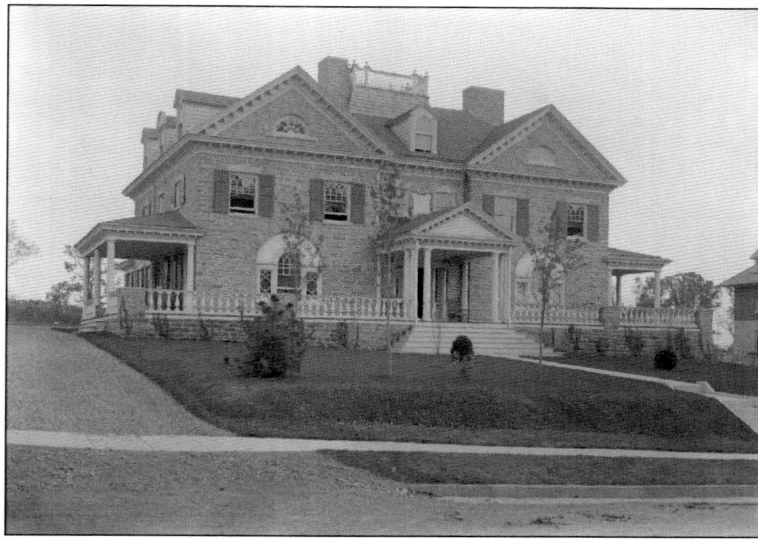

Architects and brothers Boyd & Boyd designed 5930 Drexel Road in 1894 for Robert Emory Pattison, the state's 19th (1883–1887) and 21st (1891–1895) governor. (Courtesy of Radnor Historical Society.)

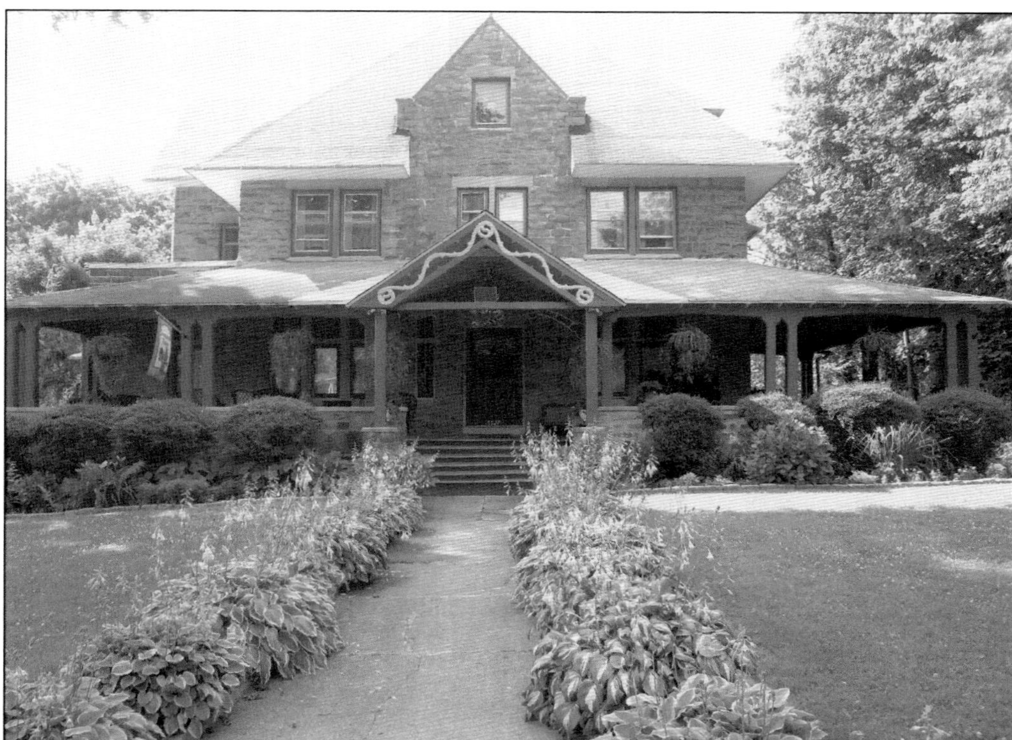

In 1894, Benjamin P. and Helen E. Obdyke purchased 5927 Drexel Road. The couple built a Gothic Revival–style house designed by architect Chester H. Kirk. Obdyke owned a prosperous building-supplies firm. He sold the property to Francis Shunk Brown and his wife, Helen, in 1899, and the Obdykes moved to a Trumbauer-designed house at 5939 Woodbine Avenue. Brown, a very prominent attorney, served as attorney general of Pennsylvania. (Courtesy of Kip Krieger.)

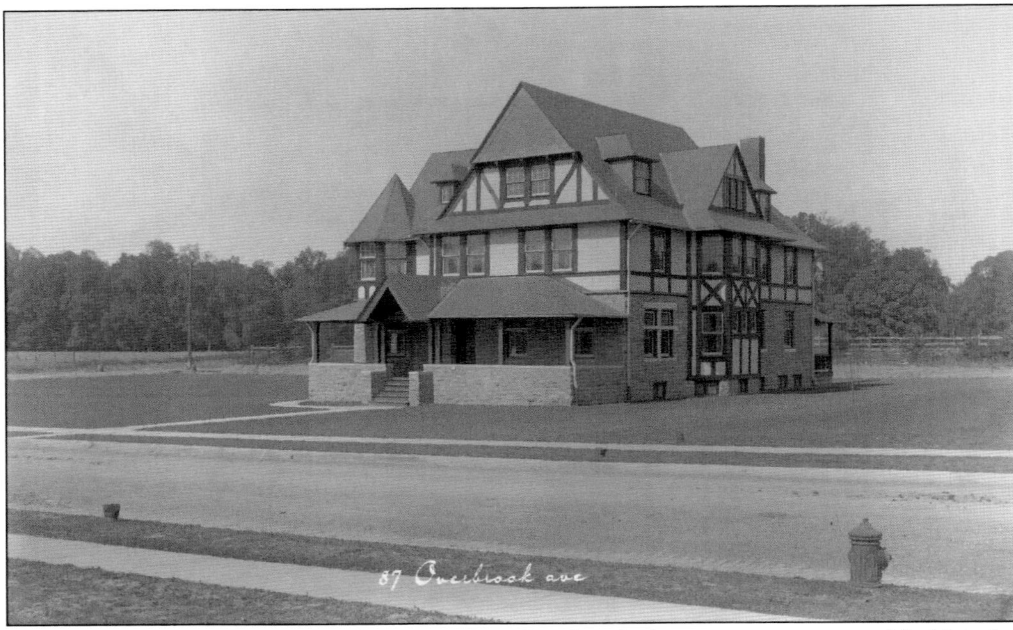

William L. Price designed this home at 6391 Overbrook Avenue as a stone and half-timber Tudor Revival in 1895. First a rental property for Wendell and Smith, it was named the Alfred Percival Smith House after its owner, a lawyer and curator of the Presbyterian Historical Society of Philadelphia. Smith purchased the home in 1913. (Courtesy of Radnor Historical Society.)

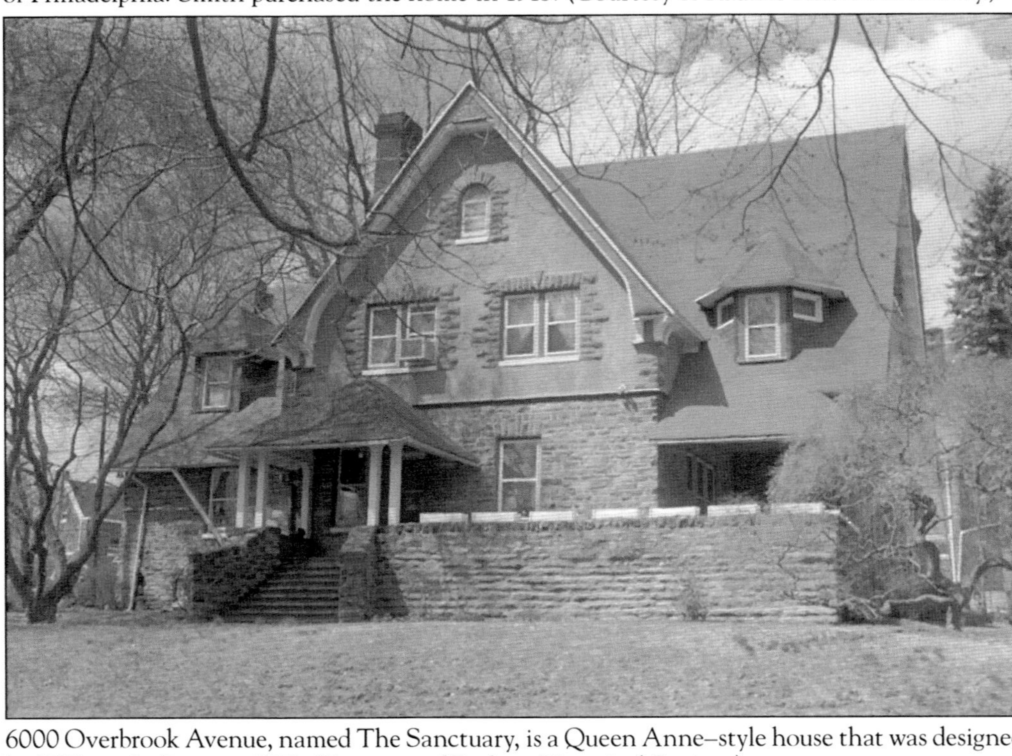

6000 Overbrook Avenue, named The Sanctuary, is a Queen Anne–style house that was designed by William L. Price in 1895. (Courtesy of Radnor Historical Society.)

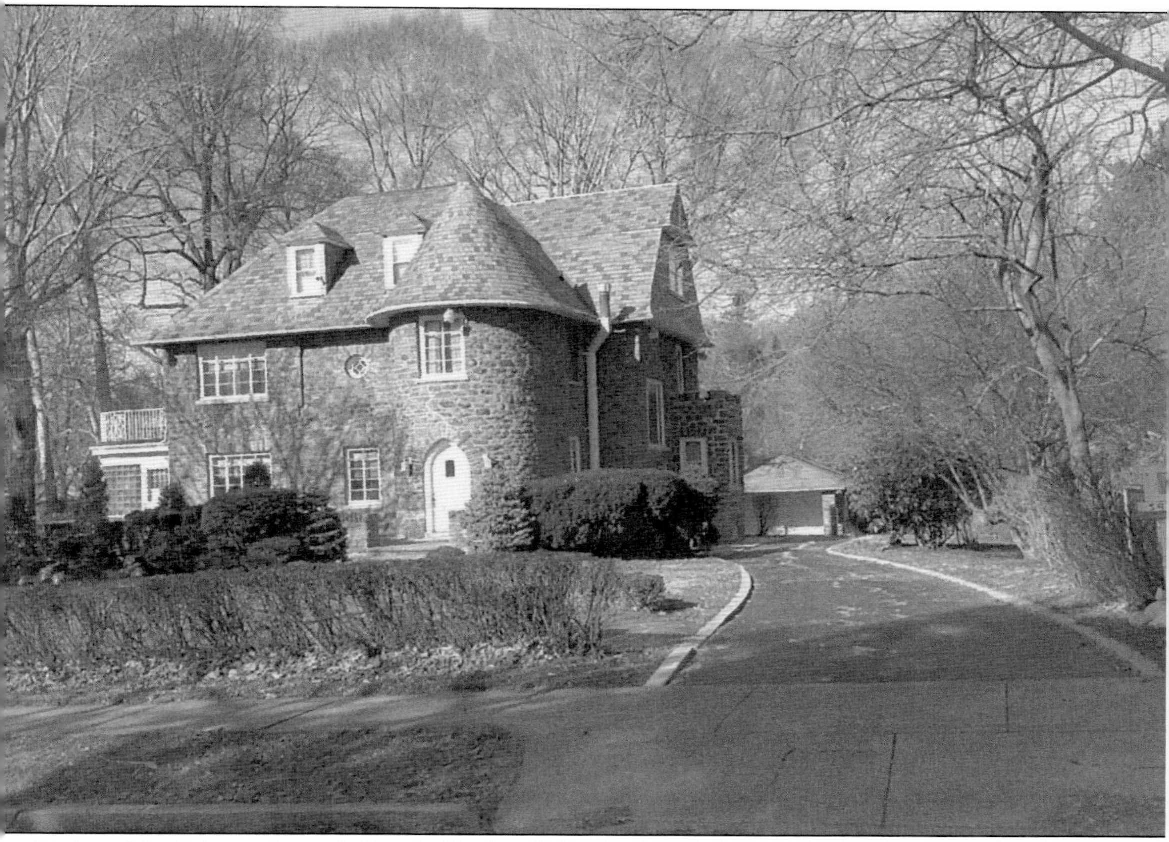

Designed by Schemerhorn & Reinhold, this 5921 Overbrook Avenue home is a magnificent example of the Normandy Revival style. Sitting on a lot of nearly an acre, the Japanese maple in the front yard predates the construction of the house. This is indicative of the care that was taken to preserve existing trees and shrubs throughout the neighborhood during the development of Overbrook Farms. (Courtesy of Radnor Historical Society.)

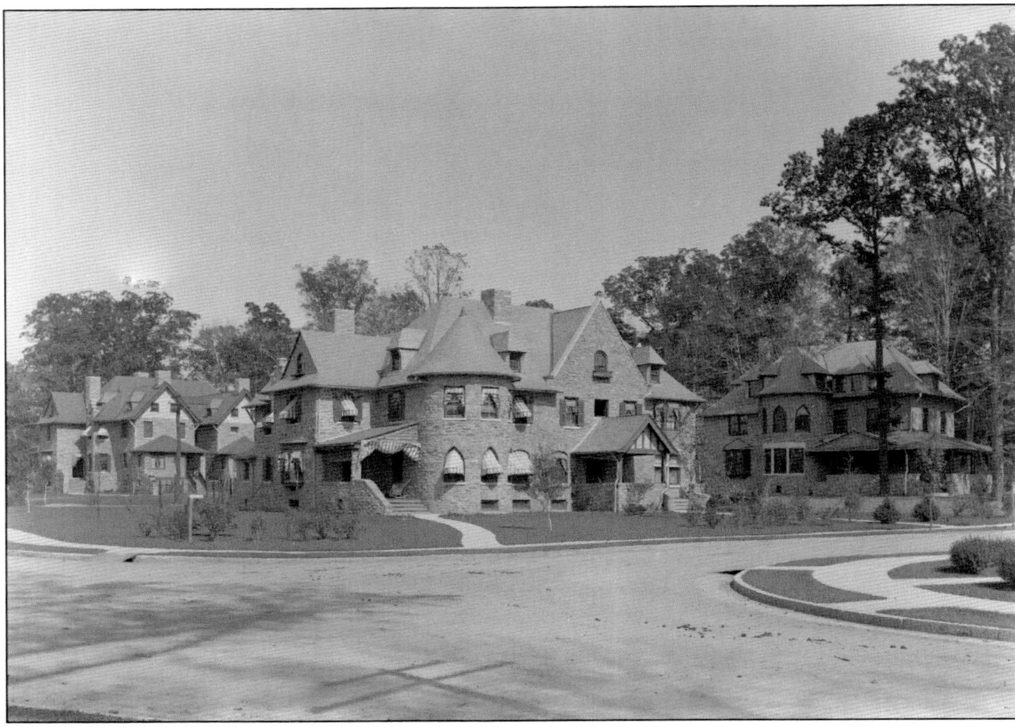

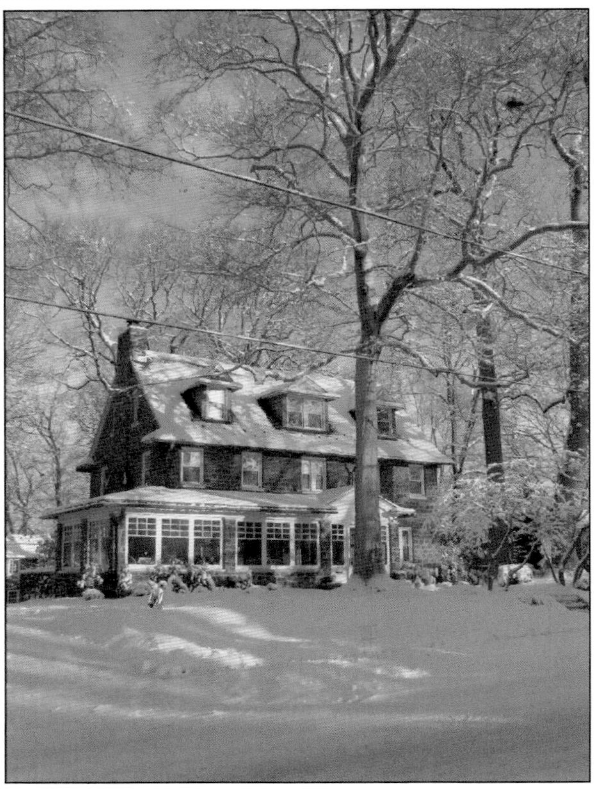

Horace Trumbauer designed the grand twins at 5979 and 5985 Drexel Road. Ida and Benjamin Ketcham lived at 5979 Drexel with their three daughters and servants. Ketcham was the owner of Benjamin Ketcham Jr. Lumber and the first treasurer of the Overbrook Farms Club. Sam P. Huhn owned 5985 Drexel and was the treasurer of the West Philadelphia Passenger Railway Company until he was indicted in 1878. (Courtesy of Radnor Historical Society.)

Walter F. Price designed this three-story, 5,300-square-foot house on Sixty-sixth Street and Woodbine Avenue. Built in 1910, it was occupied from the early 1940s until the early 1990s by the Raymond "Gus" Augusterfer family. A man of many interests and talents, Augusterfer also owned the Ambrose-Augusterfer Corp. of Germantown, mechanical contractors. (Courtesy of Kip Krieger.)

Gus Augusterfer designed and installed the neighborhood's first central air-conditioning into this home in the early 1950s. The innovation required another first, a 220-volt electrical line installed down the length of Woodbine Avenue at Augusterfer's expense. The commercial-grade chiller system had an outdoor cooling tower and two huge electric compressor pumps, each weighing hundreds of pounds. (Courtesy of Kip Krieger.)

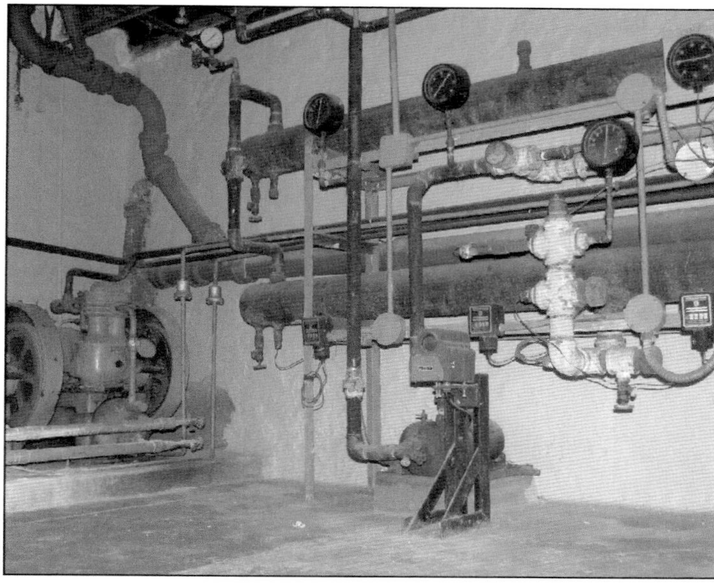

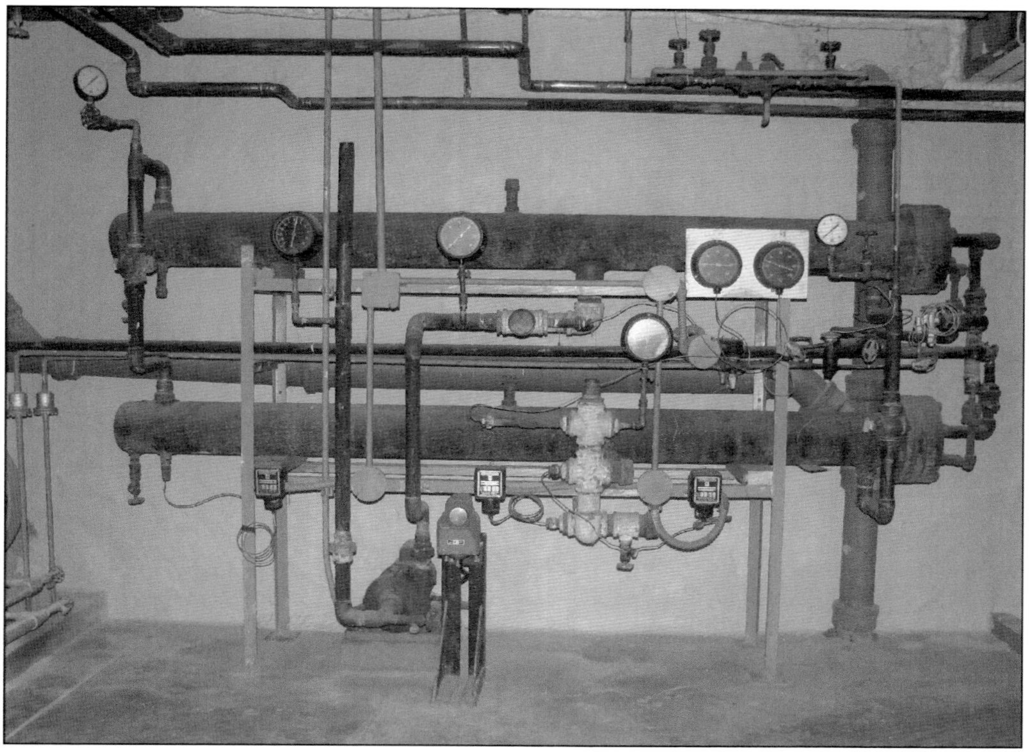

The system required an entire wall of pipes, condensation chambers, and gauges, still evident in the basement. Chilled water reached wall units in each room. The 220-volt service prevented the house from losing power during storms. Neighbors found their way to the Augusterfer home to store food in their refrigerators and freezers until power was restored. Gus Augusterfer designed and installed central air-conditioning in the chapel of Our Lady of Lourdes in the early 1960s. (Courtesy of Kip Krieger.)

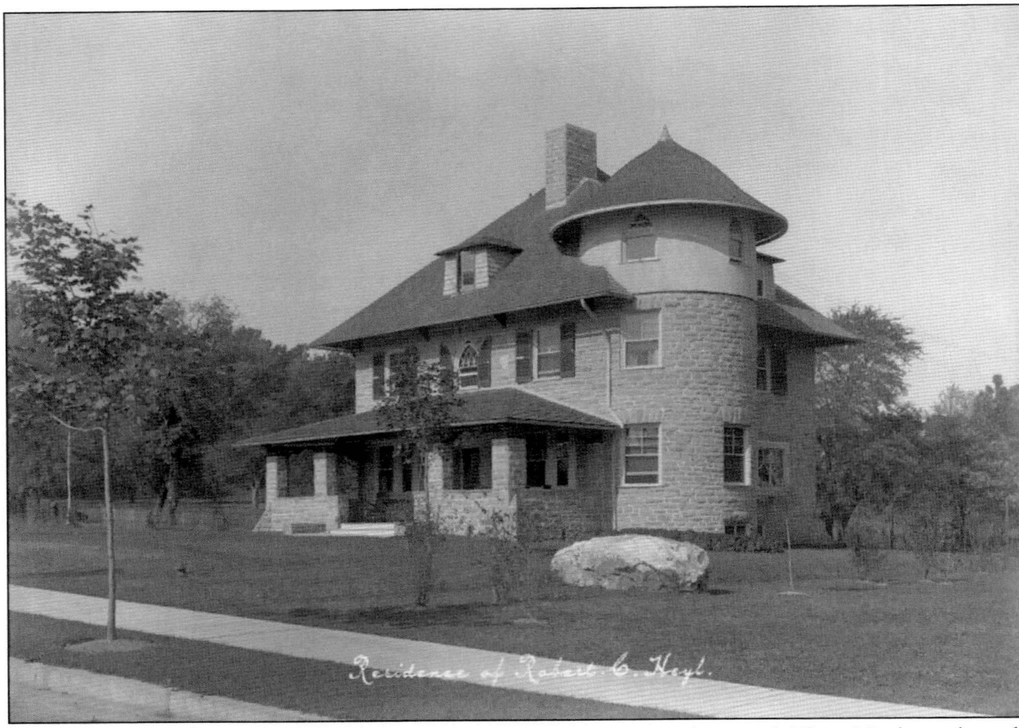

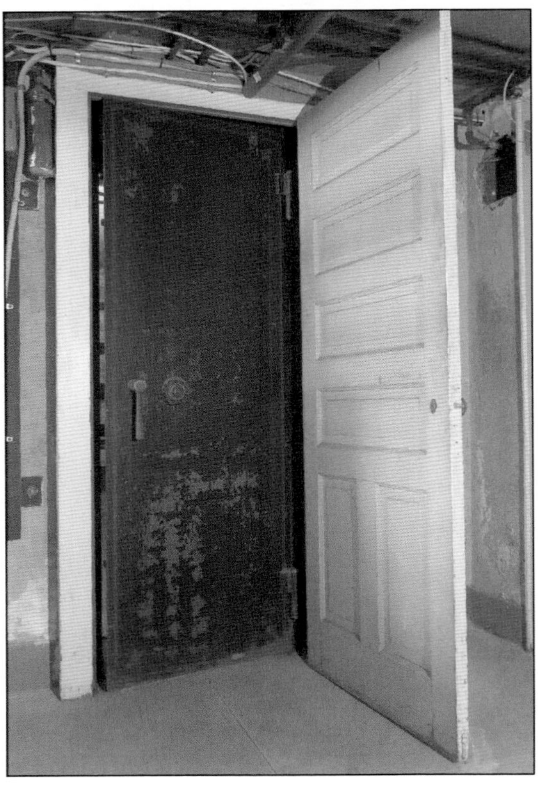

In 1894, Robert and Clara Heyl purchased a lot in the 6000 block of Overbrook Avenue and built a French Eclectic house designed by Horace Trumbauer (though some identify William L. Price as the architect). Frederick T. Chandler and his family rented before purchasing the home in 1912. Chandler was president of the Philadelphia Stock Exchange and director of Quaker City National Bank, the Securities Corporation, and the Fairmount Park Commission. (Courtesy of the Radnor Historical Society.)

The current owners believe Chandler was responsible for integrating some interesting features still found in the basement of the house, including iron bars on the basement windows that are imbedded in the foundation and a large walk-in safe with built-in shelving and a concealing closet door that, when closed, camouflages the safe. (Courtesy of Rick Pullin.)

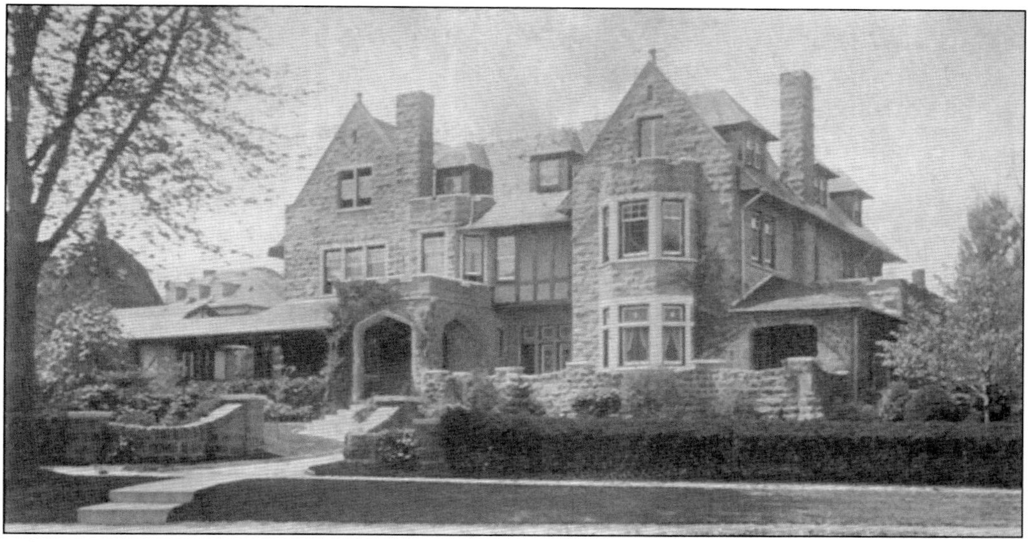

Politician and lawyer William Francis Harrity was an avid Democrat in an age dominated by Republicans. Architect Chester H. Kirk designed this grand Jacobethan Revival at 6310 Sherwood Road. Harrity supported Grover Cleveland for president in 1884 and twice helped elect his friend Robert E. Pattison, a fellow Democrat and Overbrook neighbor, to Pennsylvania's governorship (1883–1887 and 1891–1895). The house was demolished in the late 1920s and replaced by an apartment complex. (Courtesy of Radnor Historical Society.)

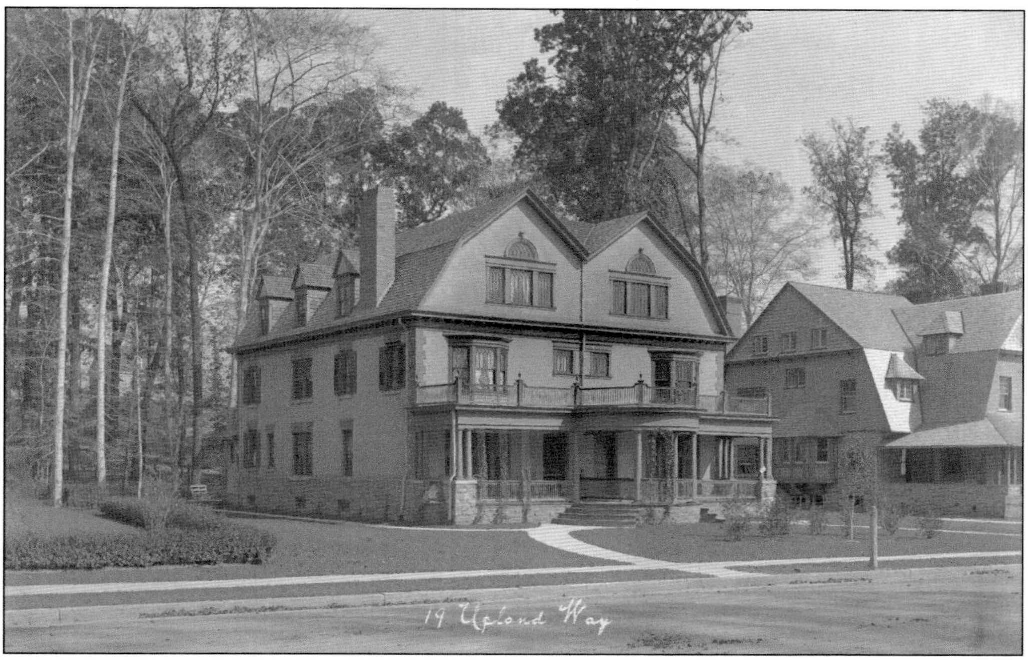

Rodney D. Allen purchased 2037 Upland Way in 1896 and lived there with his wife. The twin house at 2039 Upland Way was purchased that same year by Anna K. Harbert. Horace Trumbauer designed this Dutch Colonial Revival with his often-used gambrel roof and upper and lower front porches, with a dramatic semicircular extension of the porches. (Courtesy of Radnor Historical Society.)

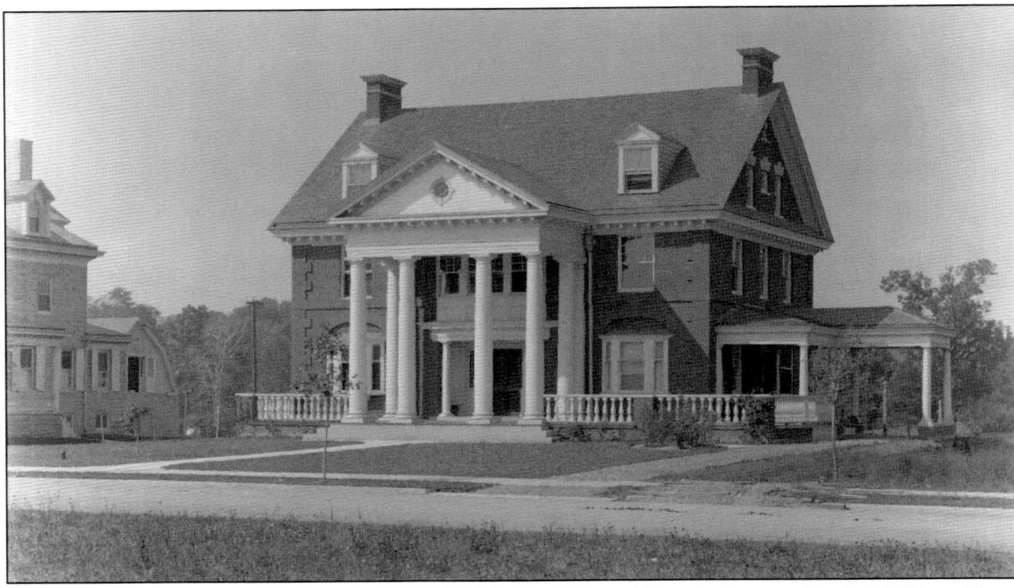

This stately Neoclassical house in the 5800 block of Drexel Road, designed by J. William Shaw, has numerous outstanding architectural features, such as modillions, a roundel window in the gable, a half-circle second-floor balcony supported by Tuscan columns, and multi-pane sidelights. Horace F. Smith purchased this home in 1894. (Courtesy of Radnor Historical Society.)

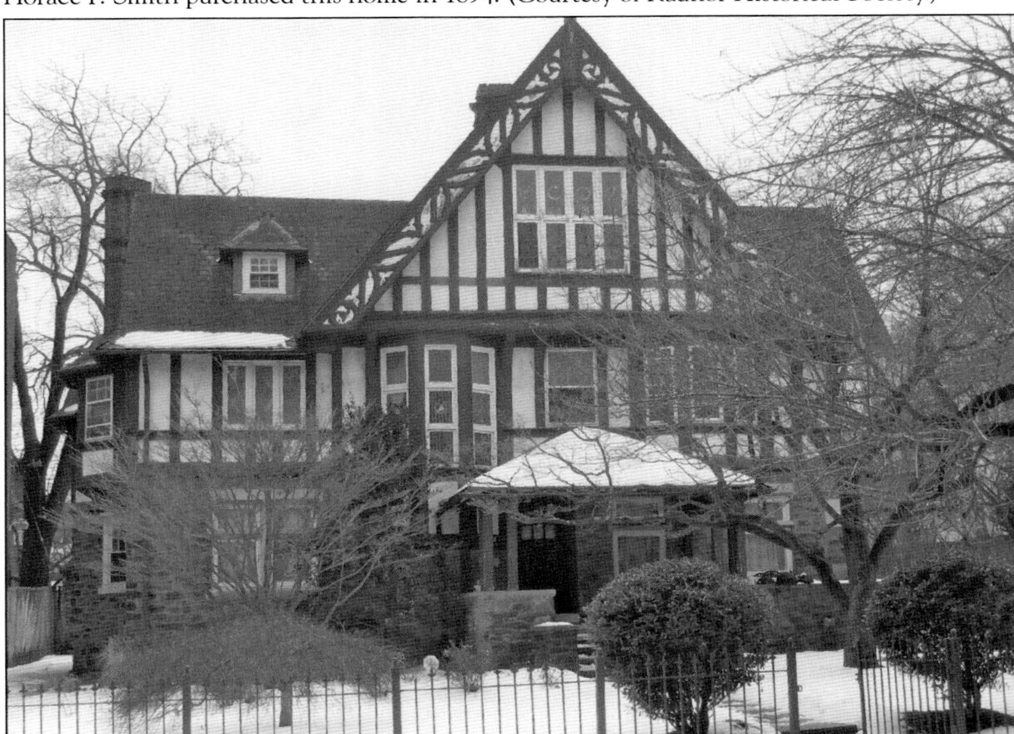

Built around 1895, this single-family Tudor Revival at 6334 Sherwood Road was designed and occupied by architect William Lightfoot Price. (Courtesy of Radnor Historical Society.)

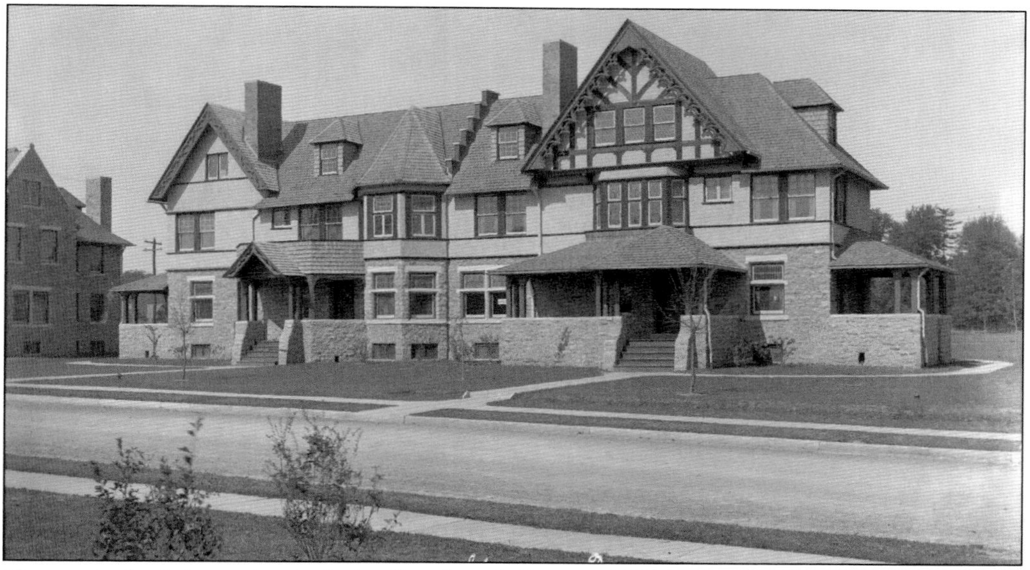

Not typical of the twins built in Overbrook Farms, 6335 and 6339 Sherwood Road were uniquely designed in 1897 by William L. Price as not symmetrical. (Courtesy of Radnor Historical Society.)

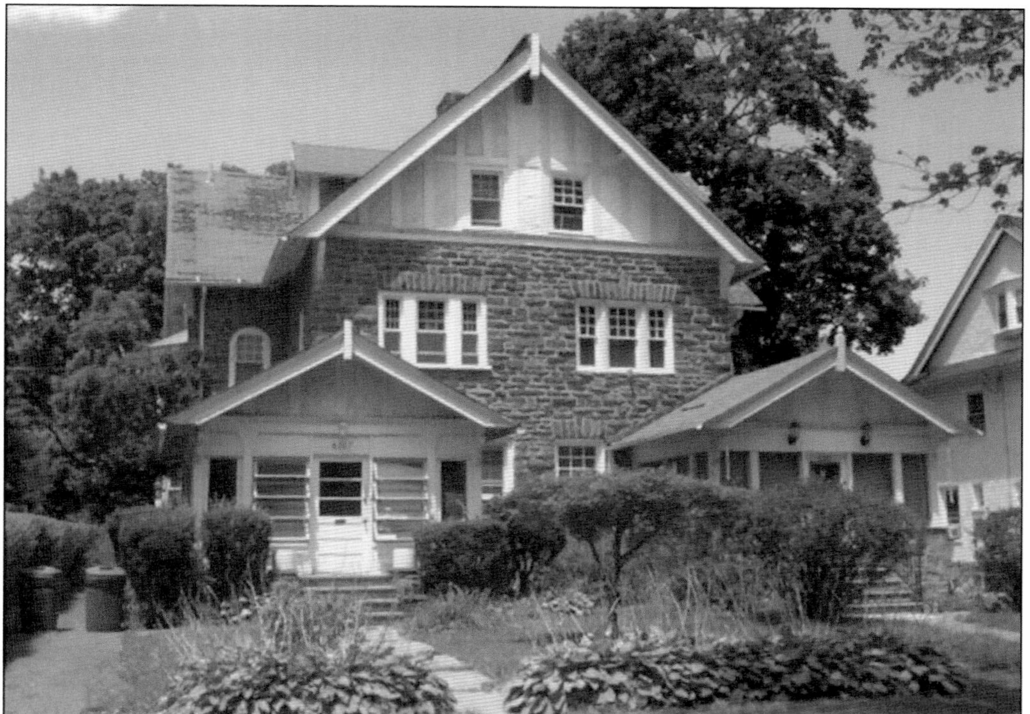

The homes in Overbrook Farms were targeted at the upper middle class and wealthy. In the mid-1890s, twin homes cost about twice that of a typical suburban house. Juliette Lamoreaux purchased 6307 Sherwood Road for $7,050. Three years later, 6305 Sherwood Road sold for $7,750 to Margaret Wendell Hess, a widow and relative of developer Herman Wendell. (Courtesy of the OFC.)

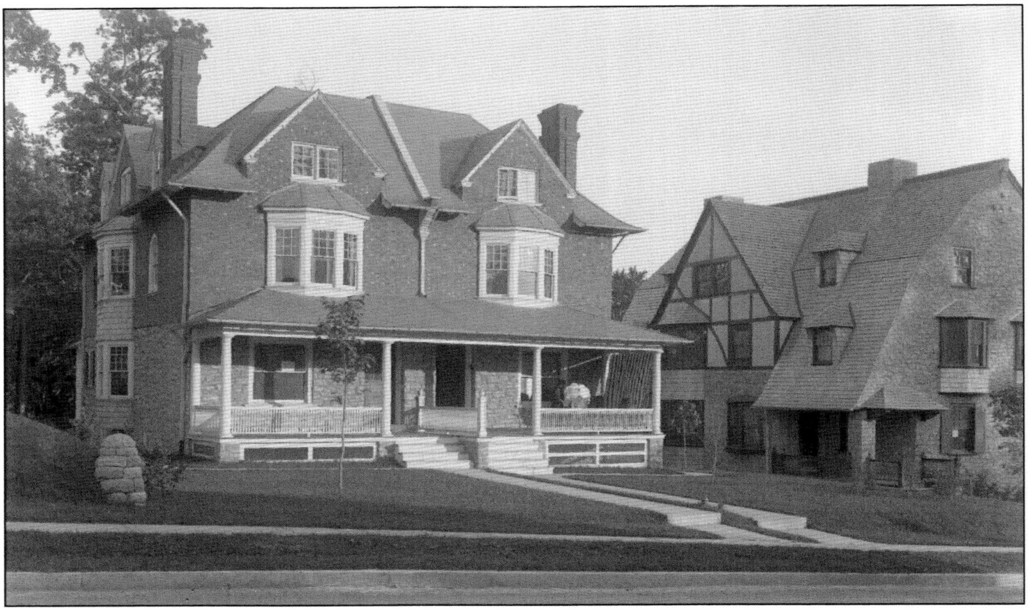

After building a large number of grand custom homes in Overbrook Farms, Wendell and Smith commissioned Horace Trumbauer to design speculative homes in several communities, including Overbrook Farms. The houses were referenced by a number. House 39 was built at 5990 and 5992 Woodbine Avenue as Tudor Revivals with stone facades, pebbledash, and half-timber side gables. The third floor was often reserved for domestic staff. (Courtesy of Radnor Historical Society.)

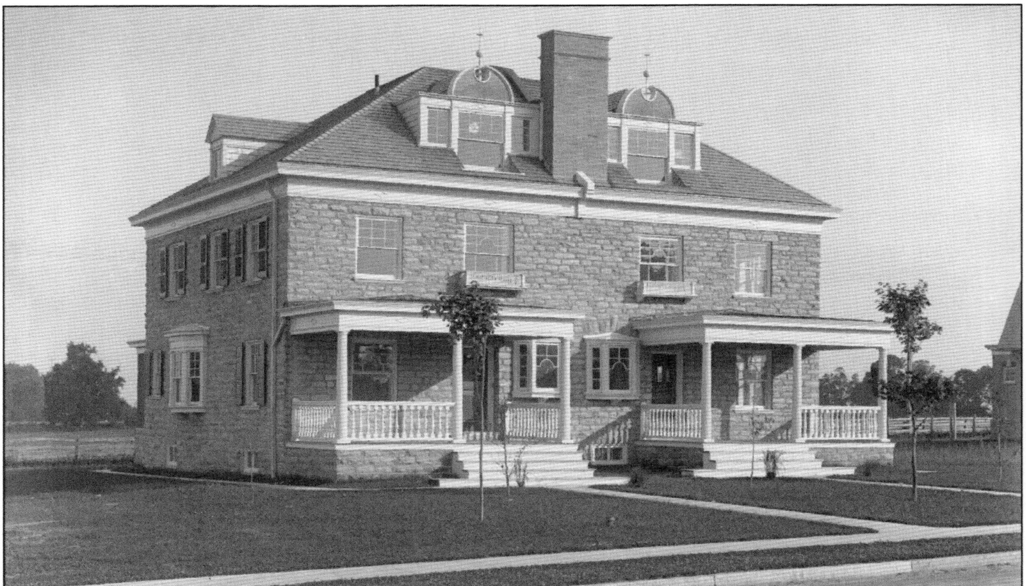

Additional standardized, speculative houses include Charles Barton Keen and Frank Mead's House 61; approximately 17 pairs were constructed in Overbrook Farms by the early 1900s. House 61 is a twin or double house that is symmetrical from a shared party wall. Some of the distinctive features of House 61 are large front porches, small detailed bay windows at the first floor, and large dormers. (Courtesy of Radnor Historical Society.)

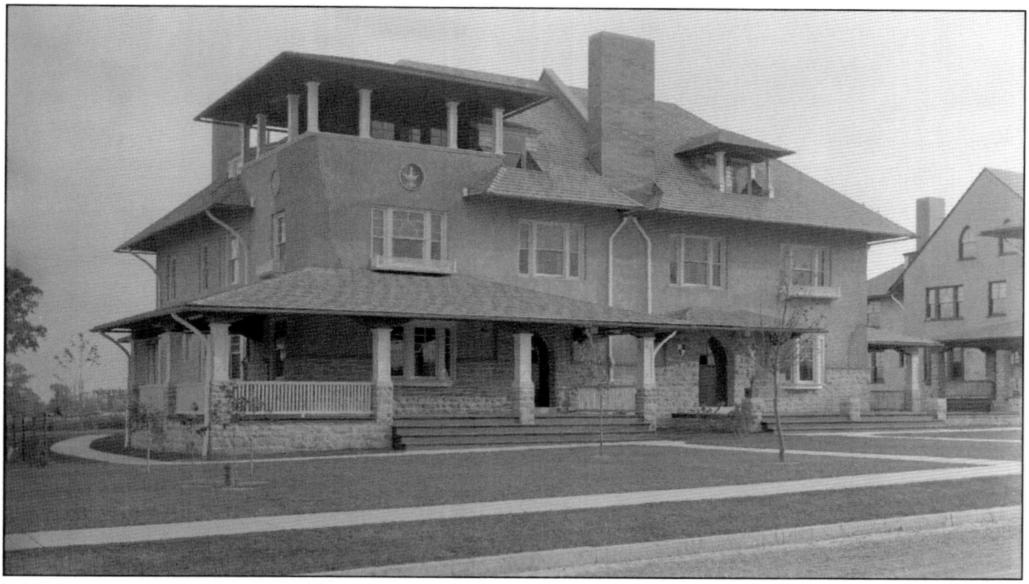

There were many varieties of the "Double Dwelling in the Spanish Style" house design, including numbers 53, 55, 57, 58, 59, and 60. These large, tall twin houses have bold projecting forms, such as turrets and towers, balconies and eaves, and unusual combinations of round and pointed arch windows and doors. In Overbrook Farms, houses of this type are on the 6300 block of Drexel Road, creating an exceptional streetscape. Albert Barnes and his wife, Laura, rented 6374 Drexel Road from Wendell and Smith upon returning from their European honeymoon. Laura Barnes posted this house in her scrapbook, which is preserved at the Barnes Foundation. (Both, courtesy of Radnor Historical Society.)

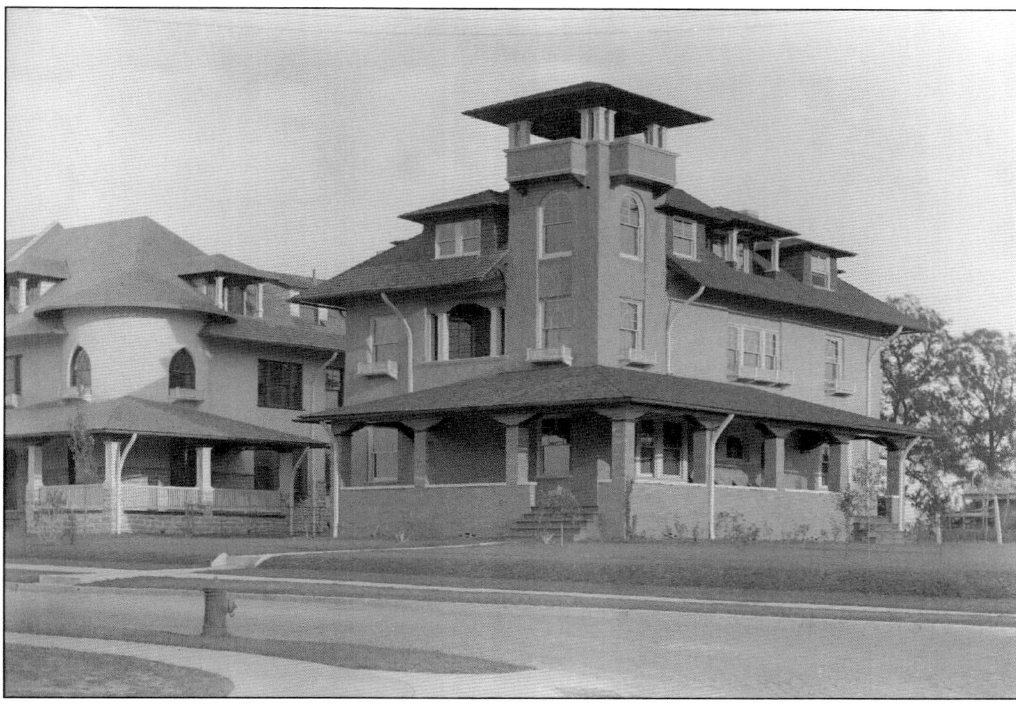

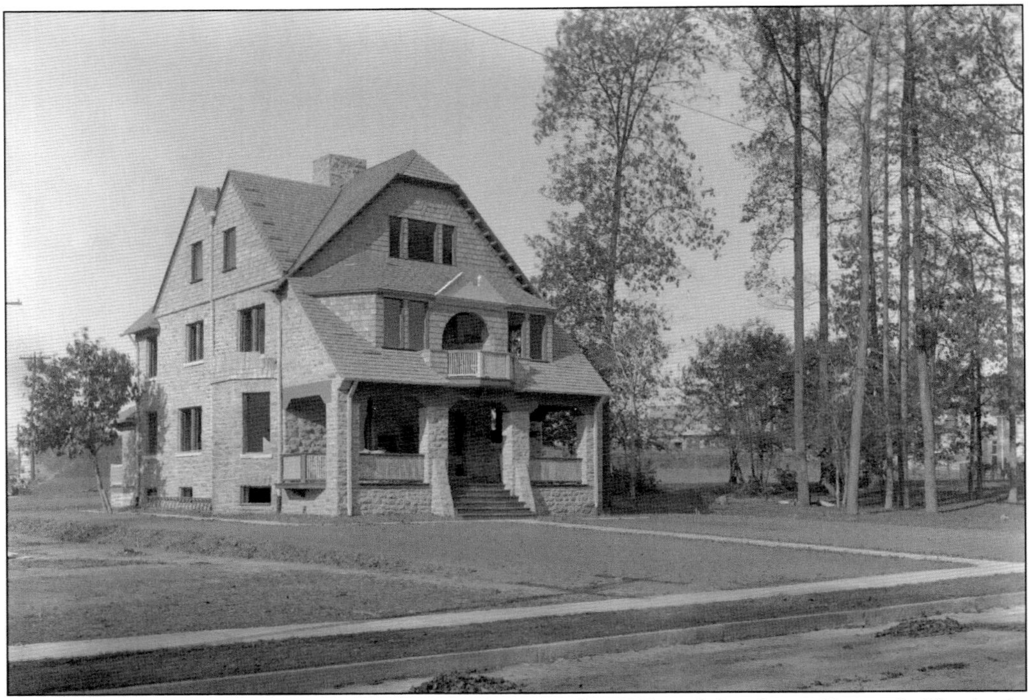

Built in 1895, 2025 Upland Way was purchased in 1896 by William Mencke and his wife, Elizabeth. (Courtesy of Radnor Historical Society.)

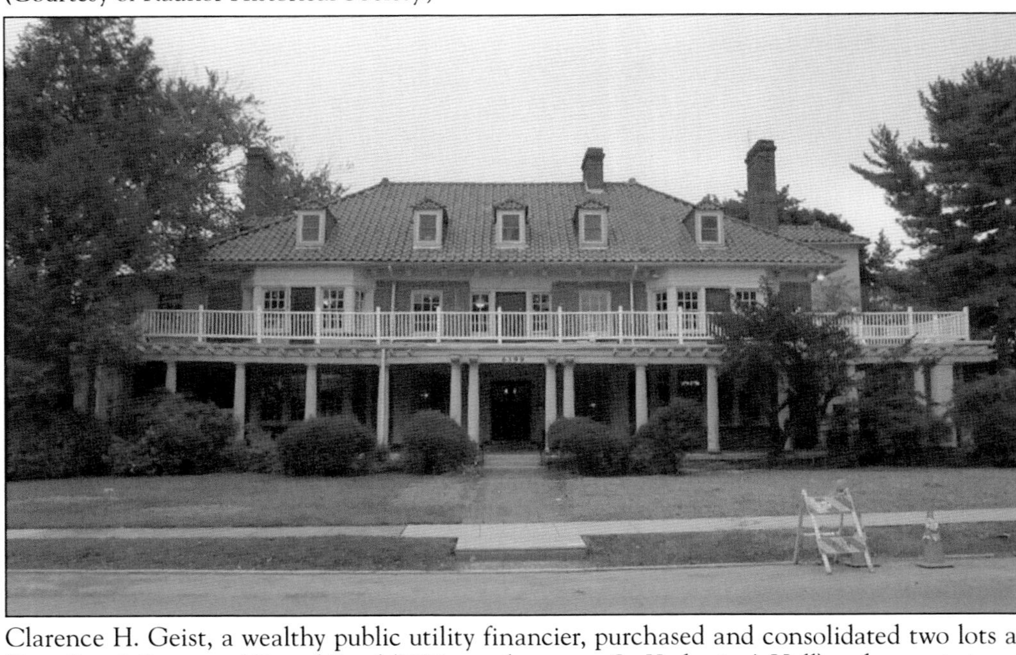

Clarence H. Geist, a wealthy public utility financier, purchased and consolidated two lots at Sixty-fourth Street and Drexel Road (6399, now known as St. Katharine's Hall) and commissioned architect Charles Barton Keen to custom design his home. Completed in 1910, its red terra-cotta tile roof and colonnaded pergola around the front and side of the house are unique in Overbrook Farms. (Courtesy of the OFC.)

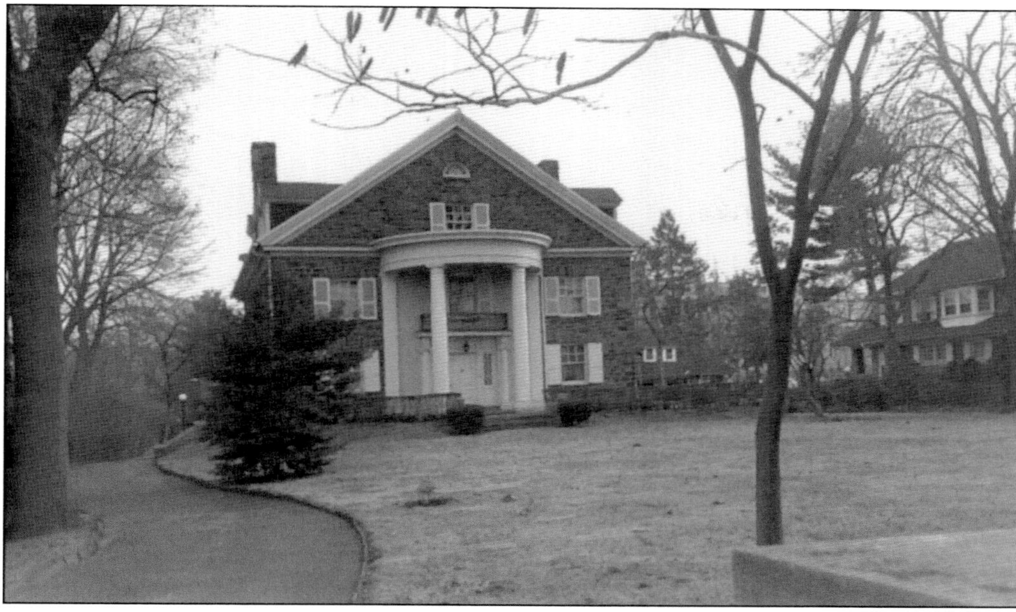

As City Avenue became a major Philadelphia thoroughfare, properties there were built on an epic scale. This Colonial Revival was designed by Westray Ladd and built in 1901. The front door and central two-story semicircular portico are located at the gable end. Its first owner was Leroy M. Lewis. His brother, well-known judge Edwin O. Lewis, would later live in the adjacent house. (Courtesy of the OFC.)

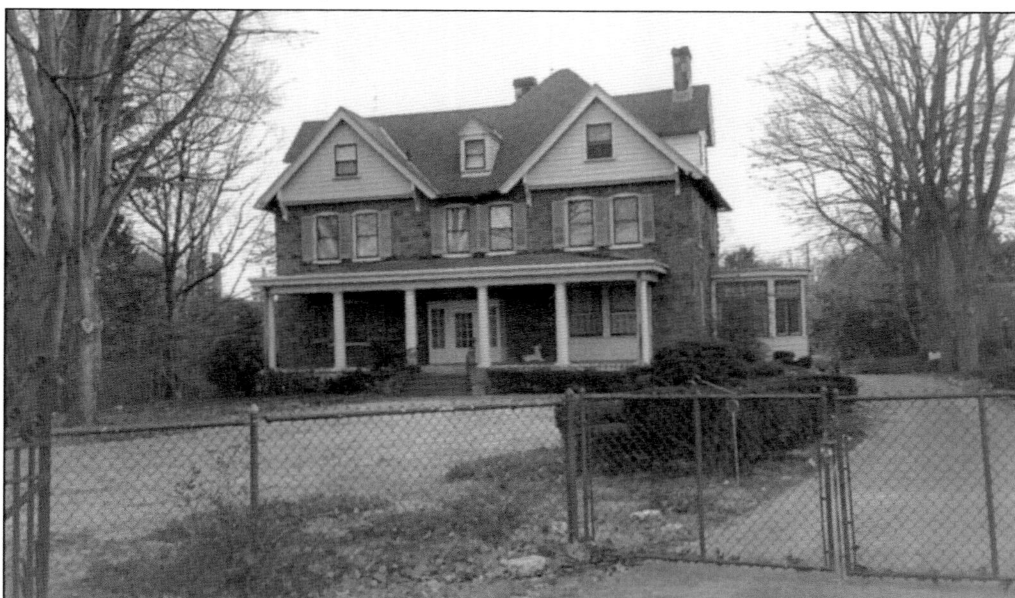

Another distinctive City Avenue property features this Colonial Revival with a one-story hipped roof porch and Tuscan columns. An early owner was Harry Harbaugh Lineaweaver, a coal operator and shipper who served as president of several companies. The house at one time featured tennis courts that were a favorite gathering place for recreation throughout the neighborhood. (Courtesy of OFC.)

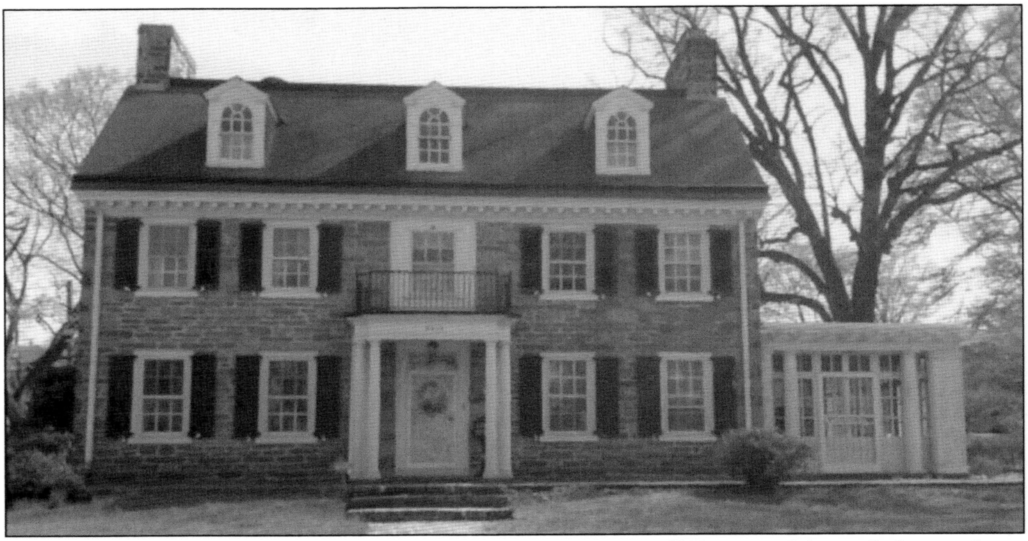

The estate of Quaker Wistar Morris was known as Green Hill Farm and formed the southern boundary of Overbrook Farms at Sixty-sixth Street. Morris's widow transferred the estate to a trust to develop the land, and Herman Wendell, this time partnered with Henry P. Wright, was hired for the development. They laid out Church Road from Lancaster Avenue to City Avenue in 1911, subdividing the property for suburban development in the manner of Overbrook Farms. Ernest Tustin, a former state senator and recorder of deeds for the City of Philadelphia, purchased the first property on Church Road that same year. (Courtesy of OFC.)

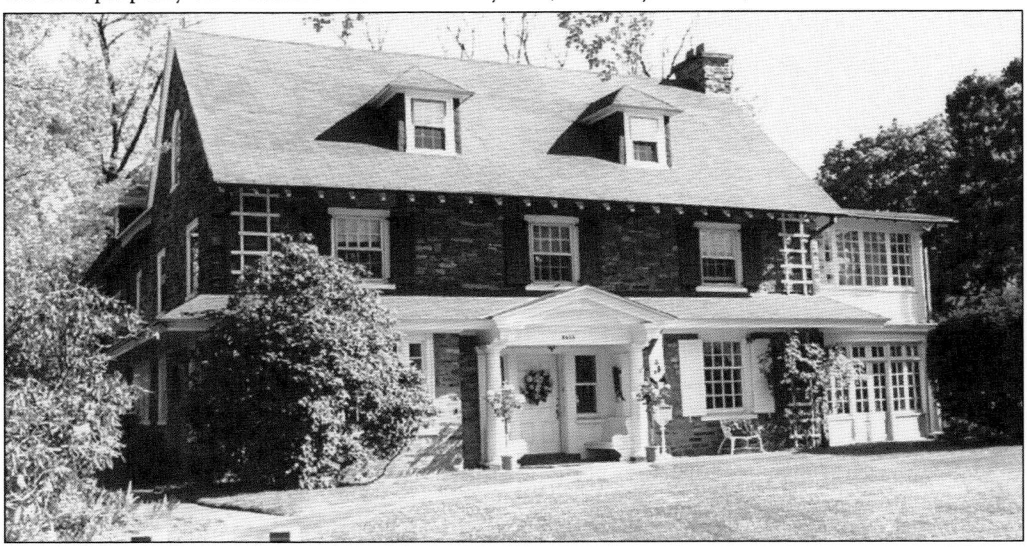

Another Colonial Revival home, this Church Road property affords a different look than its similarly designed cousin. The open eaves and the use of red, split fieldstone on the exterior are unusual in Overbrook Farms homes. Doorways were the focal point of Colonial facades; this doorway is emphasized by Tuscan columns with leaded glass windows on each side. The first- and second-floor porches deviate from its Colonial ancestors. Charles Wilson McNeely, a partner in the leather manufacturing company Perkins and McNeely, was an early owner of the property. Raymond J. Broderick, lieutenant governor of Pennsylvania from 1967 to 1971 and US district judge from 1971 until his death in 2000, was a more recent owner. (Courtesy of OFC.)

Three

Integral Institutions

Before the community had fully grown, it was graced by what remains its primary cornerstone, Overbrook Presbyterian Church. While structuring the new development, Wendell and Smith proposed giving land to Catholic, Episcopalian, and Methodist congregations. The two established that each congregation's church would be built of stone at a cost of no less than $25,000 within a year of receiving the land. Only the Catholics accepted this offer, erecting Our Lady of Lourdes Church. Founded on April 14, 1894, at the intersection of Lancaster Avenue and Sixty-third Street, it was dedicated on October 15, 1899. Thomas P. Lonsdale designed the Gothic Revival–style church, which was constructed of Port Deposit granite and Indiana limestone. Our Lady of Lourdes Church remains an active presence in the Overbrook Farms community.

Early in 1898, congregants presented a petition to the Episcopal diocese asking that a church be established in Overbrook Farms. A small Episcopal mission was formed and began holding services at Miss Sayward's School, located at 6055 Drexel Road. Land was purchased on Lancaster Avenue between Overbrook Avenue and Sherwood Road, and the Memorial Church of St. Paul was built. Designed by architect Frederick M. Mann, an MIT graduate who taught at the University of Pennsylvania, the church was built with local Wissahickon schist. It features stained-glass windows from several studios, including those of Louis Comfort Tiffany and Philadelphian Nicola d'Ascenzo. The low, decorated English Gothic building held its first service on Christmas Day in 1899.

Following decades of active community involvement, St. Paul's aging and dwindling congregation decided to dissolve, selling the building to the African Episcopal Church of St. Thomas. Originating in Philadelphia in 1792, St. Thomas is the oldest African American Episcopal Church in the United States. A chapel and stained-glass installations commemorating church founder Absalom Jones and important black saints and bishops were added in the late 1990s. The congregation continues a tradition of participation followed by all of the historic churches in Overbrook Farms.

Reflecting the diversity of the 21st century, these historic churches have been joined by a number of smaller religious institutions of many faiths.

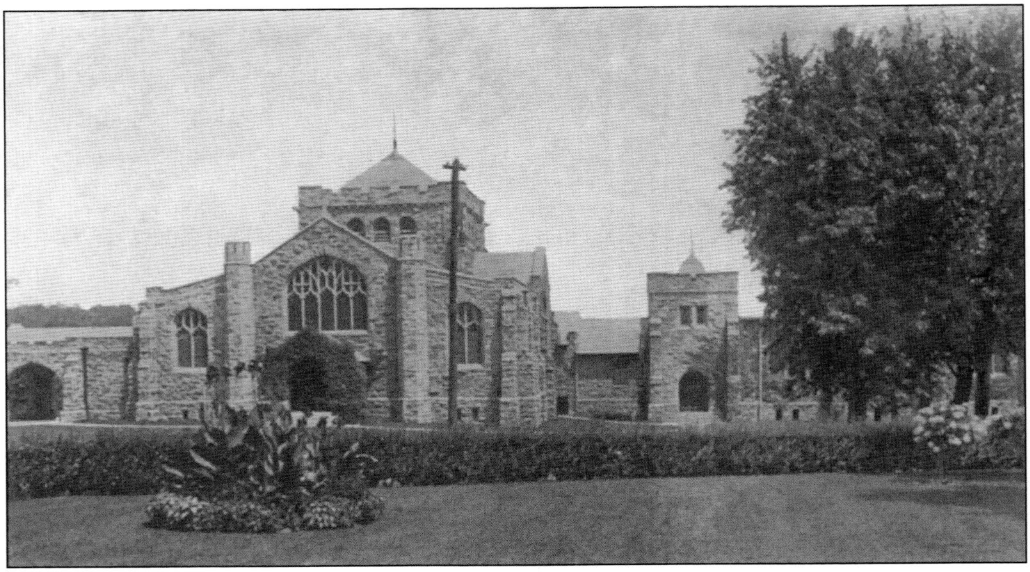

Mrs. William Simpson Jr. contributed $20,000 to erect the Episcopal church on Lancaster Avenue in memory of her husband. The Memorial Church of St. Paul held its first service in the new church on December 25, 1899. Continuing in the family tradition, the Simpsons' son W. Percy donated funds in his mother's memory for the 1920 construction of the rectory. (Courtesy of Ted Greenberg.)

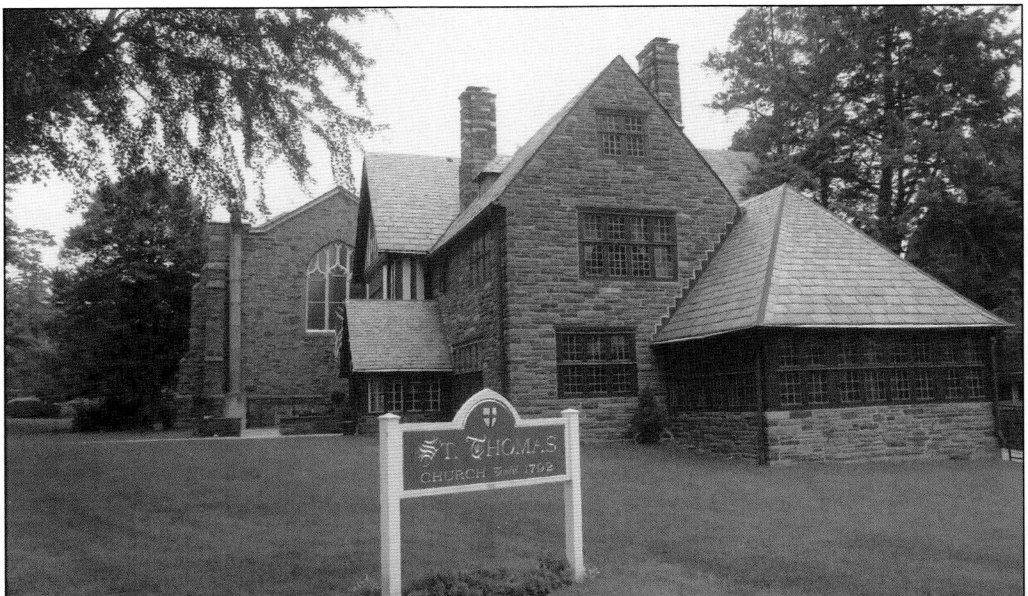

With its rich history in Philadelphia, the African Episcopal Church of St. Thomas is a fitting steward of the historic English Gothic church building formerly known as the Memorial Church of St. Paul. Since arriving there in the mid-1990s, St. Thomas has renovated the sanctuary, added commemorative stained-glass windows that reflect their congregation and founder's history, and renovated both the parish house, built in 1900, and the rectory (seen in the foreground). (Courtesy of Ted Greenberg.)

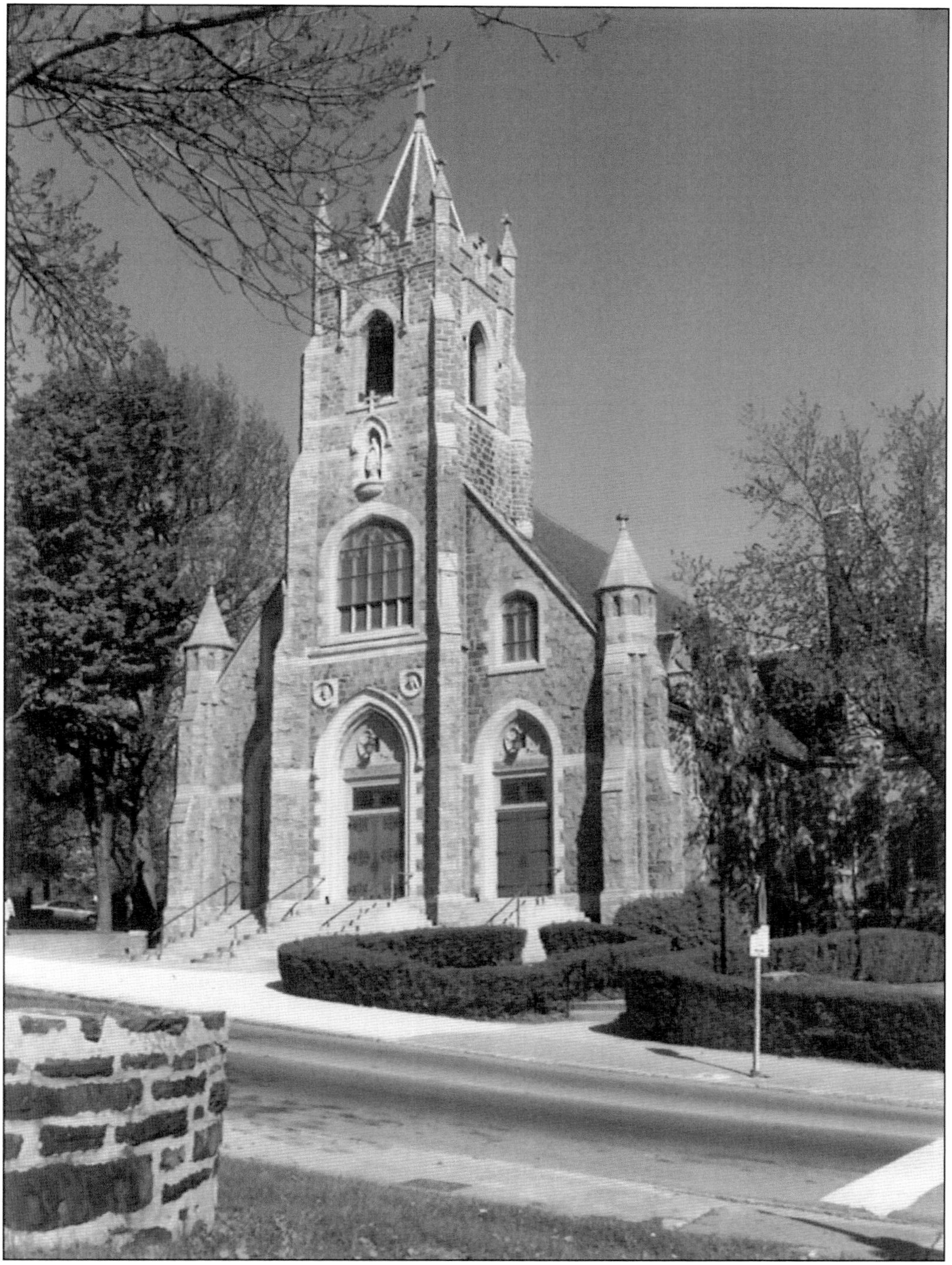

Our Lady of Lourdes Church is located on a Woodbine Avenue slope between Lancaster Avenue and Sixty-third Street, before those two major roads intersect to form a triangle. As a result, this church is a major Overbrook Farms landmark. Developers Wendell and Smith donated the land upon which the church is situated. Its Gothic spires and devoted congregants are visible from many directions. (Courtesy of Ted Greenberg.)

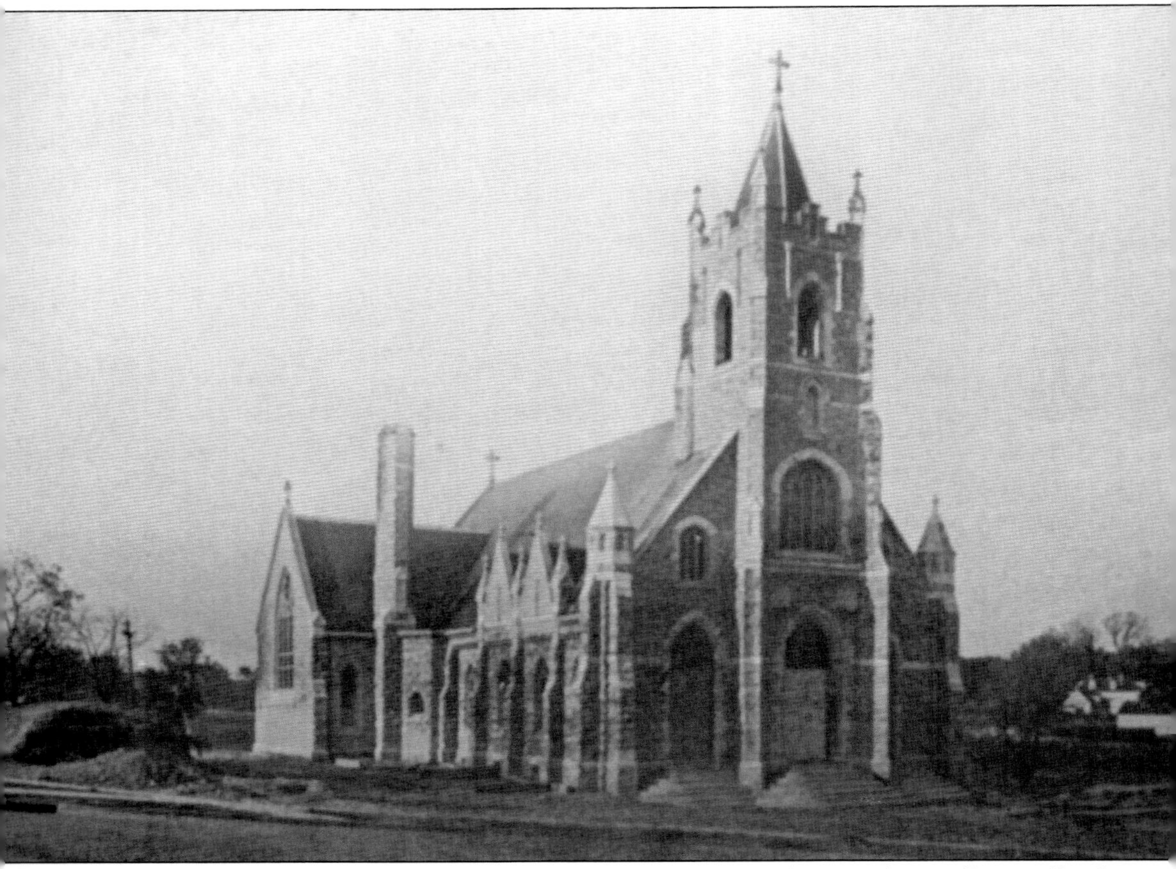

When he first learned of the new parish in 1894, Merion resident Hugh F. Sullivan offered to donate $2,000 towards the new church if it were named Our Lady of Lourdes. The archdiocese accepted his generous gift and the new name. The Reverend James A. Mullin was named the founding pastor and conducted services for the new parish at the nearby Saint Charles Seminary until the basement church opened in September 1895. The fully completed church was dedicated on October 15, 1899. The rectory was built in 1896, and a parish school was added in 1908. The Sisters of Mercy took possession of a convent built next to the school on August 15, 1914, thus completing construction for the church complex. (Courtesy of Ted Greenberg.)

Dating back to the 1700s, Lancaster Pike and City Line was an important crossroads. It was a strategic location of one of the many tollbooths on Lancaster Pike. As interest grew in developing this area in the 1880s, a meeting was held at the home of Wistar Morris to discuss the formation of a Presbyterian church. Though a Quaker, Morris supported the congregation and purchased land that he then donated to the church for this intended purpose. The cornerstone was laid in October 1889. The church, designed by Addison Hutton and built at the cost of $11,800, was dedicated in February 1890. A pipe organ was installed in 1899. (Courtesy of Overbrook Presbyterian Church.)

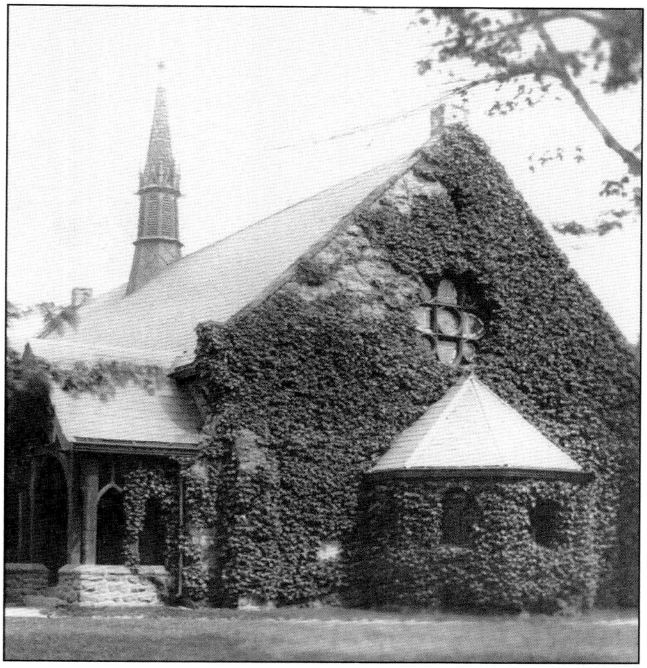

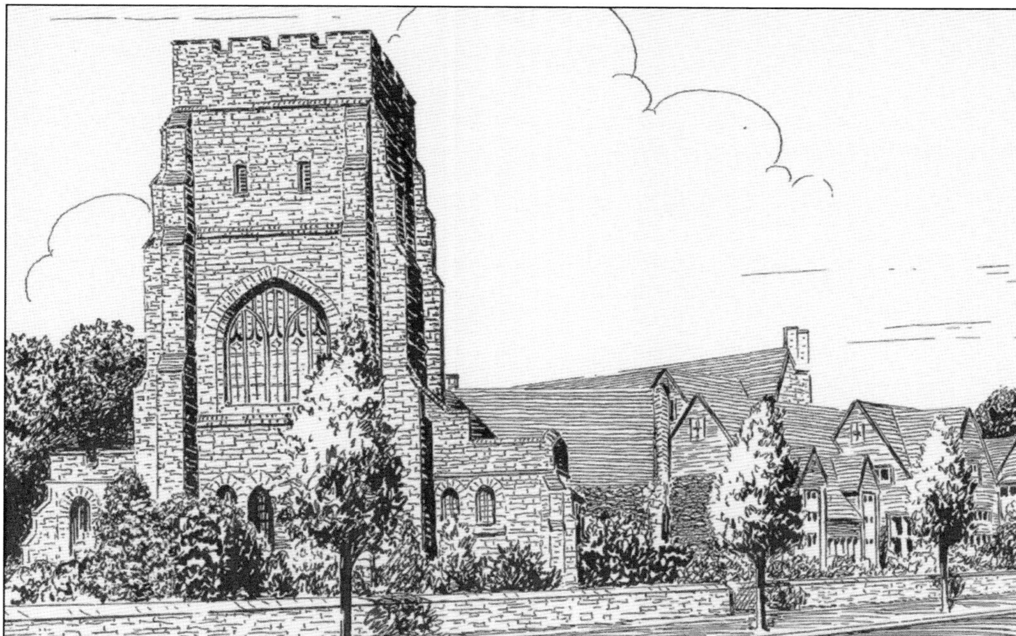

Church membership grew quickly as Overbrook Farms developed. Warren Powers Laird, dean of the School of Architecture at the University of Pennsylvania and an Overbrook Farms resident, oversaw an architectural competition for an addition to the church in 1901. Architects William and Walter Price won the competition, and the addition was completed in 1905, adding a tower facing City Avenue. The church doubled in size with this addition. (Courtesy of Overbrook Presbyterian Church.)

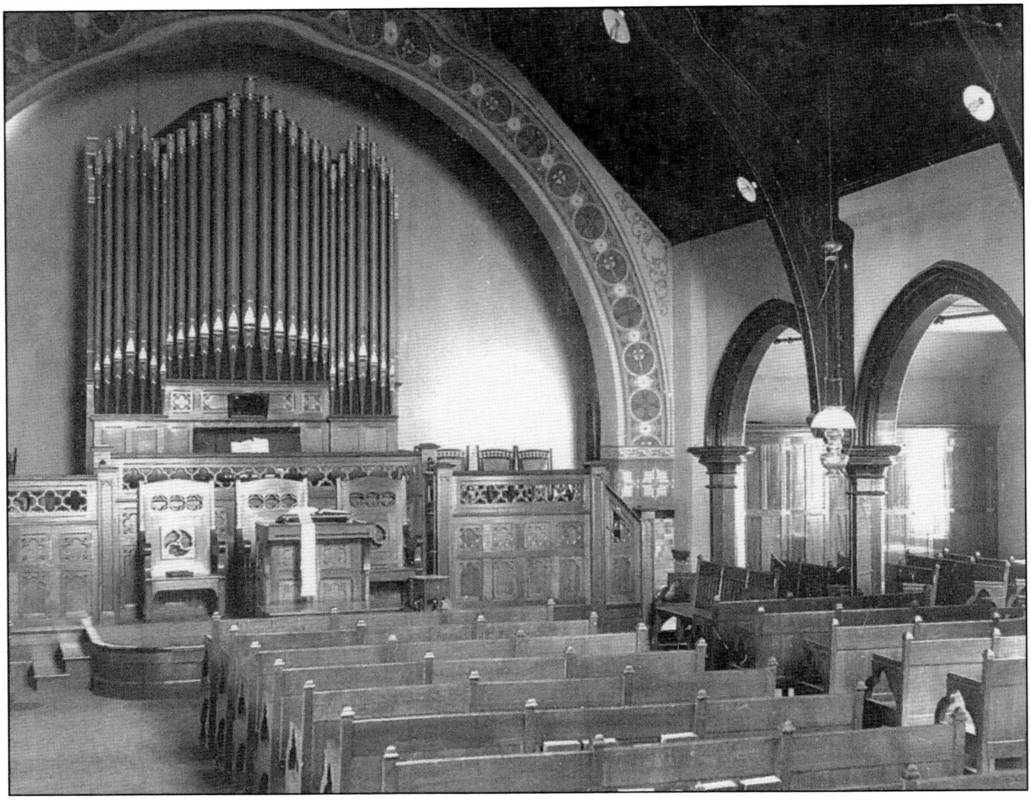

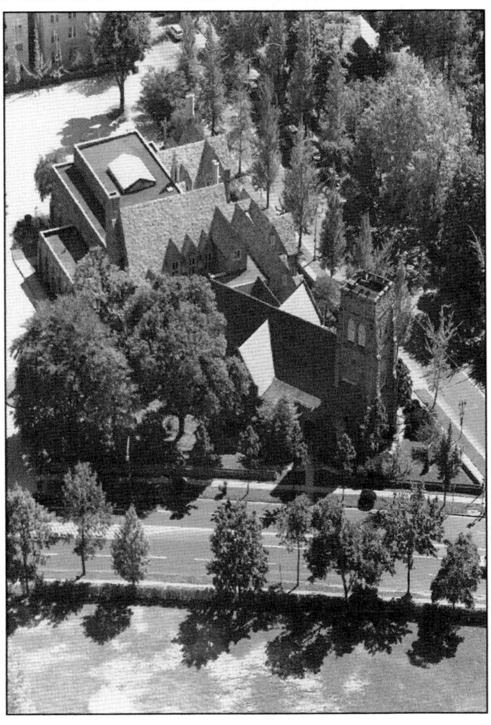

The present church house was built in 1925 and was designed to blend sympathetically with the existing church, using low gabled block in the manner of English churches. The sanctuary decorations include carvings by master woodcarver Erik Jansson and a large memorial window designed by Willet Stained Glass Company of Philadelphia. Another notable window, found in the west transept, was designed in 1908 by D'Ascenzo Studios of Philadelphia. (Courtesy of Overbrook Presbyterian Church.)

The expanded footprint of the Overbrook Presbyterian Church and its visible position at the busy crossroads of Lancaster and City Avenues is apparent in this aerial photograph. Perhaps photographed in the 1930s, this image captures the area before the removal of trees for the widening of both of these major roads. The widening of Lancaster Avenue also caused the removal of a large porte cochere that had been constructed during the renovations of 1905 and the building of a stone retaining wall. (Courtesy of Overbrook Presbyterian Church.)

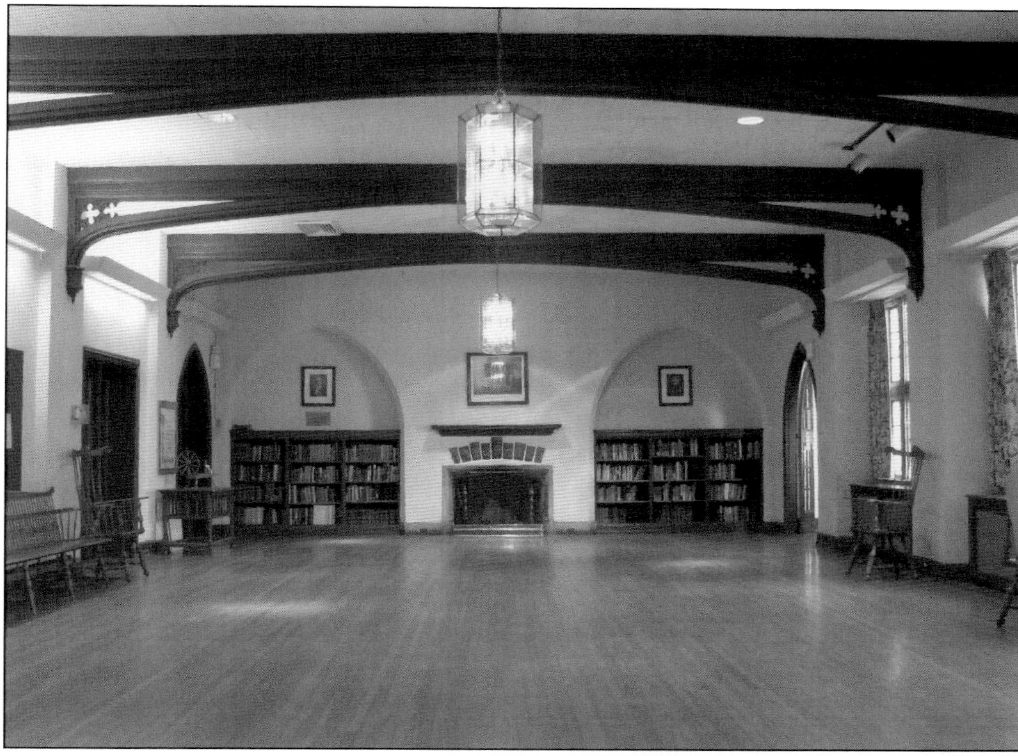

Overbrook Presbyterian Church is an active place. Not only does it host a full calendar of events for members of the church congregation, but it is also home to organizations as diverse as the Overbrook Farms Club, Narberth Community Theater, a weekly farmers' market, and a very well-established preschool. It is not unusual to see a full parking lot or groups posing for pictures commemorating their activities. (Courtesy of Adjoa Love-Dorsey.)

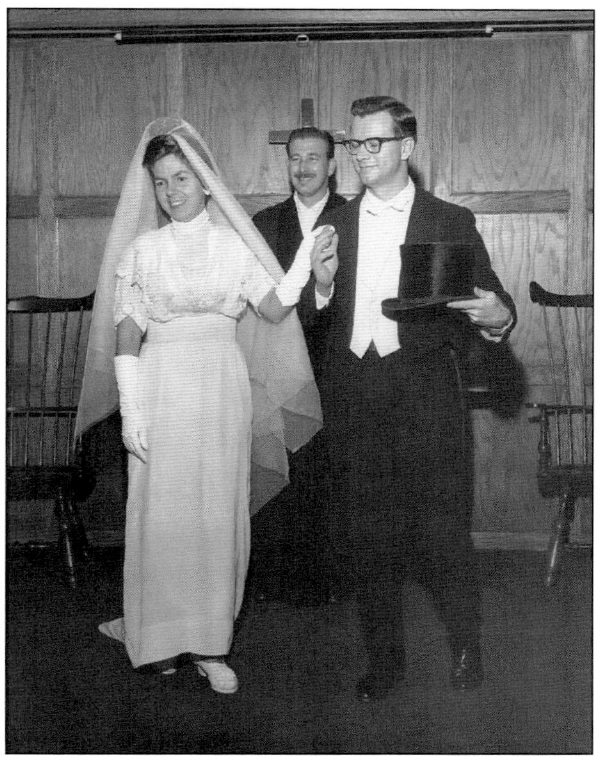

Residents and friends of Overbrook Farms respect and honor the history of the neighborhood and those who developed its grand houses and traditions. So, it is no surprise that when the Overbrook Presbyterian Church celebrated its centennial with a gala dinner, many of those who attended were inspired to dress in attire reminiscent of the Victorian era. (Courtesy of Overbrook Presbyterian Church.)

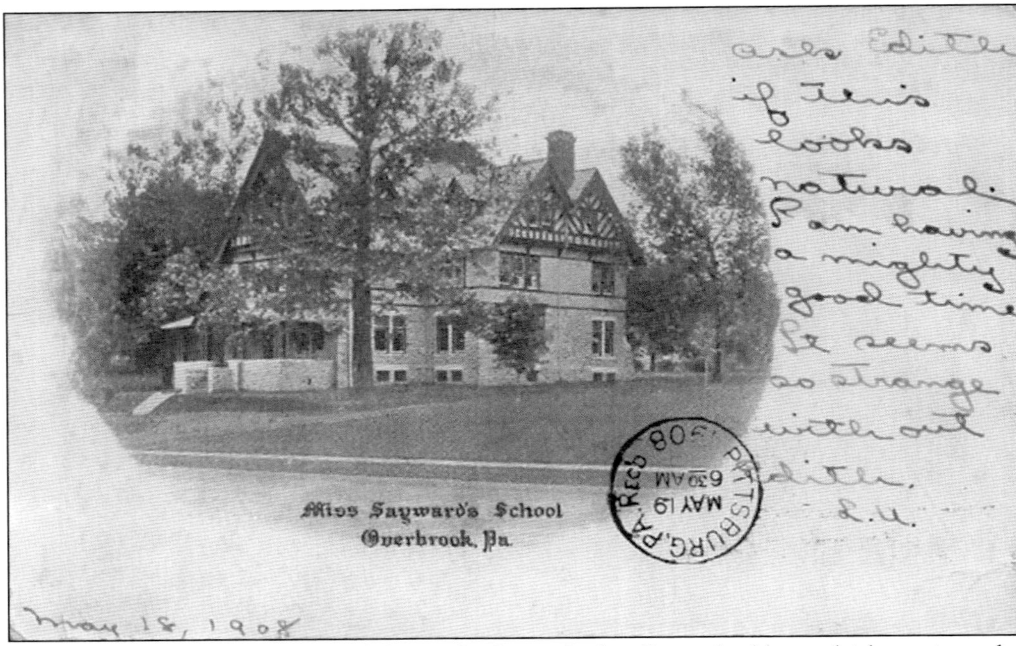

In 1895, William L. Price designed this Tudor Revival schoolhouse building, which was intended to look like a private residence for the Overbrook School, a day and boarding school for girls. The school was renamed Miss Sayward's School about 1903. The school building also served as a meeting place for community activities, including services of the new Episcopalian congregation until their new structure was constructed. (Courtesy of Ted Greenberg.)

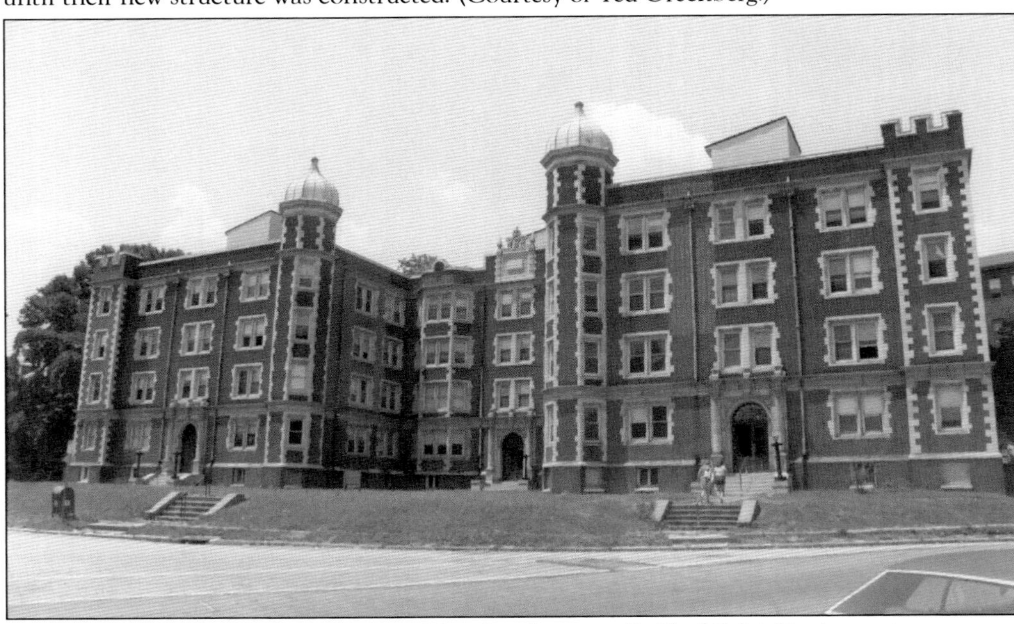

On May 25, 1909, Drexel Apartments of Overbrook, controlled by J.B. McHugh, was incorporated with the purposes of buying, leasing, and maintaining an apartment house or houses. Soon after, the corporation purchased property at 6301–6315 Overbrook Avenue, across from the Overbrook Station, and erected a Tudor Revival–style apartment building. (Courtesy of the OFC.)

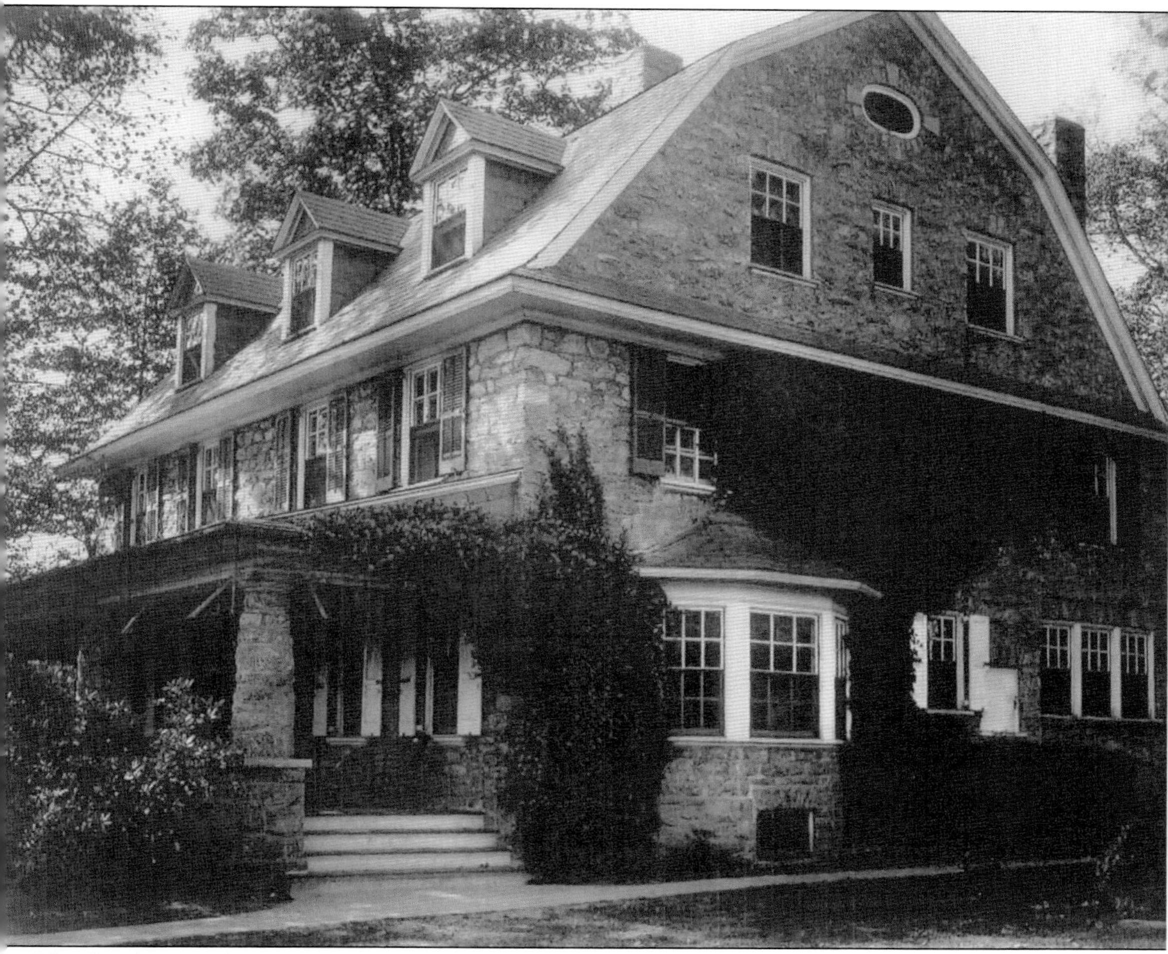

This lovely stone home at Sixty-sixth Street and Overbrook Avenue, across from Morris Park, was owned by Dr. and Mrs. Clyde A. Heller in the early 1900s. Anna Purves Heller, inspired by the growing interest in the healthful benefits of access to nature and educational experiments in Europe, founded and operated an innovative open-air elementary school for boys and girls at the rear of this home. (Courtesy of Dorothy Riday.)

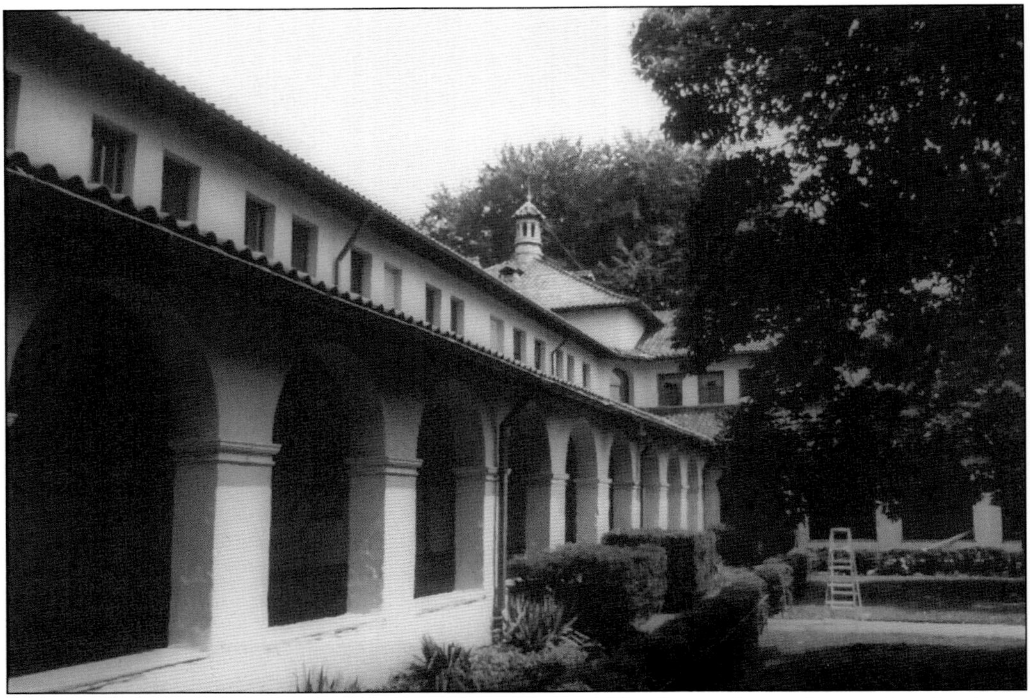

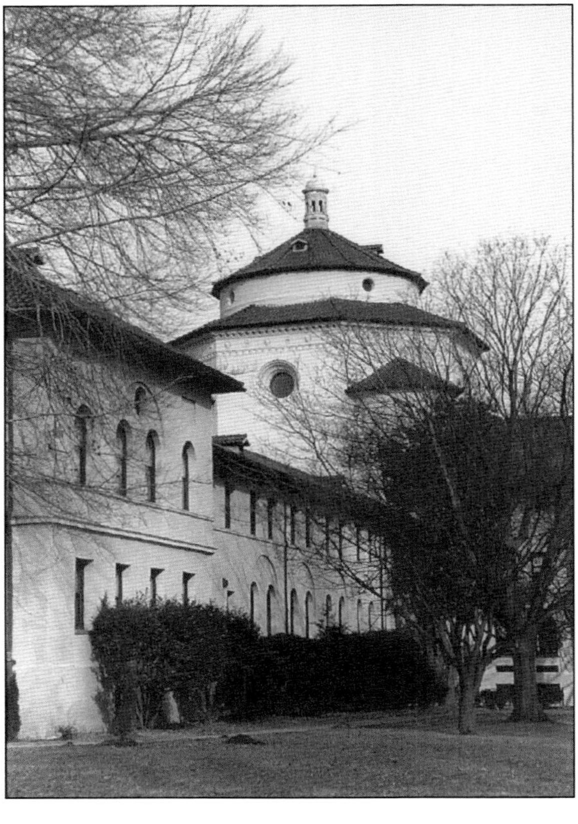

The Pennsylvania Institution for the Instruction of the Blind was founded in 1832 by Julius Friedlander. Moving from its original Center City location to a new campus in Overbrook Farms, the school assumed its residency in a Spanish Renaissance–style building with two interior cloisters in 1899, and the campus was renamed the Overbrook School for the Blind. Designed by the firm of Cope and Stewardson, the architecture was so innovative that the school and its architects were invited by the US government to display their plans at the Paris Exposition in 1900. The campus, though not part of the National Historic District, forms the eastern boundary of Overbrook Farms and has been a significant neighbor through the decades. (Both, courtesy of OFC.)

The Overbrook Fire Department, Engine 54, is notable as the third-oldest firehouse in Philadelphia. Erected in 1907, it has never moved from its original location at Sixty-third Street and Lancaster Avenue. (Courtesy of the City of Philadelphia Archives.)

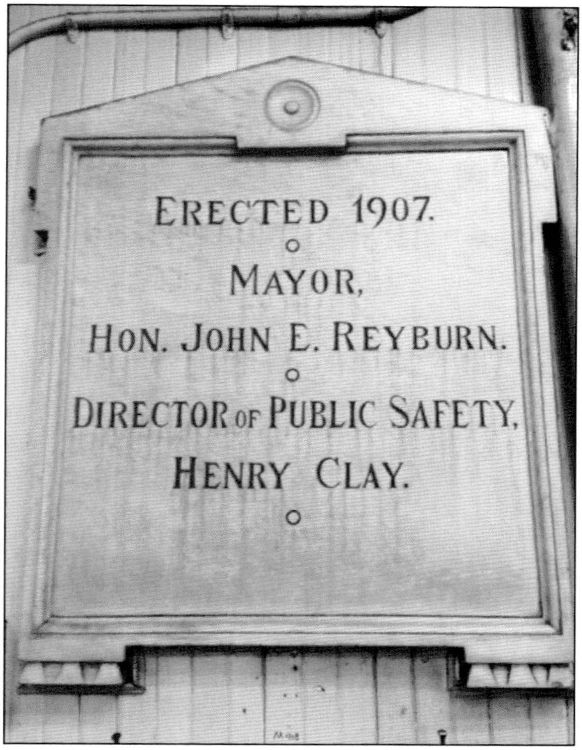

Early days saw the station fitted with a hook and ladder wagon and a horse-drawn steamer pump. The steepest streets, Woodbine Avenue and Drexel Road, required that engines travel up Sixty-third Street and cross City Line (recently christened City Avenue) in order to climb the grade and attend to the fire. Some young residents assisted with pushing these engines up the hills. (Courtesy of the City of Philadelphia Archives.)

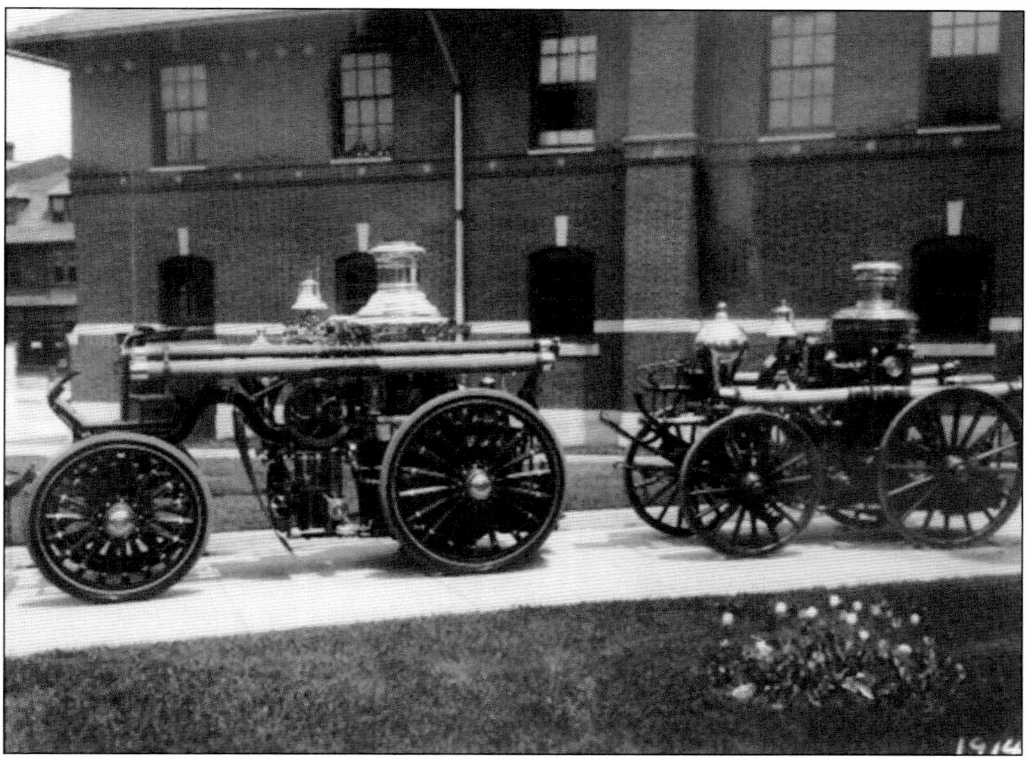

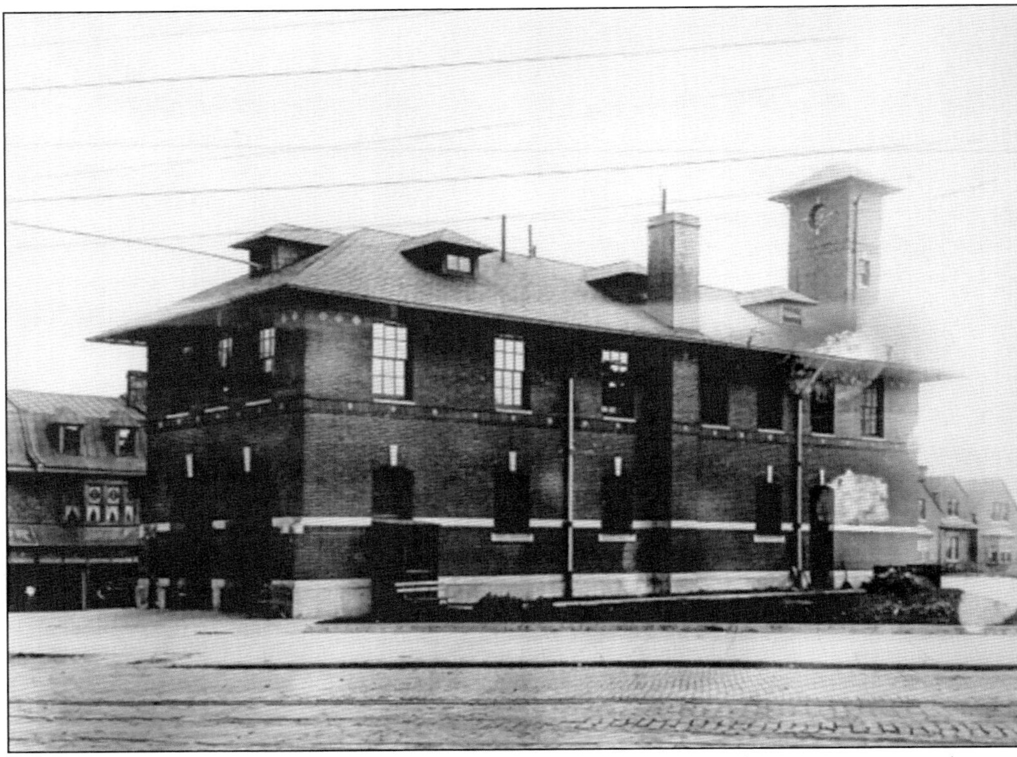

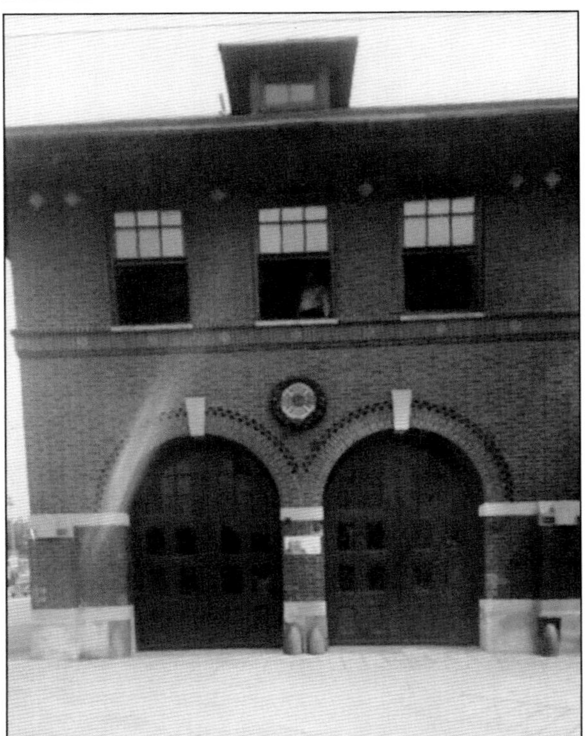

Two years after its erection, and shortly after the fire company moved into their newly opened station, the area witnessed its largest fire. The firemen were forced to call for help from the West Philadelphia companies, but the Overbrook Garage and several cars stored in its Sixty-third Street and Overbrook Avenue location burned to the ground. (Courtesy of the City of Philadelphia Archives.)

The original firehouse had two doors for the horse-drawn steamer pump. In later years, those doors were retrofitted to accommodate the new fire trucks and automatic opening doors. (Courtesy of the City of Philadelphia Archives.)

Four

Overbrook Farms Businesses

Commerce clustered around the Sixty-third Street corridor, adjacent to the rail tracks. Perhaps the most popular in appeal was a post office located at the Overbrook railroad station until 1917. The station agent served as postmaster. Just outside the train station facing Sixty-third Street was the neighborhood's first store, Lafferty's, later joined by the adjacent Hines bakery. The second floor above Lafferty's held the well-known community gathering spot Overbrook Hall, where in addition to social and cultural events, OFC board business was conducted. Dr. Theodore Campbell's drugstore opened nearby.

Many people owned their own horses, but others hired them from Herald's Livery Stable, located on the corner of Woodbine Avenue and Sixty-third Street. And while the rails afforded many residents an easy walk home, taxi companies had their beginnings in these horse-and-buggy days. Their hacks were familiar sights at the Overbrook railroad station, awaiting possible riders. Eventually, restaurants, large apartment buildings, medical and dental offices, and real estate and service offices would align themselves along Sixty-third Street.

Critical to the neighborhood was a facility that served Overbrook Farms from 1894 until its demolition in 1976—the Overbrook Farms Steam Heat Plant, located at Woodbine Avenue and Upland Way.

Scattered among the community were other businesses and services, including the 52,000-square-foot, three-story brick building erected for the Raub Supply Company in 1927. The plumbing and heating supplier served active construction in the vicinity of Overbrook Farms. A two-story, 8,000-square-foot addition was erected a decade later. Designed by architect Isadore Levin, a Russian immigrant who studied at Central High School and Drexel Institute, it facilitated a rail spur line alongside the building to receive deliveries from freight trains. Over the years, a number of businesses used those successively vacated buildings—including Nevins Drug Company; Philco Distributors, Inc.; Pennsylvania Company for Estates; Scriptomatic, Inc.; and a small firm for the manufacture and repair of computers and electronics—before it again became vacant and was subsequently redeveloped by contemporary visionaries.

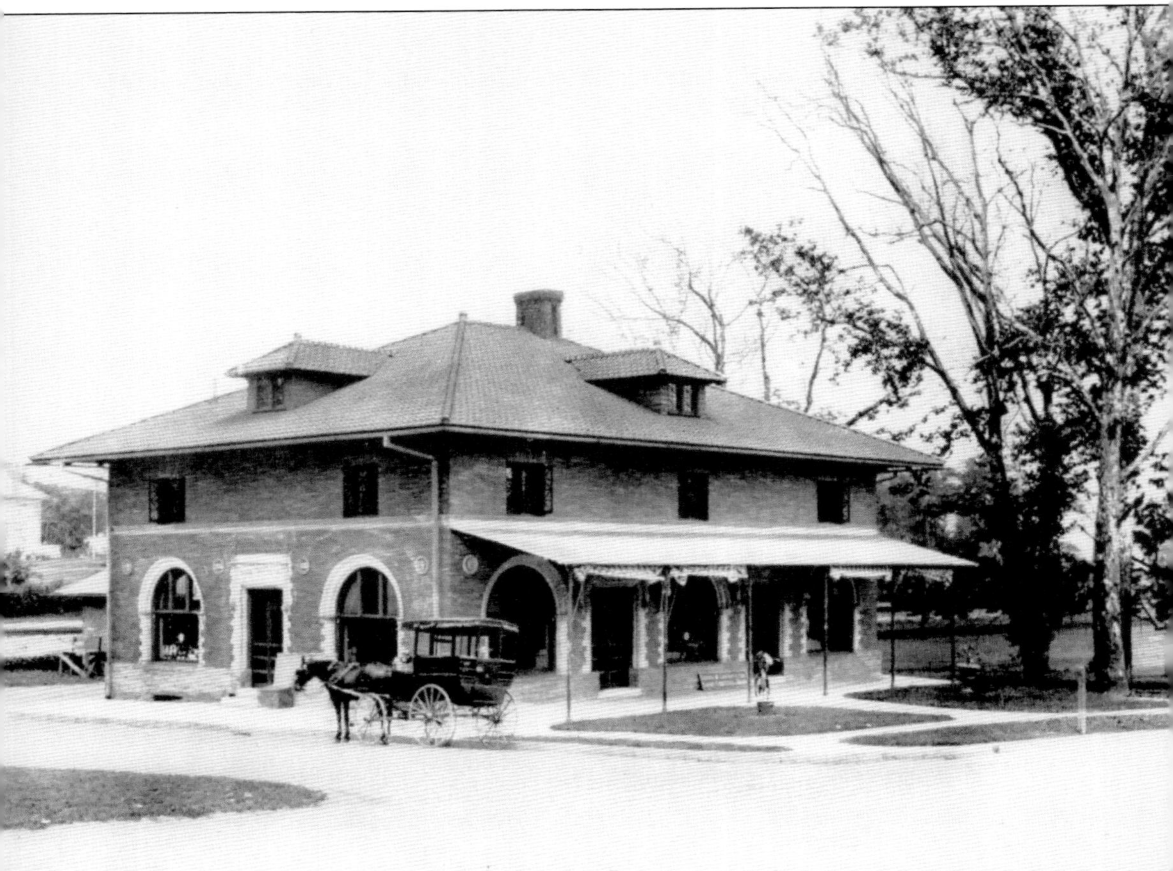

The first commercial building was Lafferty's Market, constructed in 1894 and located along Sixty-third Street near the Overbrook Station. This Pompeian brick Italianate-style building still operates today. (Courtesy of Radnor Historical Society.)

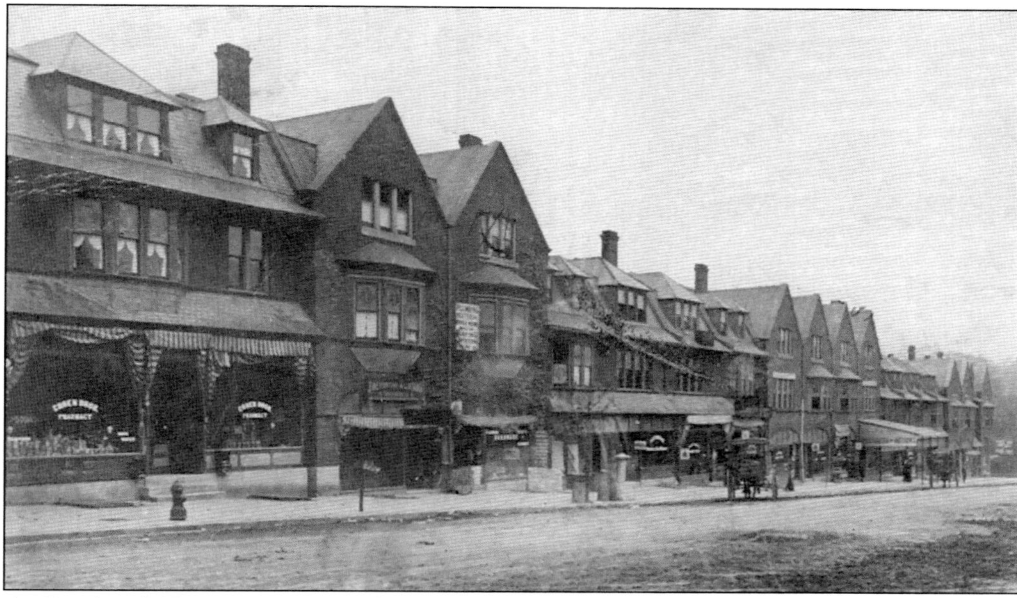

As Overbrook Farms grew, many shops aligned down the length of Sixty-third Street serviced the new community. (Courtesy of Ted Greenberg.)

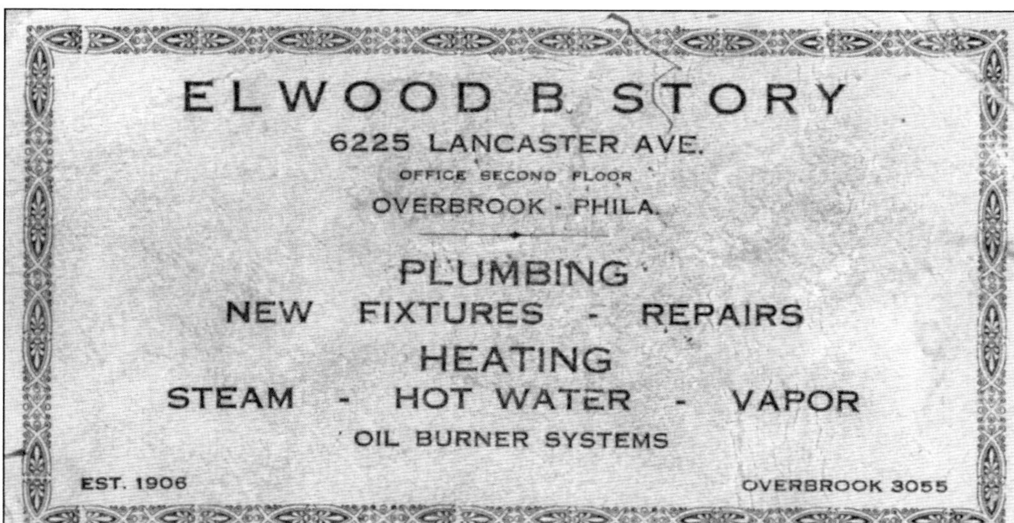

Many of the contractors and other businesses advertised their services. Established in 1905, Elwood B. Story was a plumbing and household supplies general business. The business serviced and supplied homes in the area. (Courtesy of Ted Greenberg.)

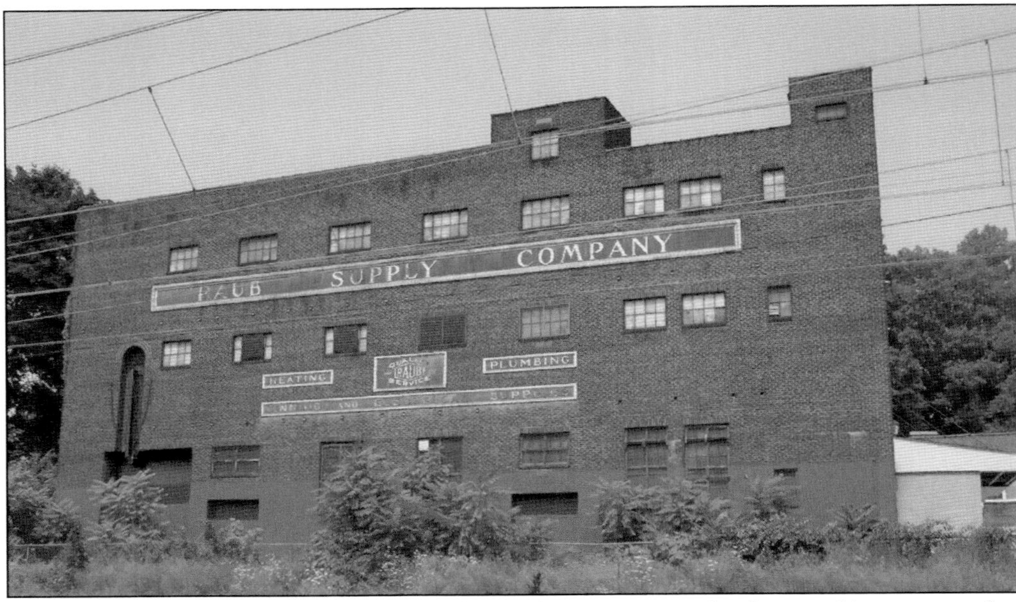

Located along the railroad tracks, the Raub Supply Company, a plumbing and heating supplier, served active construction in the vicinity of Overbrook Farms. The complex was built in 1927. (Courtesy of Blake Ingram.)

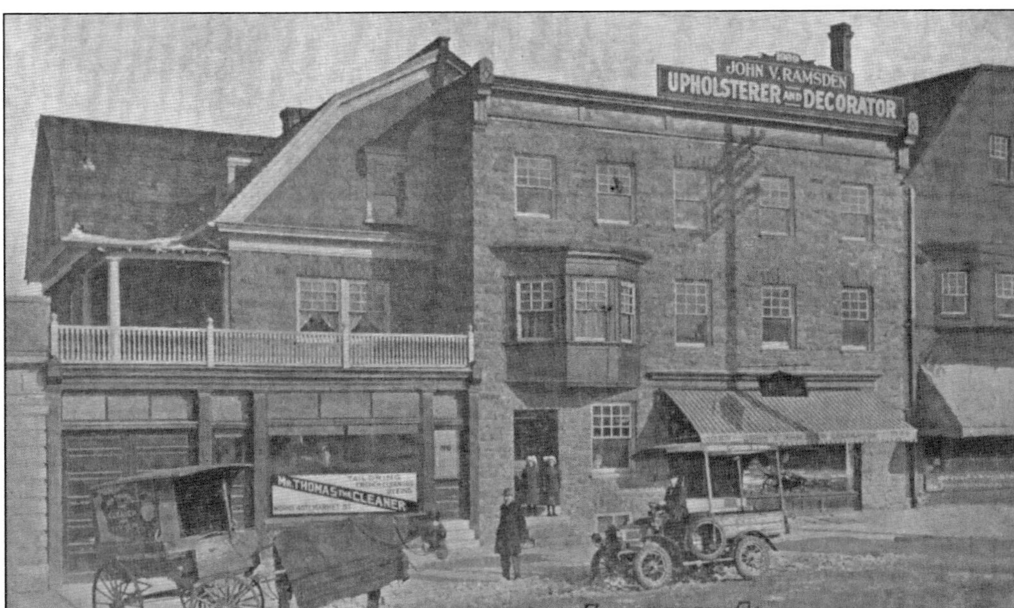

Upholsterer John V. Ramsden found work in many of the Overbrook Farms parlors, delivering finished commissions to those who ordered from his business. (Courtesy of Ted Greenberg.)

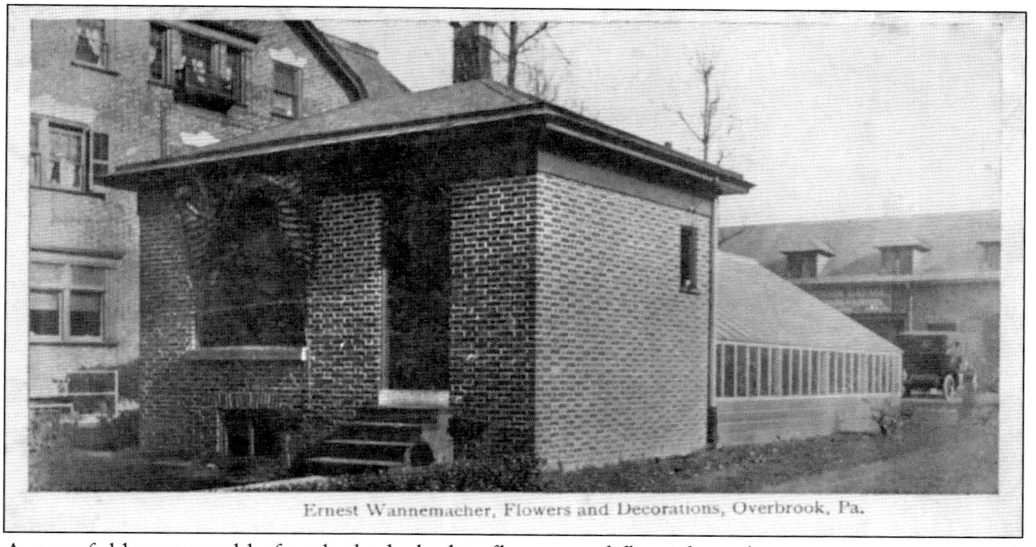

A graceful home would often be bedecked in flowers and flourishes when guests were expected. Ernest Wannemacher was ready with a supply. (Courtesy of Ted Greenberg.)

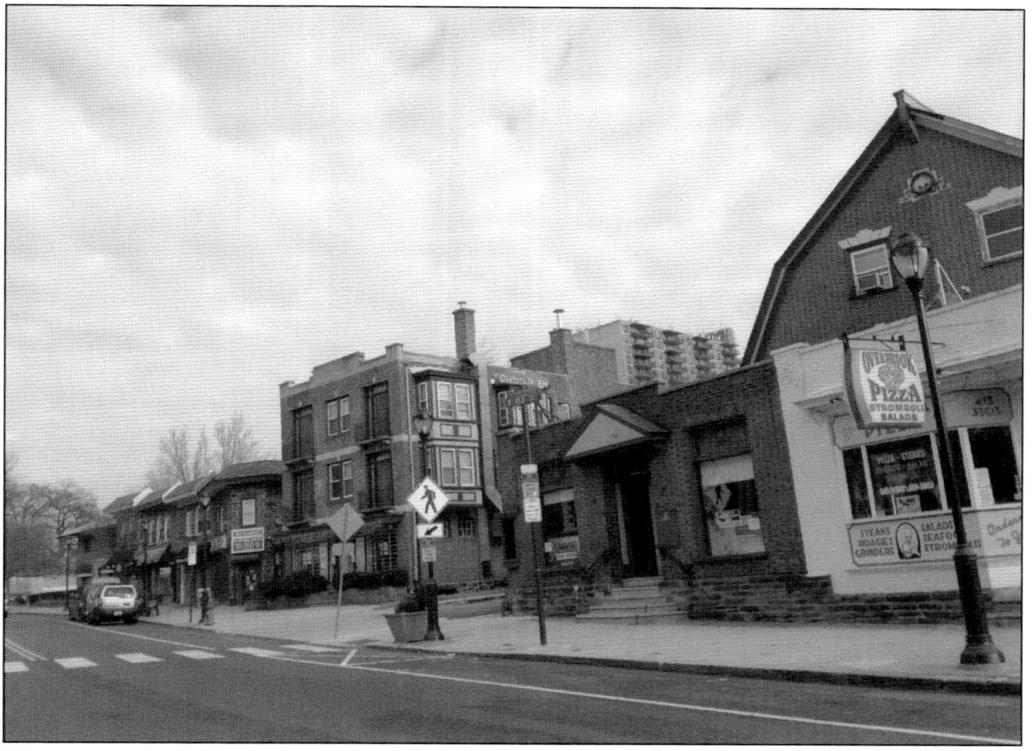

The existing businesses along Sixty-third Street continue to serve Overbrook Farms residents. Some have been at their location for more than 33 years, including Overbrook Pizza, actor Will Smith's favorite pizza shop. Another, Bill's Market, has been providing groceries for more than 30 years. (Courtesy of Victoria Wilson.)

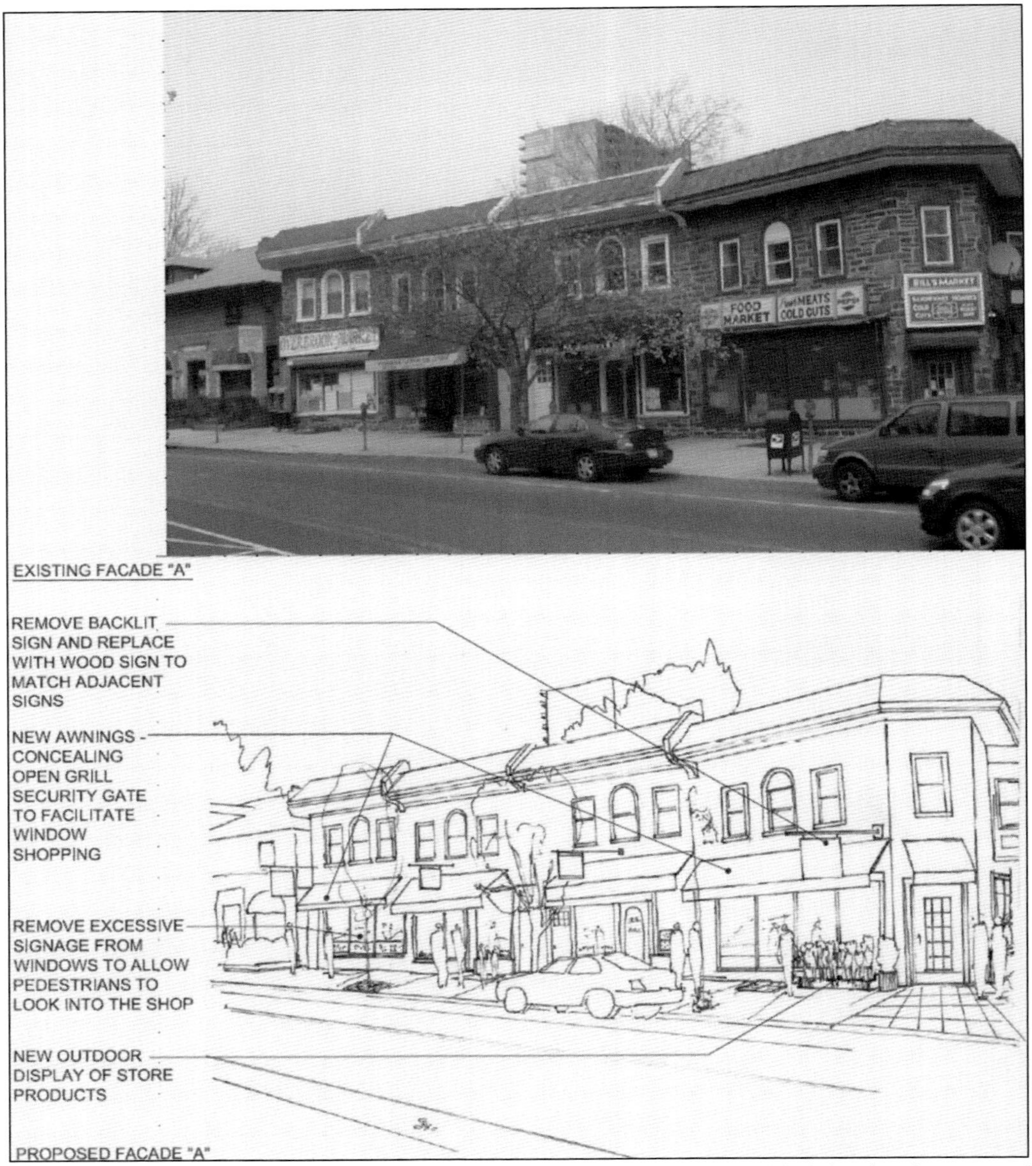

Grant-funded support from the Community Design Collaborative enabled the development of a master-plan strategy for commercial-corridor improvement of Sixty-third Street. This image shows the recent Sixty-third Street facade with a rendering of proposed changes, some of which have already been implemented. (Courtesy of the OFC.)

Five

Sportin' Life

Emblematic of the Gay Nineties, Overbrook Farms residents had their roles to play in making sure their homes and gathering places could be used in what was a celebrated era of galas, dances, lectures, musical revues, masquerade balls, teas, and other forms of collective entertainment. Adults were as eager for spaces to gather socially and enjoy recreation as their children were to experience an open-air school, dance lessons, and neighborhood friendships.

A number of Overbrook Farms households were attended by servants, many of whom were of Irish or African descent. Their local entertainment would often feature trolley dances, where the streets at Sixty-third Street and Lancaster Avenue were roped off and housed a band in a trolley car.

As early as the 1890s, a small tennis club began, which whetted appetites for more outdoor activity options. Leased land allowed for an athletic field that accommodated tennis, cricket, quoits, and croquet, and on the Fourth of July, sponsored fireworks paid for by subscribing residents. Not long after, a demand for a golf club emerged, and couples soon began taking to the links. Ah, but the bicycle captivated everyone, and the Wheel Club snared most of the neighborhood's residents. Never a nation to avoid competition, local residents even sponsored bicycle races. Of course, winter created opportunities for sledding and skating and, afterwards, the thrill of cocoa and an open fire to warm cold extremities.

During the horse-and-buggy days, the most traveled and passable roads were located near tollbooths. A great pastime was hitching up teams to travel the farthest distances in the suburbs without paying tolls. Rough, ready, and willing to jostle were the only rules of that game. Families also hired huge horse-drawn wagons from Kennedy Farms for moonlight hayrides.

Because a thick ribbon of forested land bordered the Sixty-sixth Street edge of Overbrook Farms, there were ready and proximate opportunities to hike, ride horses, and otherwise enjoy nature.

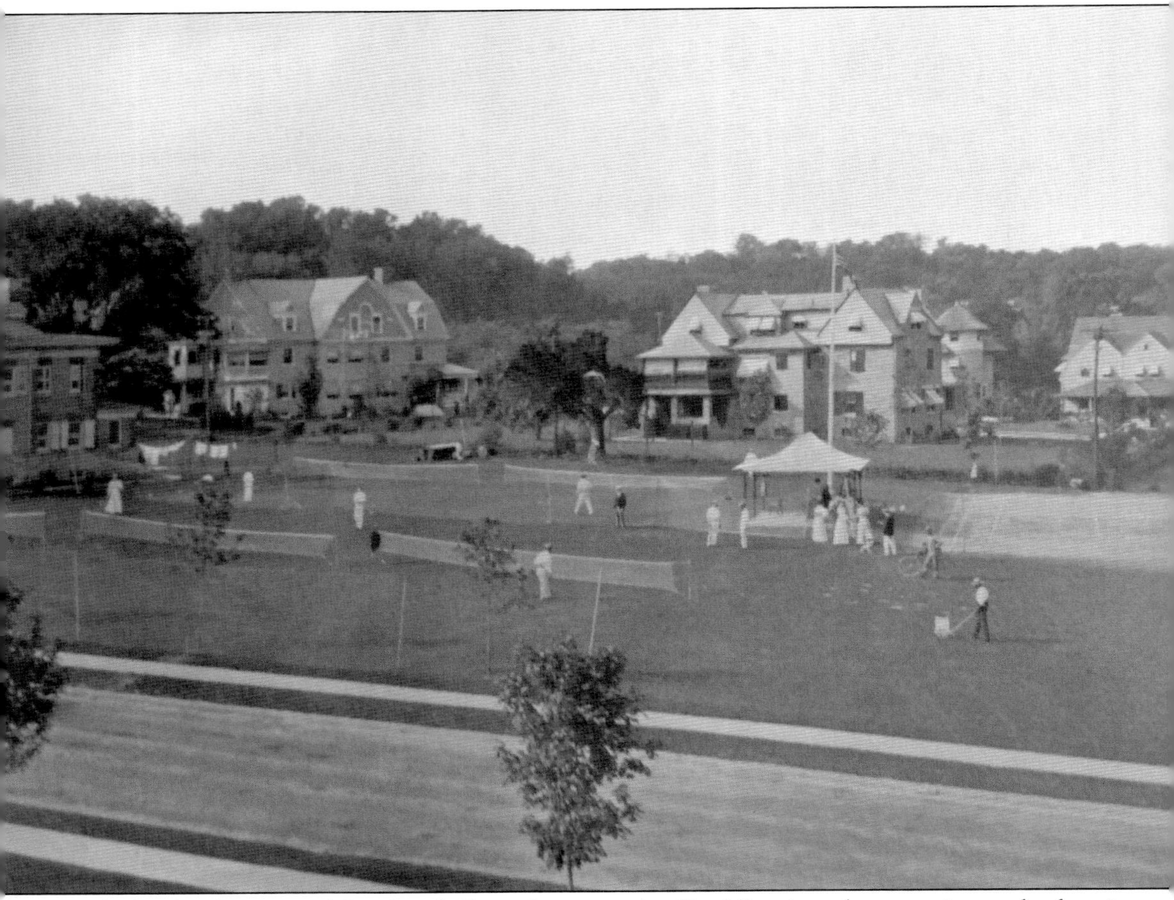

The development of Overbrook Farms began in the Gay Nineties, when tennis was the favorite sport, so a tennis club soon formed. Courts located on Drexel Road hosted many spirited matches. As interest grew, the Overbrook Farms Club sought subscriptions to lease property at Upland Way and Woodbine Avenue. An athletic field sported five tennis courts, a cricket field, and spaces for quoits and croquet. (Courtesy of the OFC.)

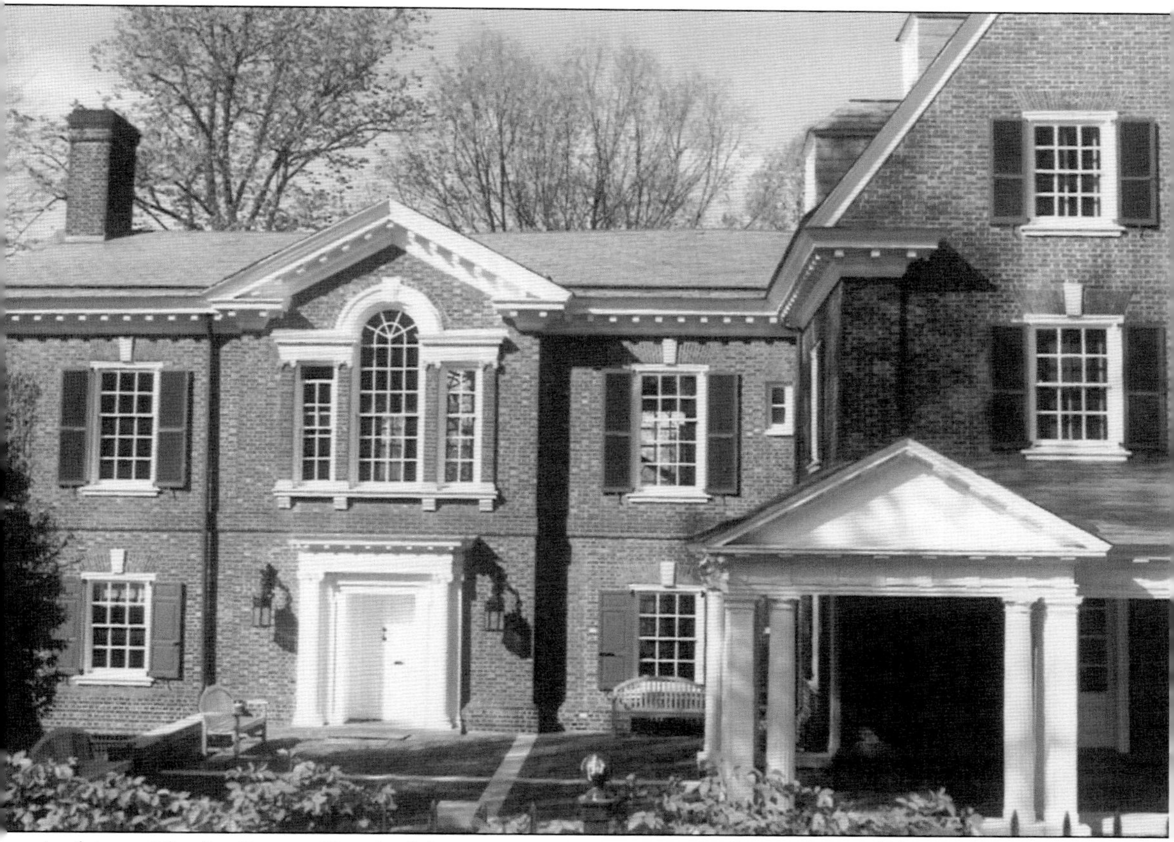

Architect Charles Barton Keen's elaborate commission is tucked into the middle of Lancaster Avenue. Its hand-painted ivy-leaf-motif skylight lent Ivy Hall its name. Judge Charles Y. Audenreid, an early owner, served the Court of Common Pleas from 1896 to 1917. He served as vice provost of the Law Academy of Philadelphia and was a director of the Athenaeum. (Courtesy of the OFC.)

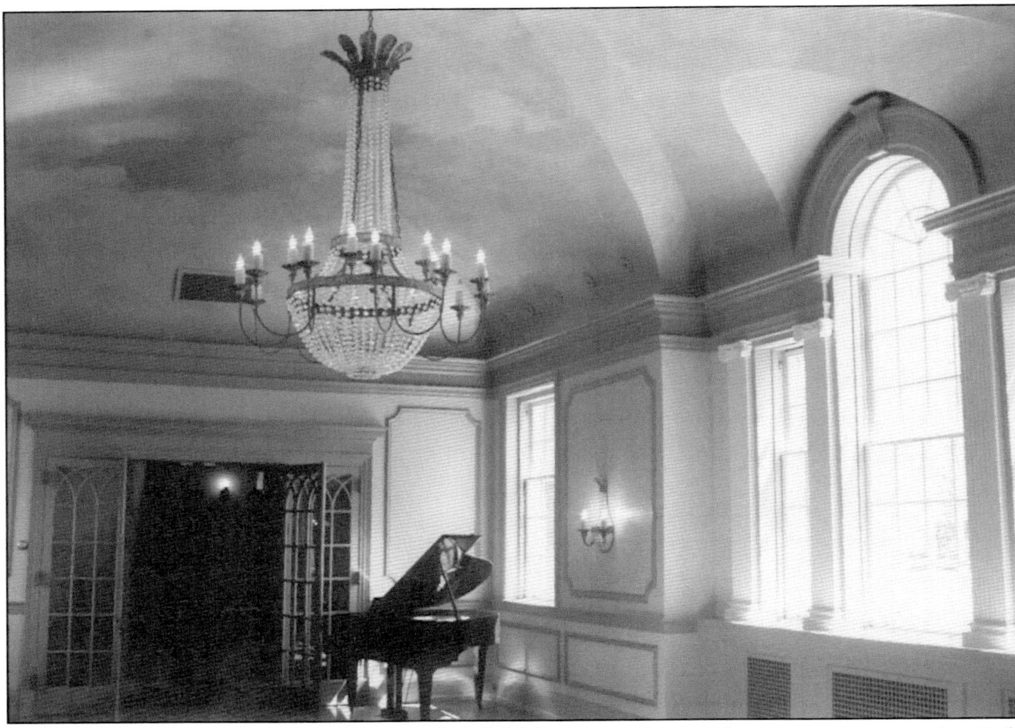

The famed ballroom wing was constructed in 1926. It attracted a significant arts pioneer to Ivy Hall. Dance prodigy Florence Cowanova taught her first class at age 11. When moving to New York, the family fell in love with Philadelphia. Cowanova opened her first studios downtown beginning at the tender age of 18. She later moved her studio to Ivy Hall. (Both, courtesy of the OFC.)

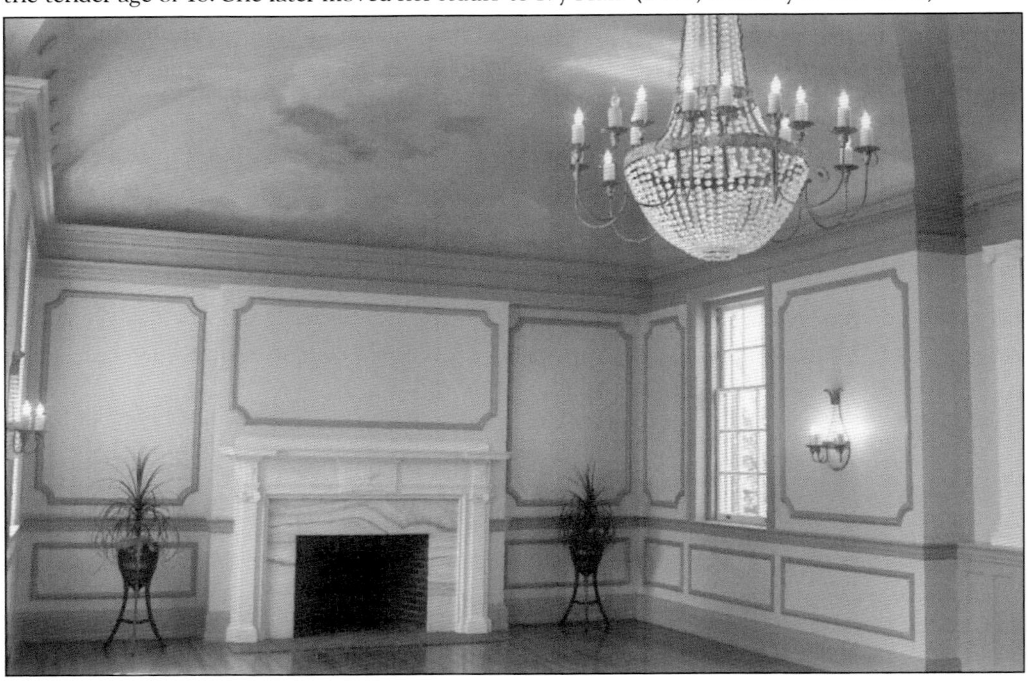

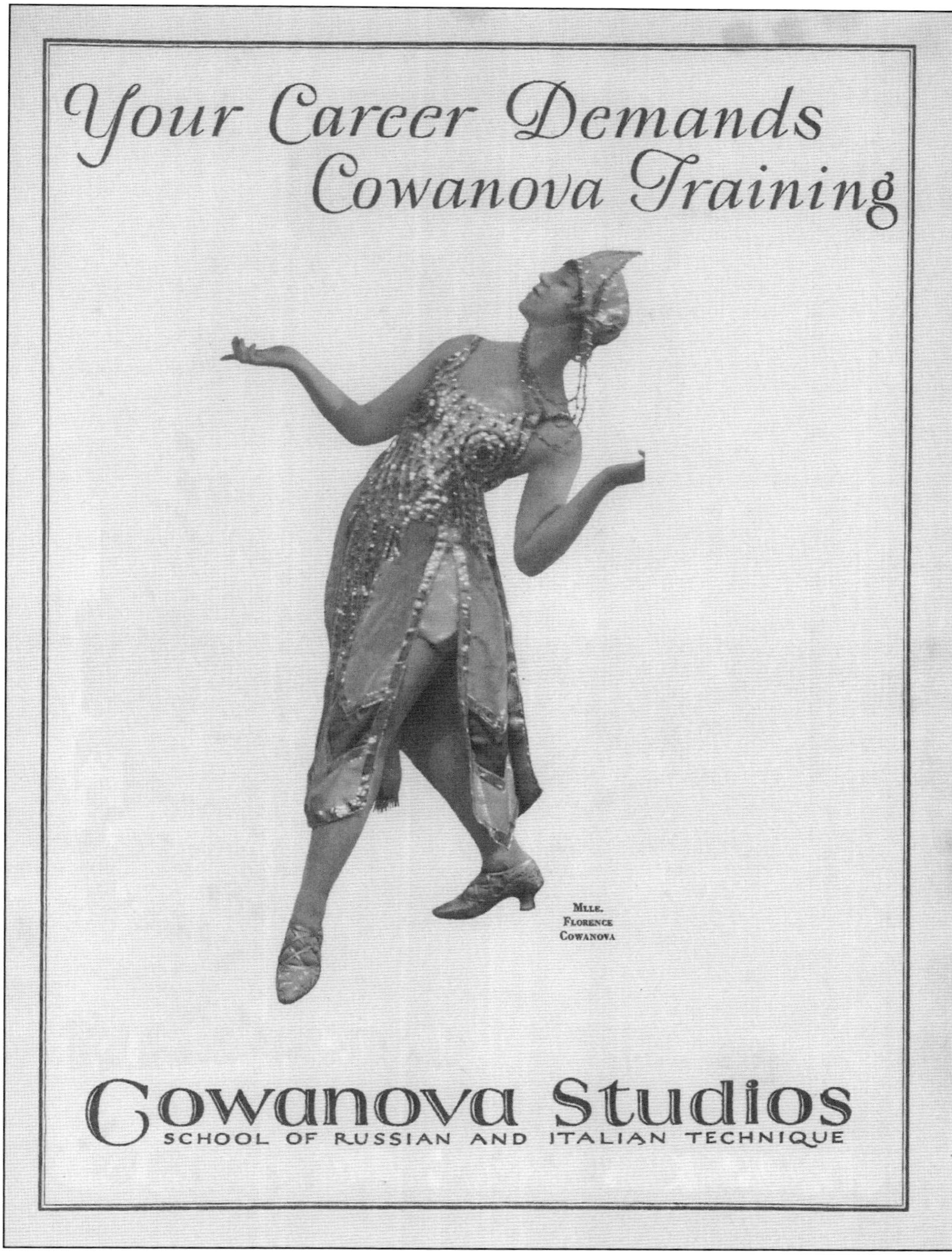

Cowanova taught and encouraged all dance forms and is credited with bringing the serious study of ballet to Philadelphia. Her young dancers were the first to perform with the Philadelphia Orchestra. For over 50 years, she staged a spring review at the Academy of Music, replete with a full orchestra and professionally made costumes. Graduates included Ice Follies performers, comedian Imogene Coca, and Grace Kelly. A grand ballroom's grande dame, Cowanova died at the age of 90 at Ivy Hall. Her obituary—posted on February 17, 1992, by the *Philadelphia Inquirer* staff writer Michael B. Coakley—described her as "one of America's most acclaimed dance instructors, whose pupils filled social registers and covered theater marquees." (Courtesy of the OFC.)

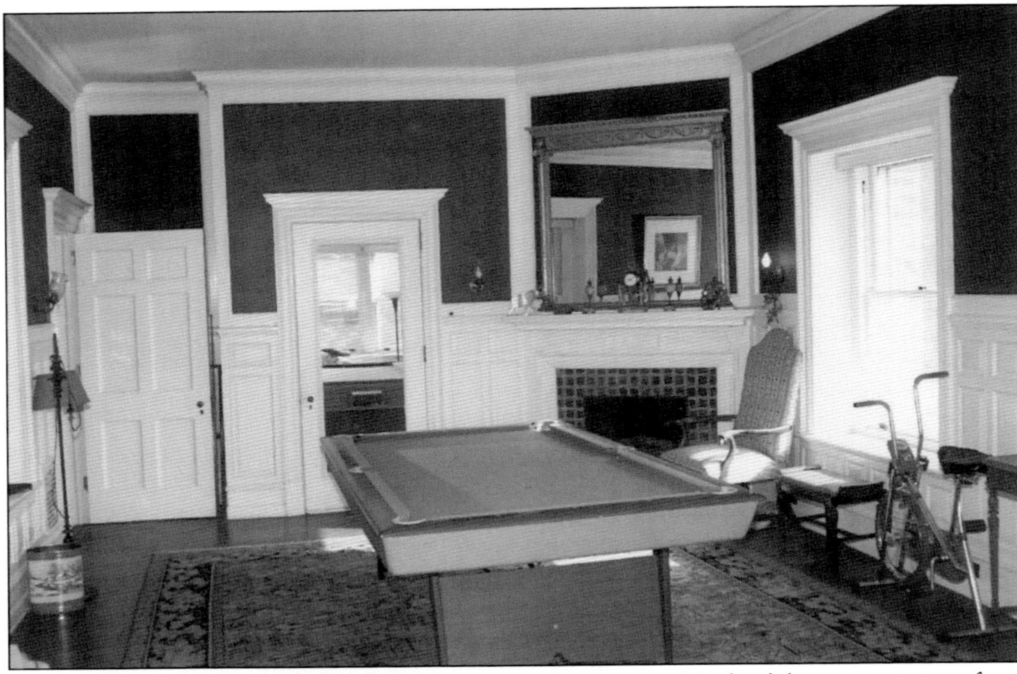

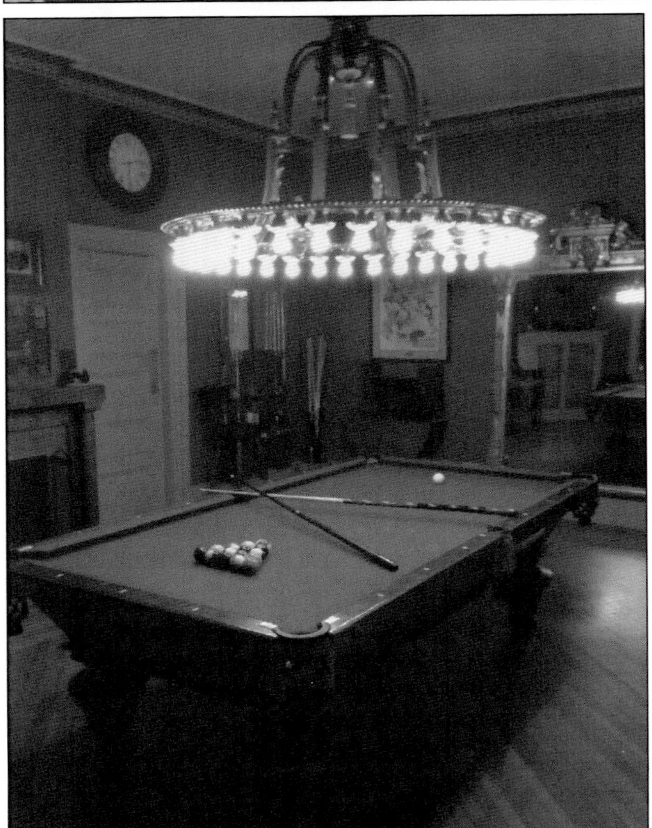

Much of the entertaining of the era was done in the home. Many owners built or designed rooms to indulge their special interests. Billiards was popular, and several homes had rooms whose walls bristled with billiard cue racks. Elaborate chandeliers provided light over the tables. Several original billiard rooms remain in use today. (Above, courtesy of the OFC; left, courtesy of Adjoa Love-Dorsey.)

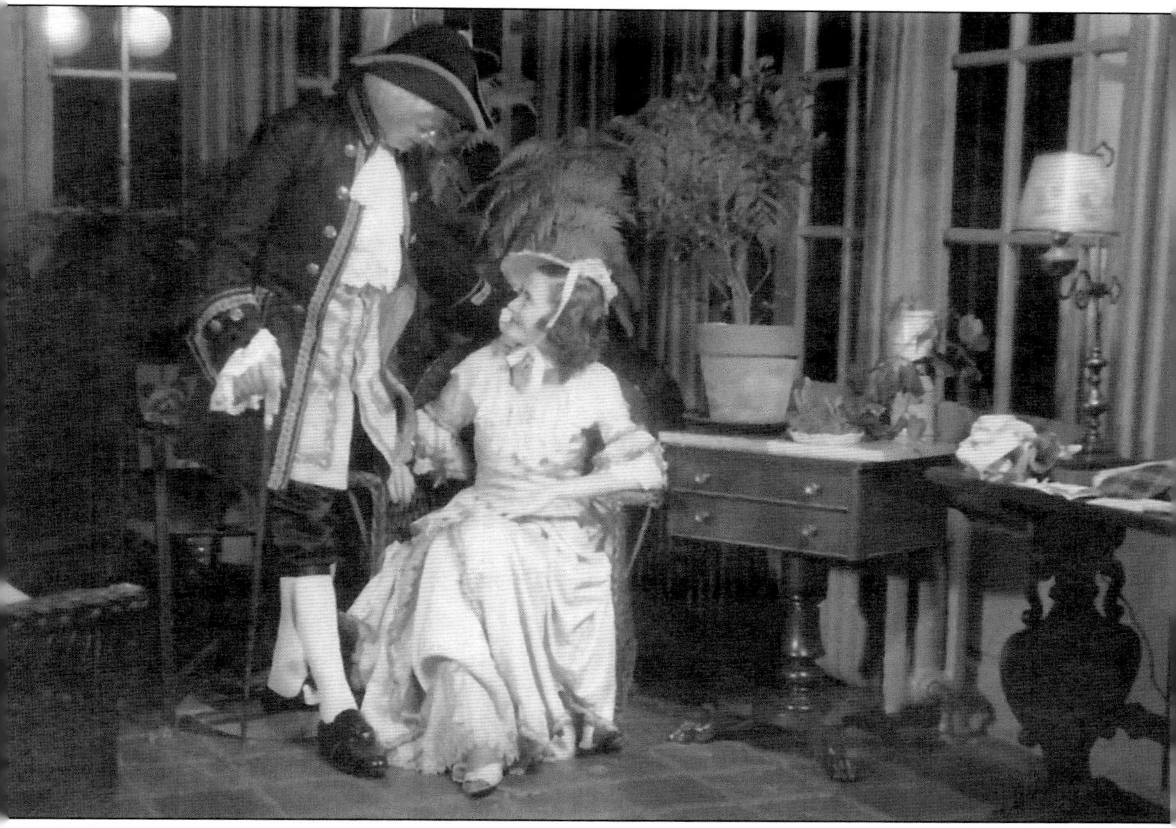

The houses of Overbrook Farms were built with an eye toward entertaining—spacious rooms to permit the easy flow of guests, windows and French doors to assure plenty of light, fireplaces to warm winter nights, and sunporches and lovely gardens for enjoying spring and summer days. Entertainments included themed soirees, as in this photograph taken during a masquerade party on Church Road. (Courtesy of the OFC.)

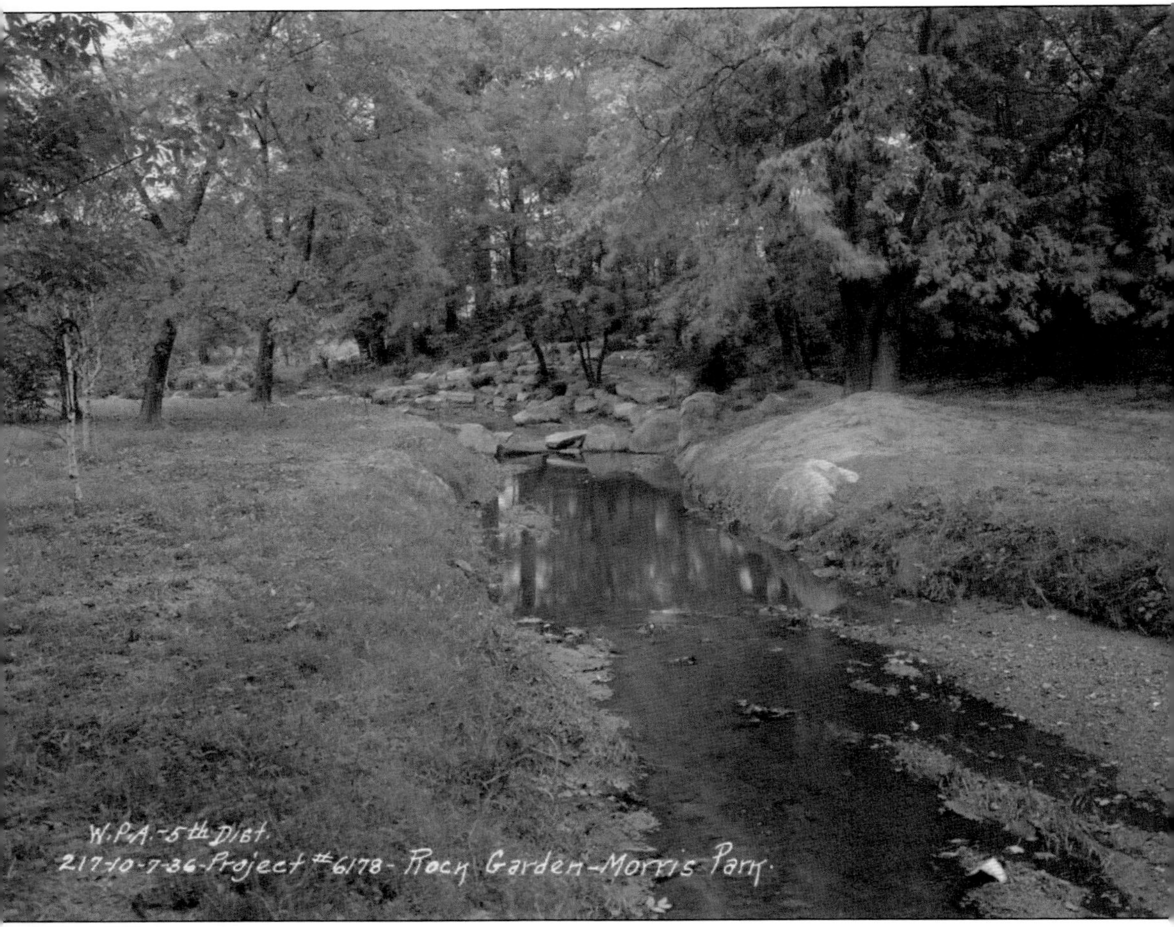

Following Wistar Morris's death, his widow transferred the property into a development trust. A portion was sold to complete the boundary of Overbrook Farms along City Avenue to Sixty-sixth Street. A tract along Indian Run (in center of photograph) was dedicated to the City of Philadelphia in 1911. This land formed Morris Park. (Courtesy of the Fairmount Park Historic Resource Archives.)

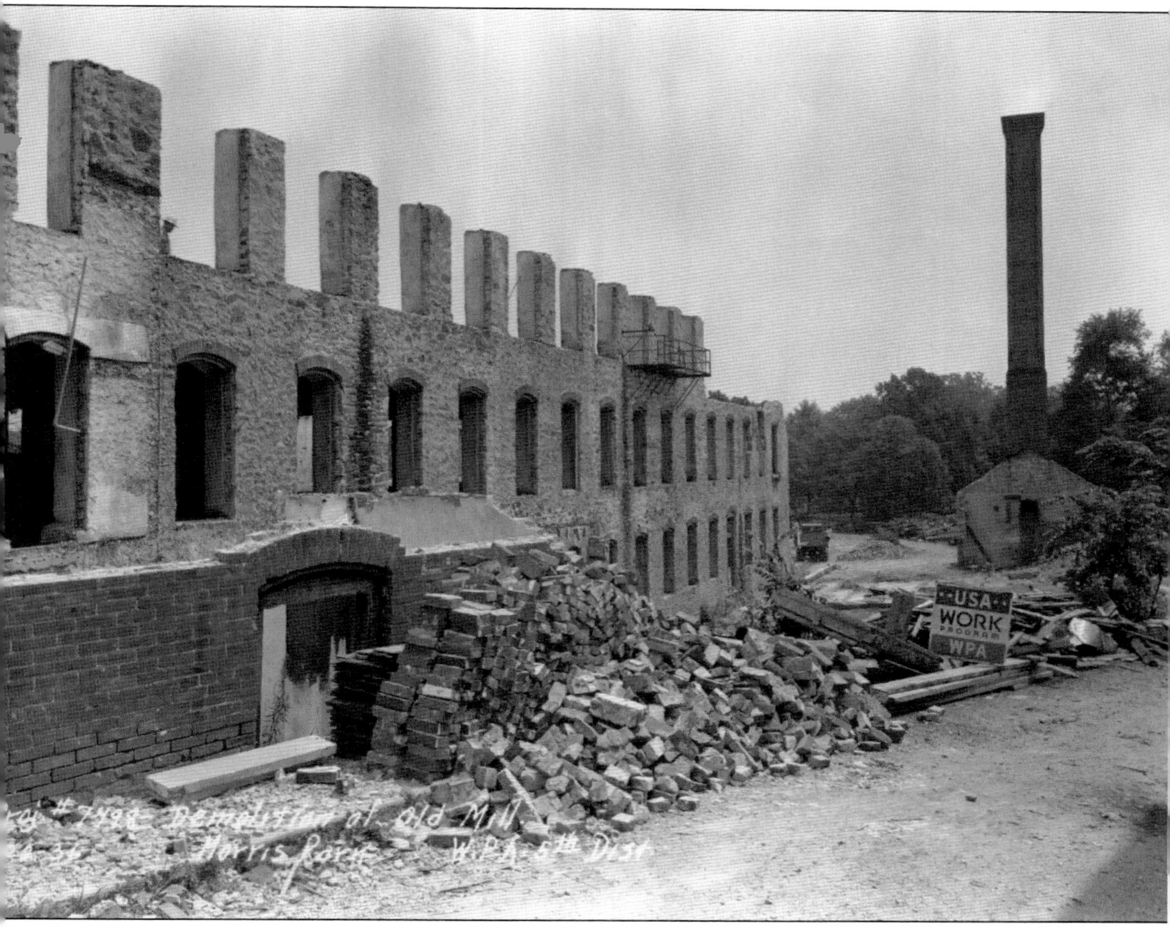

The West Branch of Indian Run flows into Cobbs Creek and once supported dozens of waterpowered mills, beginning with Philadelphia's first, built by Swedish settlers in 1642. Flour, paper, and textile mills also sprang up. Factories converted from waterpower to steam power, and these outdated mills disappeared by the mid-20th century. Located along Indian Run, this mill was demolished under Fairmount Park Commission supervision. (Courtesy of the Fairmount Park Historic Resource Archives.)

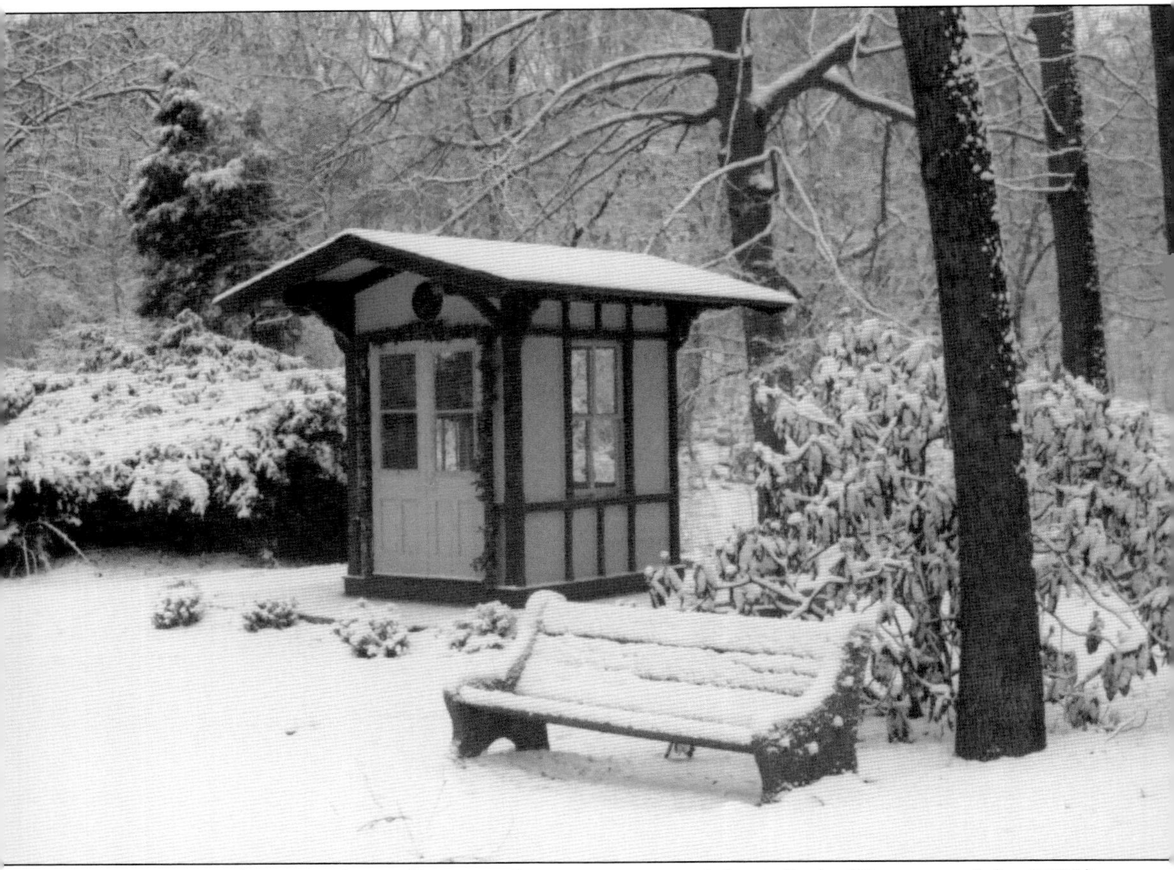

This recently restored guardhouse welcomes visitors to Morris Park. (Courtesy of the OFC.)

Six

The Overbrook Farms Club

The Overbrook Farms Club's initial purpose, as stated in the club's charter, was "[T]o promote friendly intercourse; to encourage field and other athletic sports, and to afford opportunity and means of cooperation and concerted action in matters of local interest which affect the community at Overbrook." The club's early interest in athletics resulted in the formation of a tennis association as well as a cricket team and the Wheel Club, with field space maintained on Upland Way from Fifty-ninth Street to Woodbine Avenue. In 1900, a golf club was organized, with grounds located on what is now Lankenau Hospital.

By 1915, the club had moved towards civic activities, many of which were initially performed by the Civic Club of the 34th Ward, an Overbrook Farms women's group formed in 1900 and disbanded in 1926. Their activities included establishing zoning, obtaining extra policing in the community, and securing street signage for the area.

For more than 70 years, the club took responsibility for snow removal from the sidewalks and purchased and maintained brooms and then snowplows, first using horses and then modern equipment as it became available to do the job. Overbrook Farms had central steam heat until the mid-1970s. It arranged a hearing in Harrisburg in 1917, securing a rebate from the steam-heat company for assessing excessive charges. The club thereafter maintained oversight of the service until its demise in the mid-1970s and the razing of the steam plant in the 1976.

The Overbrook Farms Club has sponsored both new and time-honored activities during its tenure. The Garden Club, operated for many years, has recently been revived. The beautification committee is alert to improving the neighborhood's appearance. There are property, marketing, and communication committees. Santa in the Park, an annual Easter egg hunt, and a neighborhood summer picnic are all opportunities for family fun. The Overbrook Farms Open House Tour and Tea, offered for decades each spring, is a time to open the beautiful homes to region-wide appreciation. The more recent farmers' market now operates in the neighborhood as a result of a joint effort between the club and The Food Trust.

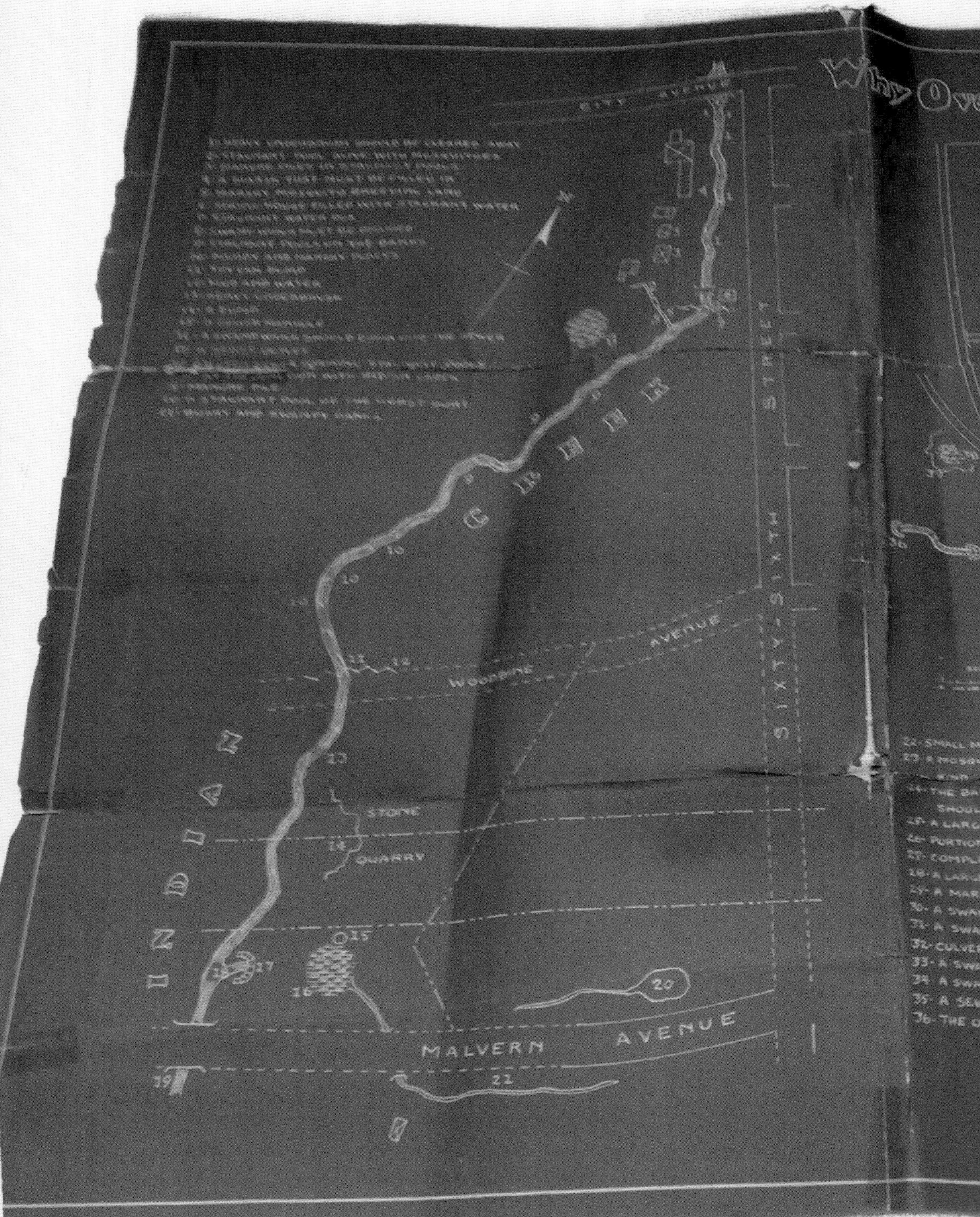

CITY AVENUE
SIXTY-SIXTH STREET
INDIAN CREEK
WOODBINE AVENUE
STONE QUARRY
MALVERN AVENUE

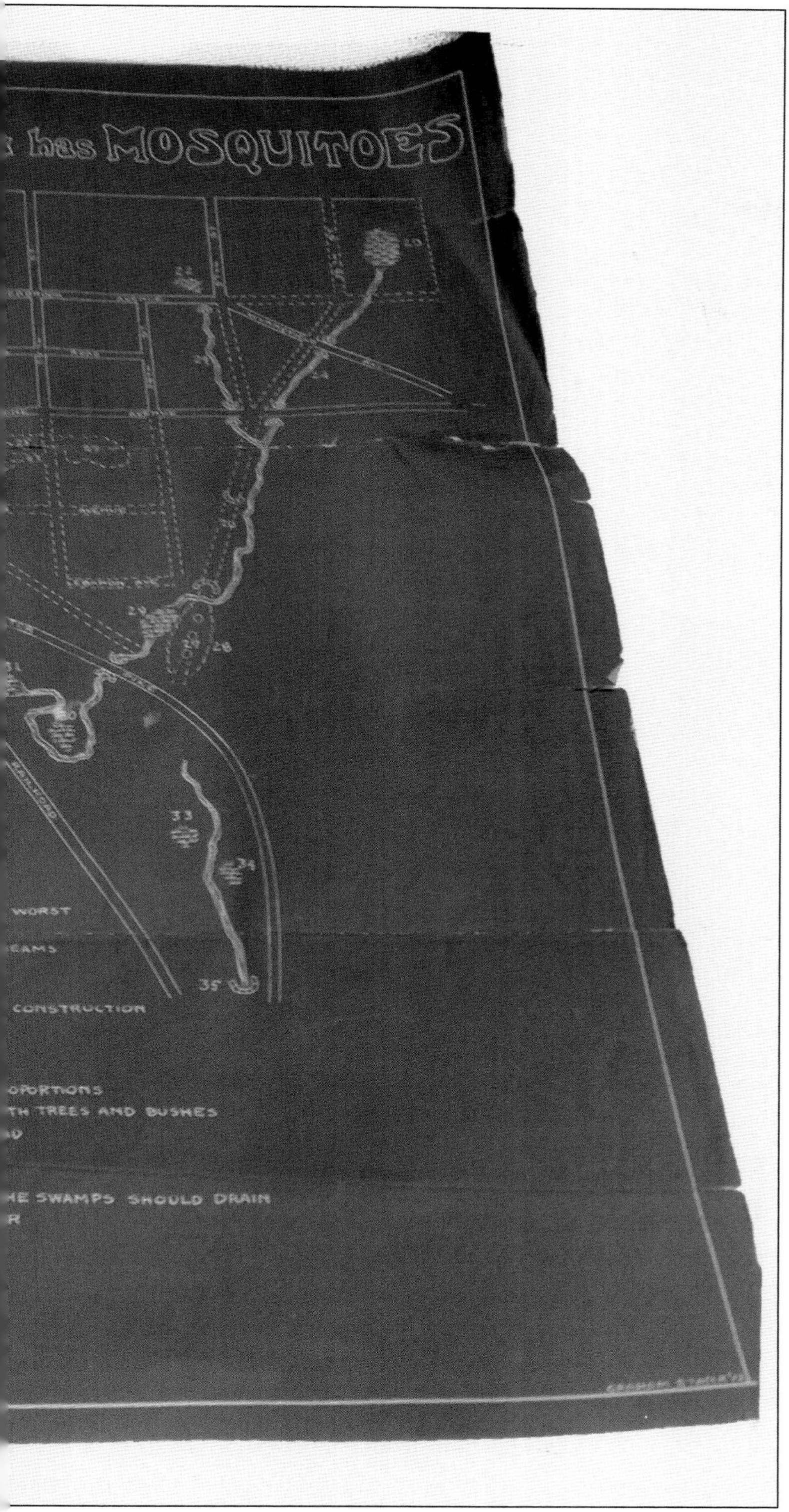

From its beginnings to the present day, the OFC addresses challenges that affect the welfare of neighbors and neighborhood. An early example was a committee formed to "abate the mosquito nuisance in Overbrook." A final report, submitted to the board in November 1912, indicates its efforts "met with a considerable degree of success, but with experience gained this season, more thorough work can be done another year." A map pinpointed some 36 breeding places, and nearly 150 trouble spots were treated. The city's director of public works assigned laborers to these troublesome spots. A neighborhood canvass suggested measures residents could take to further reduce the problem, apparently with little success. Informational pamphlets promoted the goal "that this community can be freed of mosquitoes." Their cost was $245, with a remaining balance of $157! (Courtesy of the OFC.)

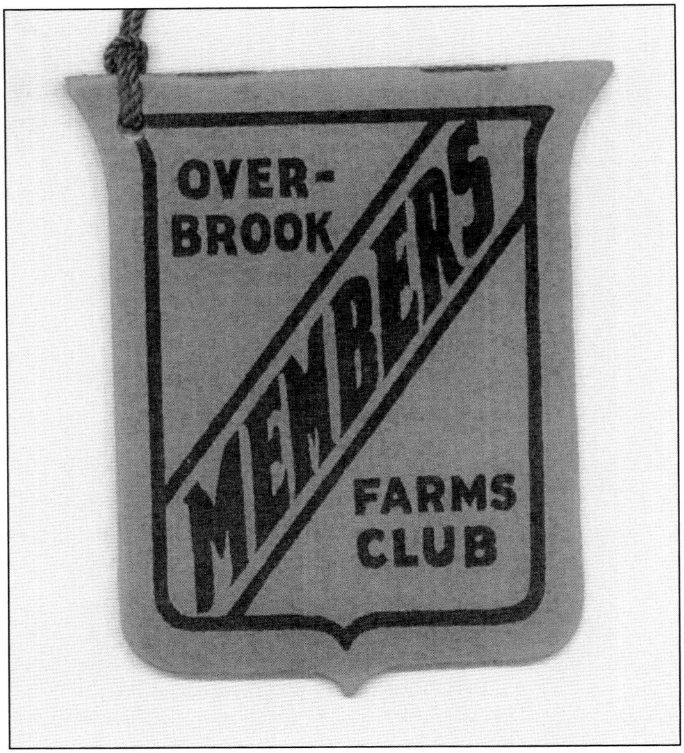

The Overbrook Farms Club was chartered by the Commonwealth of Pennsylvania in 1896 to "promote friendly intercourse, to encourage field and other athletic sports, and to afford opportunity and means of cooperation and concerted action in matters of local interest." Led by a board of directors, it remains an active presence in the community, sponsoring activities ranging from representing residents in zoning matters to organizing community gatherings. (Both, courtesy of Jean Tracy.)

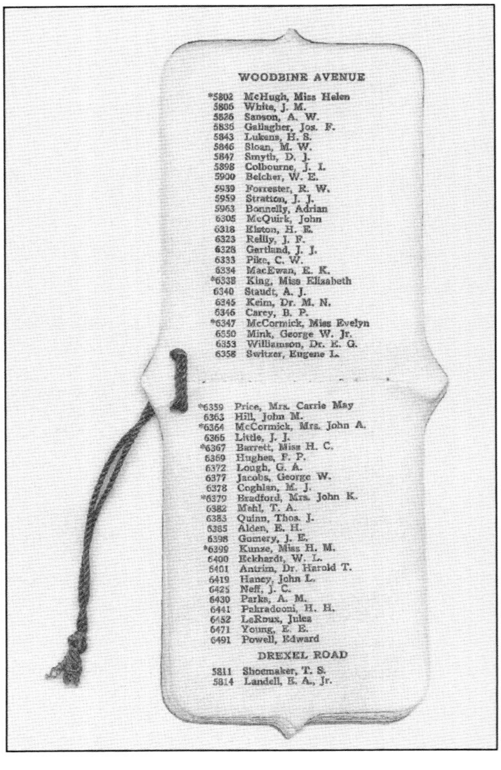

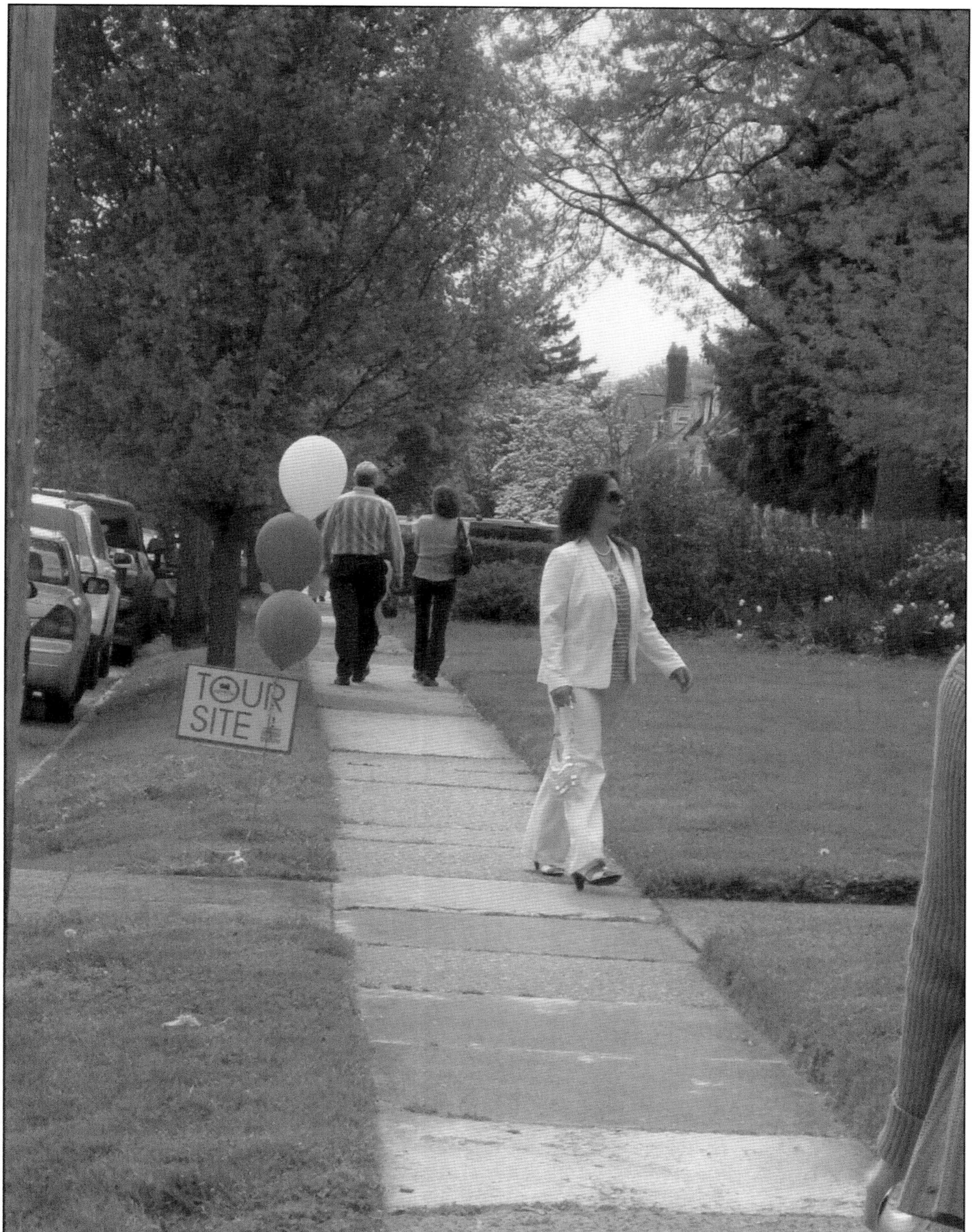

For 25 years, the OFC has sponsored the Overbrook Farms Open House Tour and Tea to showcase "The Suburb Deluxe." Each spring, ticketed tour-goers are invited to visit a selection of homes that highlight the work of the "Astral Architects." Docents point out the unique features and history of each property. (Courtesy of the OFC.)

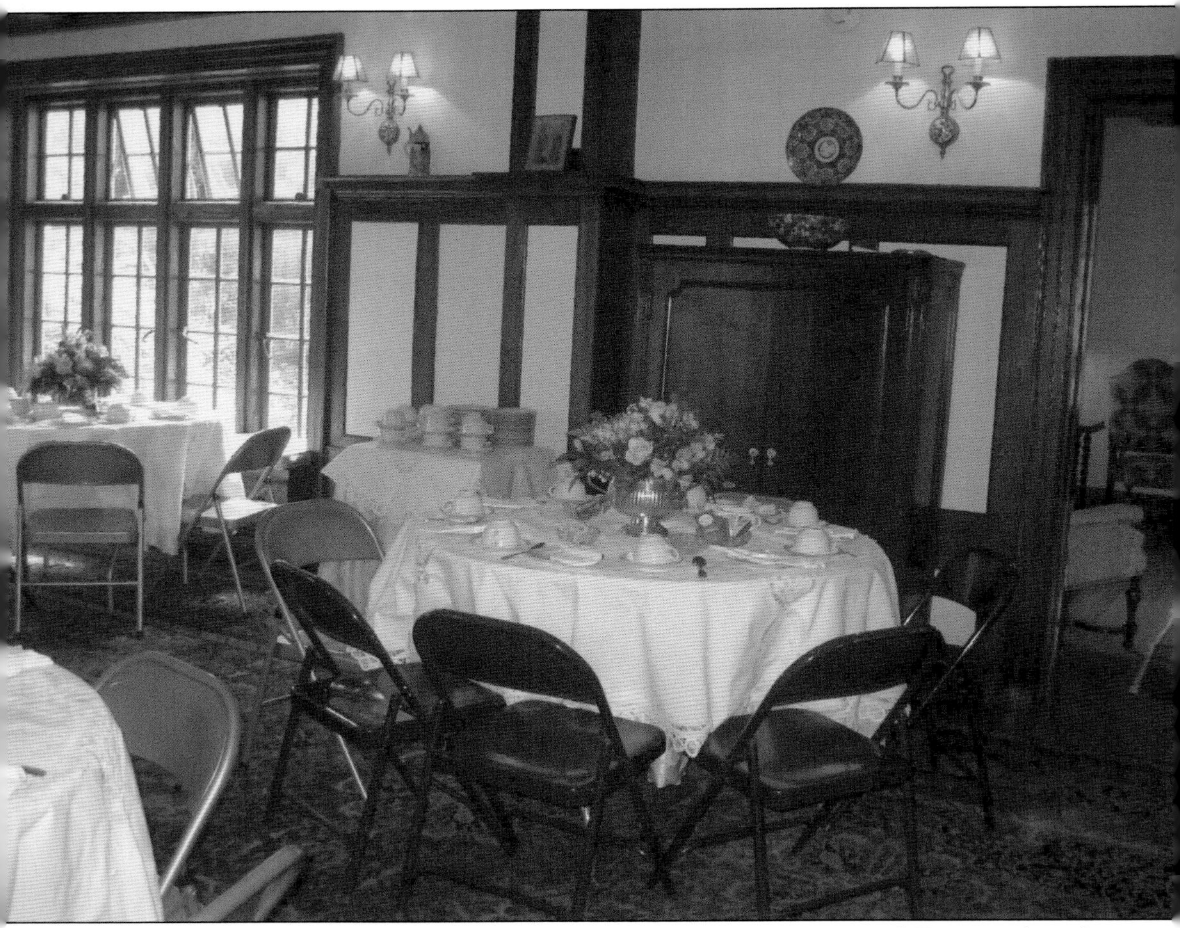

For many, the highlight of the Overbrook Farms Open House Tour and Tea is its formal tea. Held in one of the larger historic homes, it features lace tablecloths, floral centerpieces, china tea service, and tiered trays with tea sandwiches and finger desserts. (Courtesy of the OFC.)

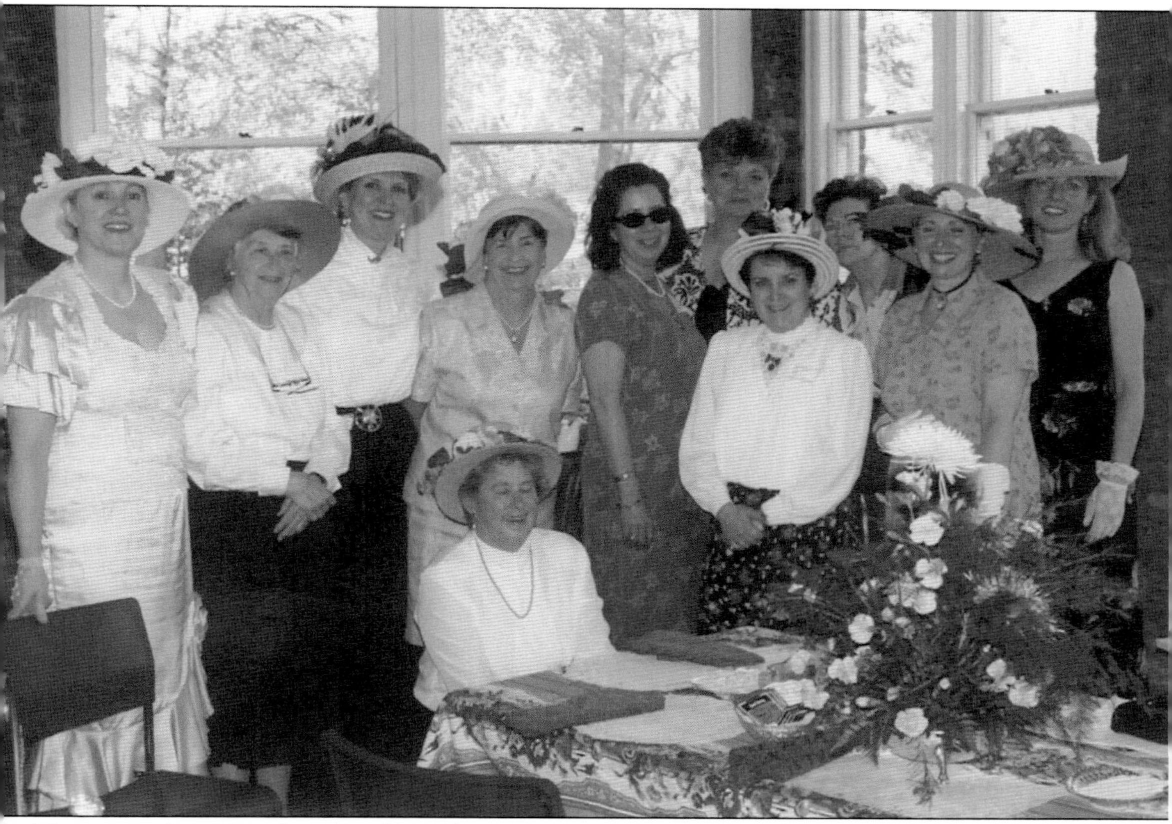

The tour is planned and produced by volunteer committee members who often dress in Victorian-era attire to promote the event. People come from near and far for the history, the architecture, and to see how these homes have been adapted to 21st-century living while maintaining the best features of their 19th-century roots. (Courtesy of the OFC.)

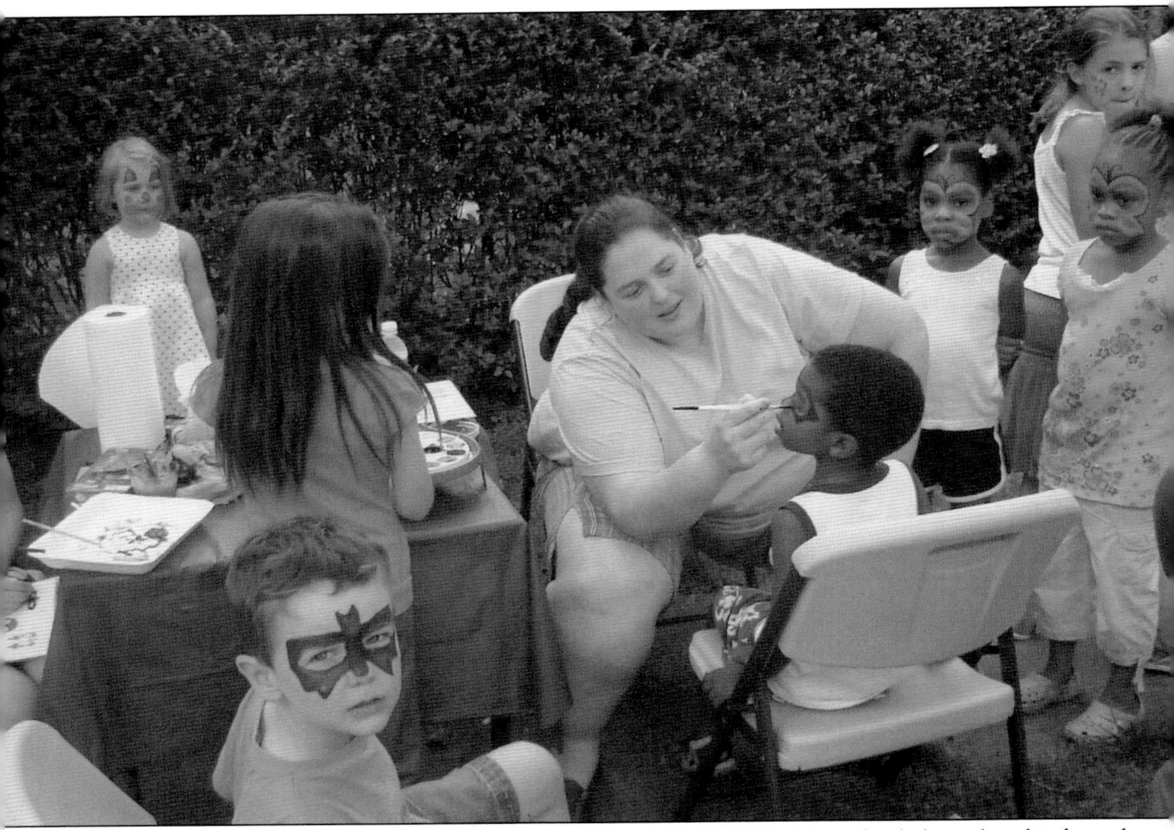

Since its inception, the Overbrook Farms Club has sponsored activities, both formal and informal, for its members. In the early years, they included lectures and readings, Fourth of July speeches and fireworks, and athletic competitions. In more recent years, the club has sponsored formal community meetings with welcoming receptions in the spring and fall of each year. (Courtesy of the OFC.)

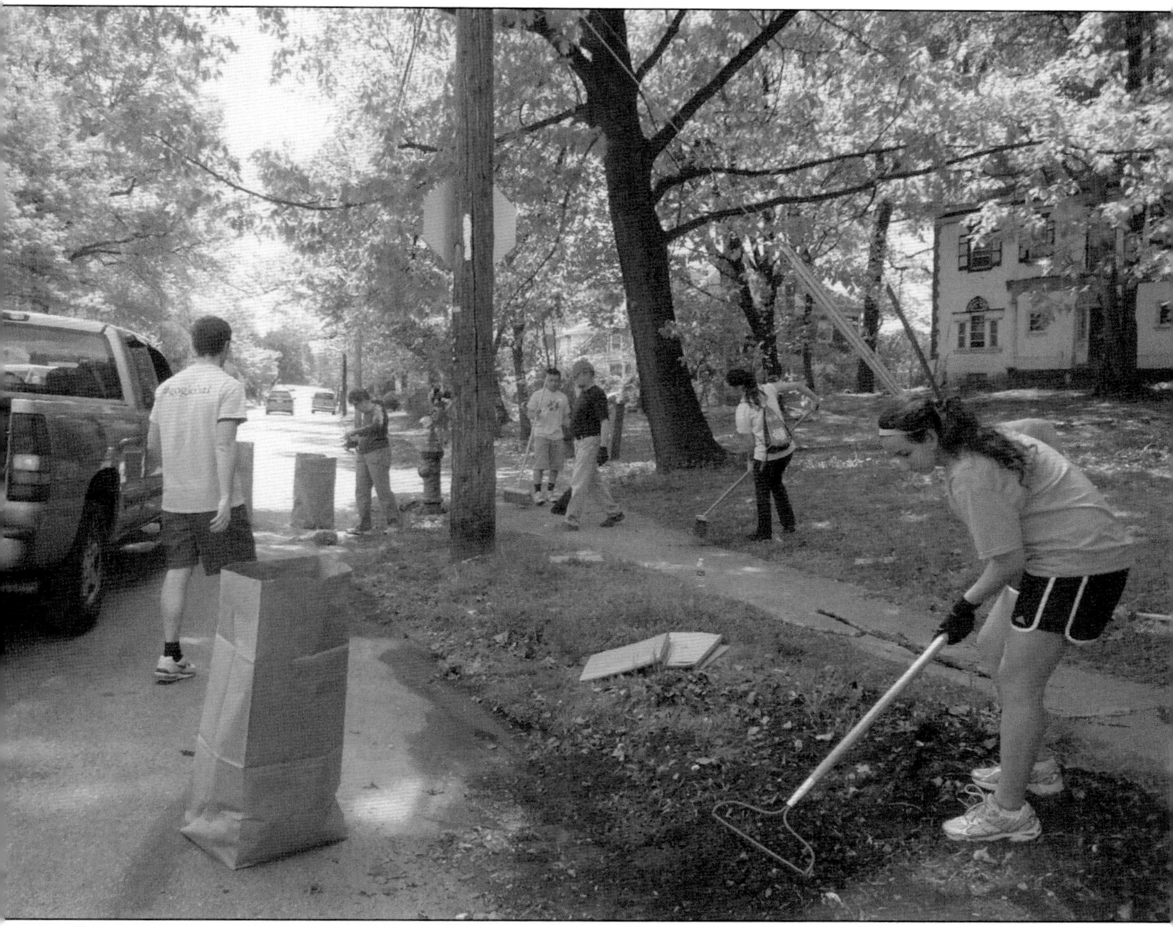

At least twice a year there are "work days" for residents to gather and help with neighborhood beautification projects. Among the volunteers are students from St. Joseph's University, who team up with members of the community to clear, repair, and replant target areas. (Courtesy of the OFC.)

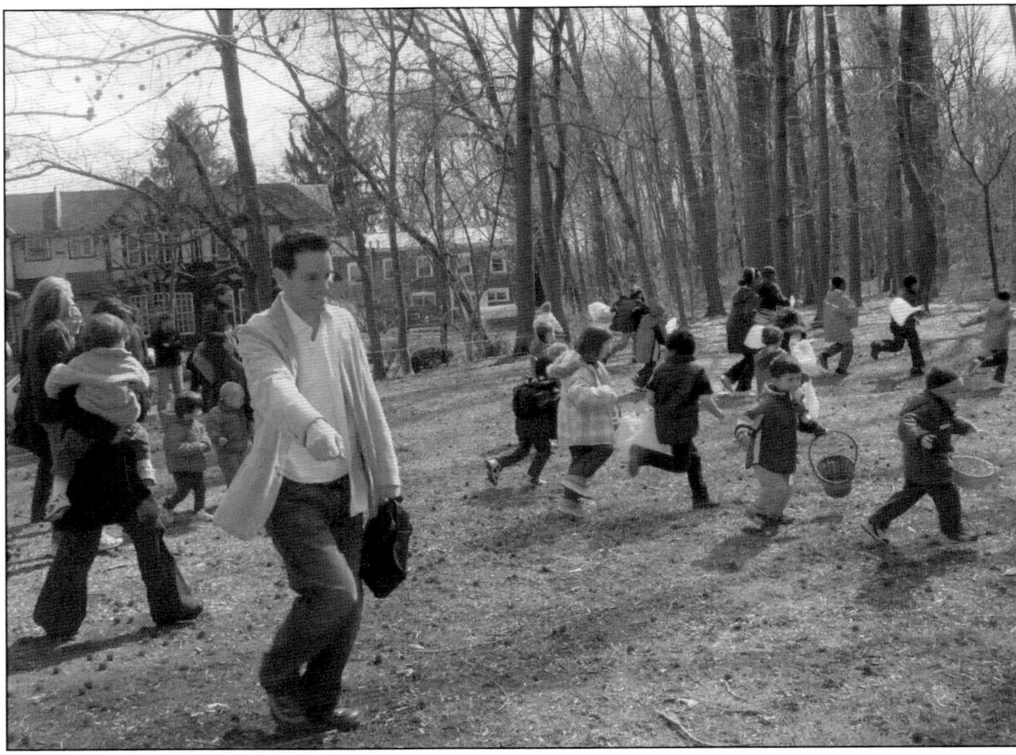

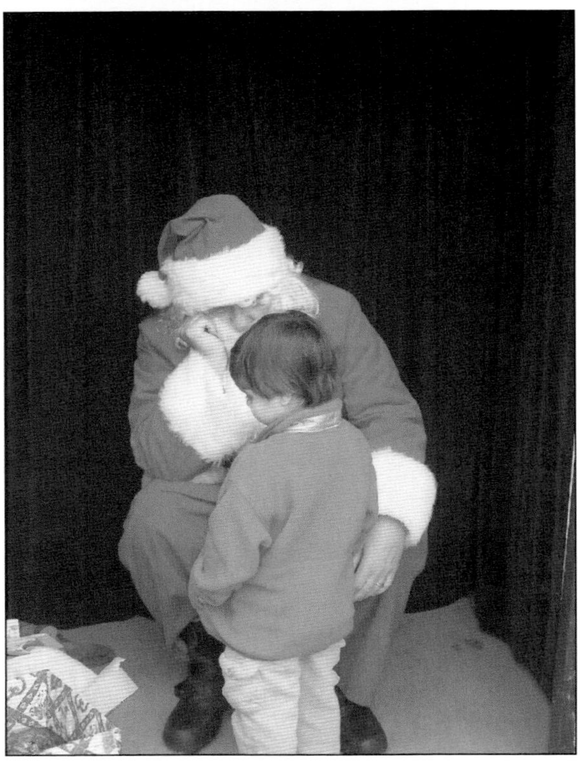

The area's most popular activities are those geared toward fun for all, especially for the children. Pictured here are two of those events, an Easter egg hunt held in Morris Park (above) and Santa in the Park (at left). A perennial favorite is the summer potluck picnic held in the park or on a street closed to traffic. (Both, courtesy of the OFC.)

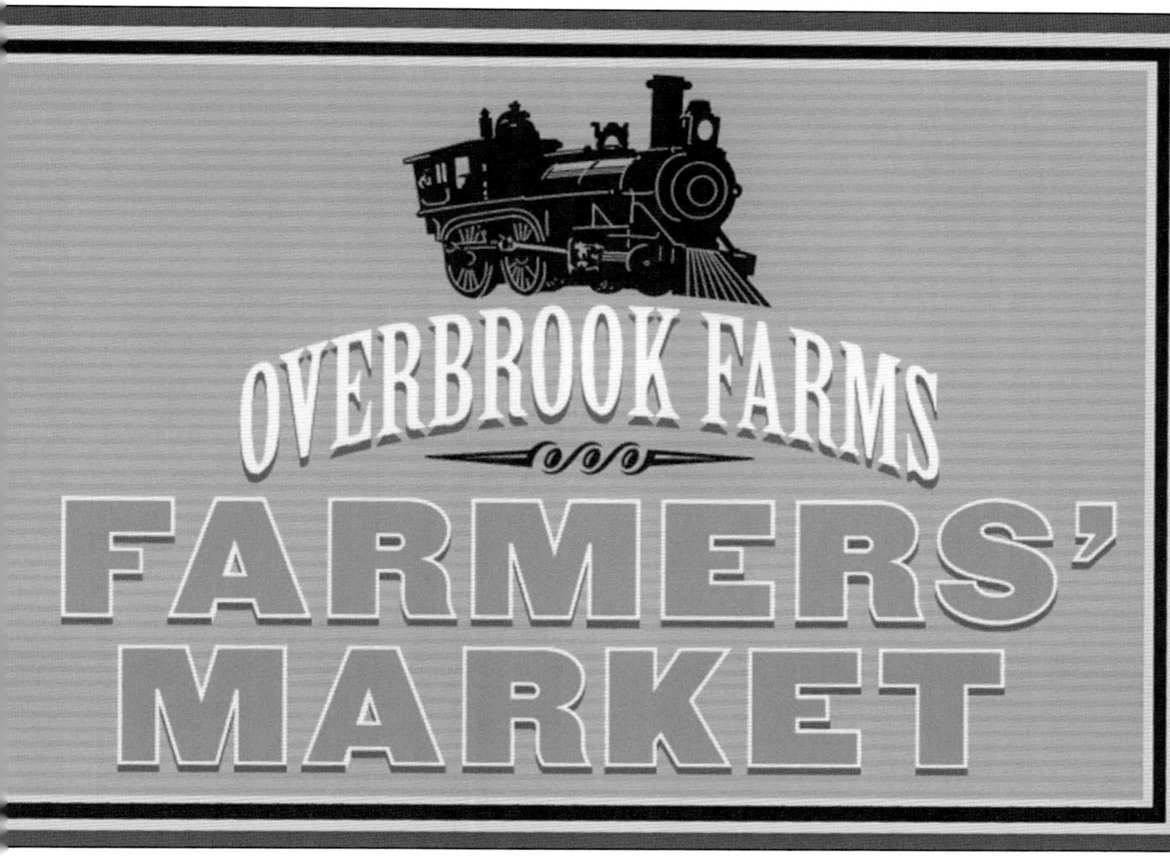

The OFC partnered with The Food Trust to bring farm-fresh fruits and vegetables, baked goods, and other products to the neighborhood. Established in 2007, the farmers' market is open every Saturday between mid-May and Thanksgiving in the parking lot of the Overbrook Presbyterian Church. While providing a source of fresh, nutritious food, it has become a neighborhood meeting place on Saturdays, and the vendors have become friends. (Courtesy of the OFC.)

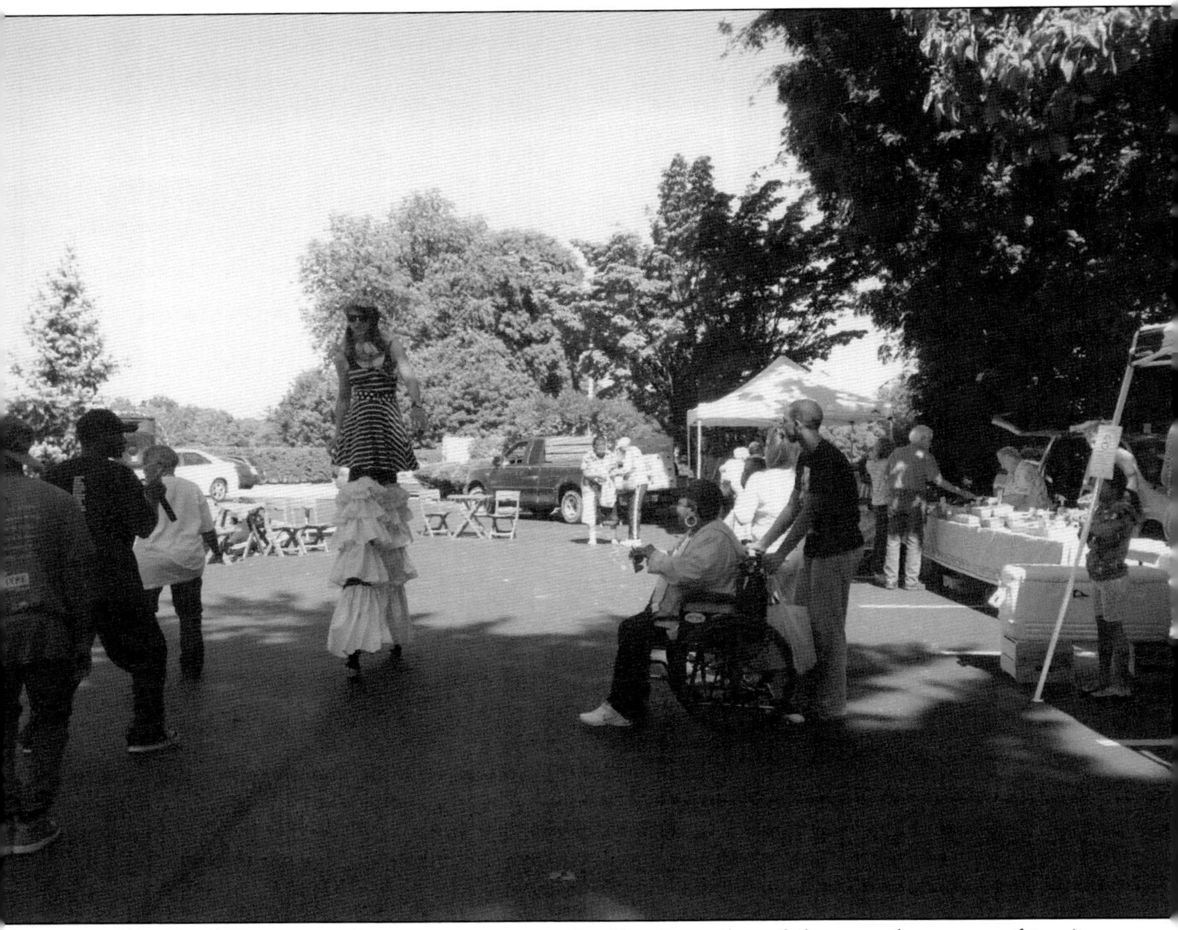

The Food Trust provides entertainers on the first Saturday of the month as part of its Art at Market program. One such first Saturday, a stilt walker/juggler, a rapper, and some dancers found their way to the market to the delight of many shoppers. (Courtesy of the OFC.)

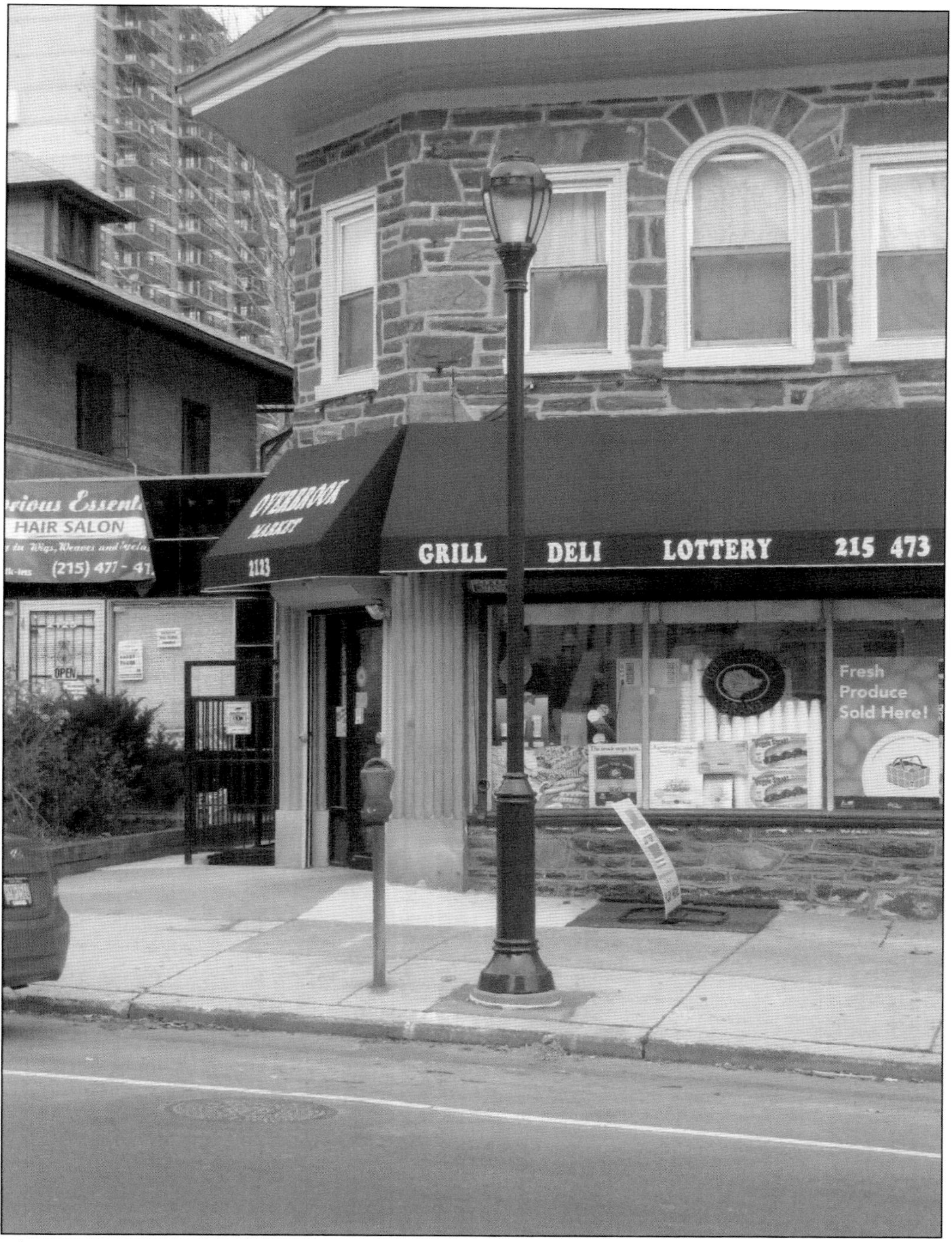

The City Avenue Special Services District collaborated with the City of Philadelphia and the Township of Lower Merion to enhance their conjoined public and private sectors. Extending west on City Avenue from the Schuylkill Expressway to Sixty-third Street and Wynnewood Road, the project, completed in 2013, created a curb extension along the north side of Overbrook Avenue. Now, residents enjoy a shorter, safer pedestrian crossing. (Courtesy of City Avenue Special Services District.)

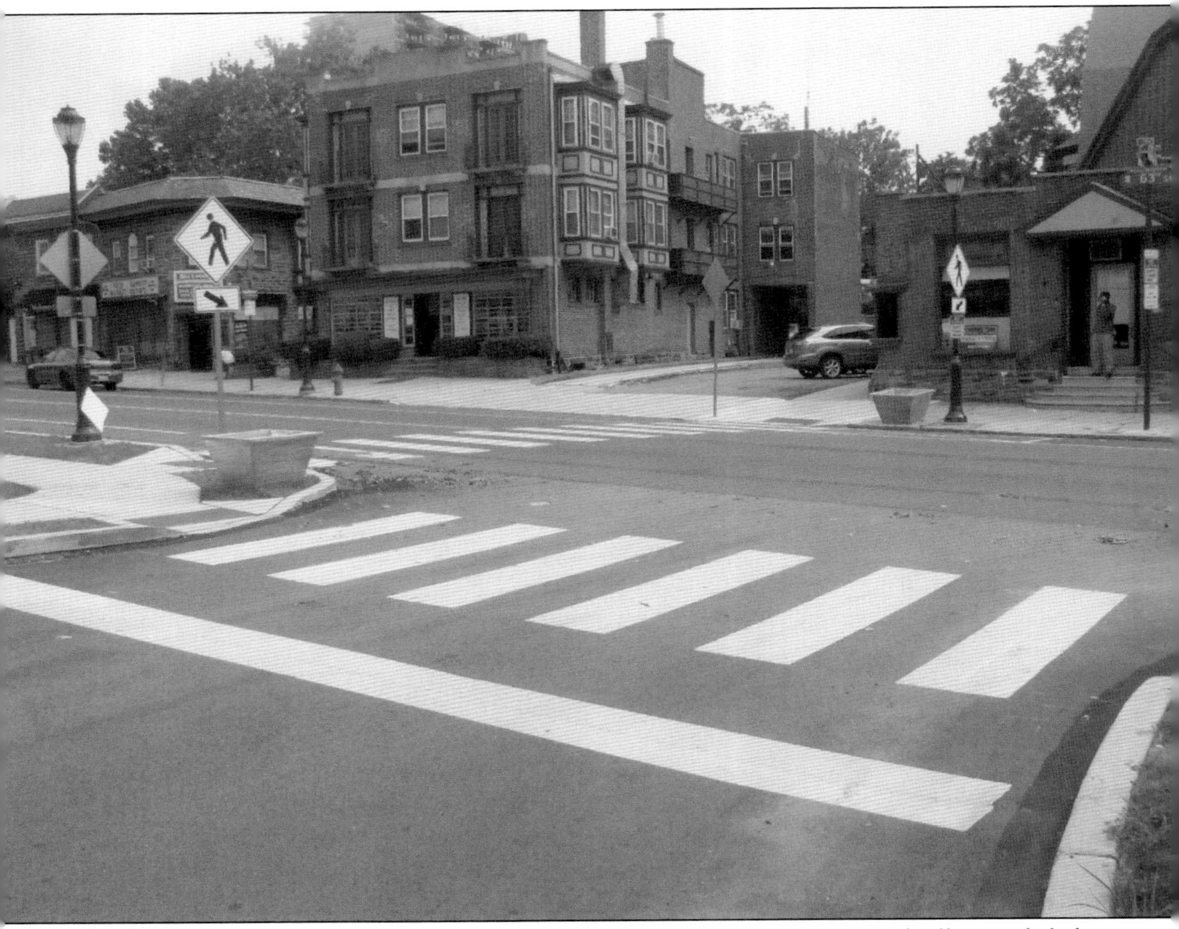

Newly painted pedestrian crosswalks serve to calm traffic, while ornamental village-style lighting will illuminate the corridor at night. This project supplements the work performed by the Overbrook Farms Club commercial-district redevelopment plan and subsequent traffic study. (Courtesy of City Avenue Special Services District.)

Seven

Enduring Overbrook Farms

Wendell and Smith's 1898 promotional brochure *A Little Talk with the Home Seeker* assured prospective owners that they could "either build a home according to an owner's own ideas," or offered "a lot and finished house at a definite price."

Hoping to make these finished homes the likely buyer's choice, the developers promised that these homes would nevertheless feature painstaking details, quality materials, and distinctive finishes, while at the same time saving their owners the unanticipated expenses that might arise with customization.

Even their so-called "finished house" featured interior and exterior architectural refinements that set each apart. A cursory view of the Overbrook Farms neighborhood shows that each home reflects the pains taken to create distinctive flourishes to the properties and surrounds. Some of the modifications occurred with early owners, while others happen daily. Since horse-and-buggy transportation reigned during the neighborhood's beginning days, architecturally compatible garages in the earliest-built homes came significantly later, with no small number featuring carriage houses inhabited by household staff members. Glazed and tiled porches or patios were added to some homes. Inside homes, heating sources were modified, electricity replaced gas lighting fixtures, and other refining amenities became increasingly popular.

Easily viewed in a simple neighborhood walk are outcroppings of mature trees and shrubs, grotesqueries, carved-stone or heraldic medallions, ponds and pools, statuary, terraces, carriage houses, porches, patios, and vestibules and foyers, as well as Palladian, fan-shaped, leaded, and stained-glass windows and sidelights. Inside, a proliferation of cove and exposed wood-beam ceilings, ornate plaster and wood moldings, exquisite wallpapering, dizzyingly spiraling stairways, billiard rooms, libraries, and elaborate fireplaces are places where these distinctions are apparent throughout these homes.

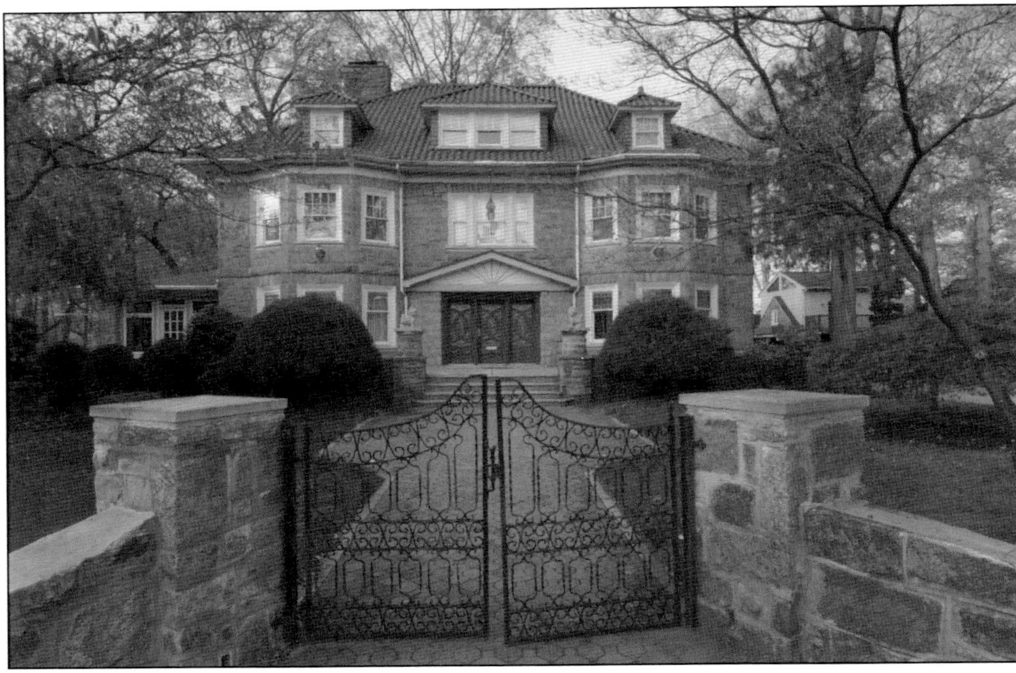

Tom Stafford visited many neighborhoods in 1988, seeking a location close to the city and nearby suburbs and looking for evidence of close-knit neighbors. He stumbled upon an area of large well-maintained homes with manicured lawns and tree-lined streets. Stafford immediately fell in love with Overbrook Farms. Walking its streets, he smelled food cooking and heard the laughter of families having fun. He felt he was in the suburbs. (Both, courtesy of Rick Pullin.)

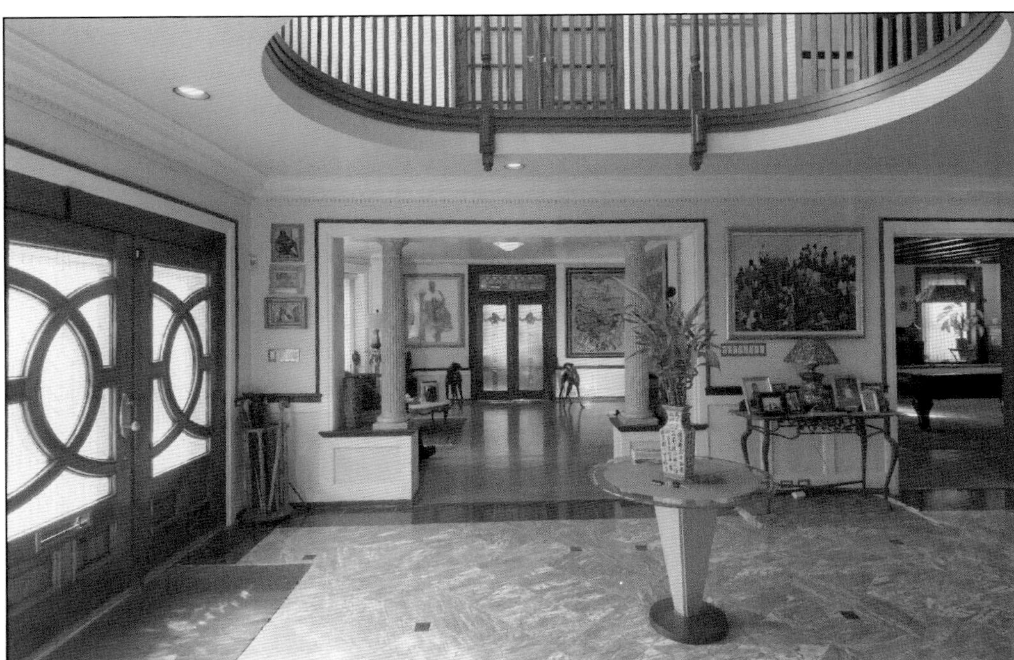

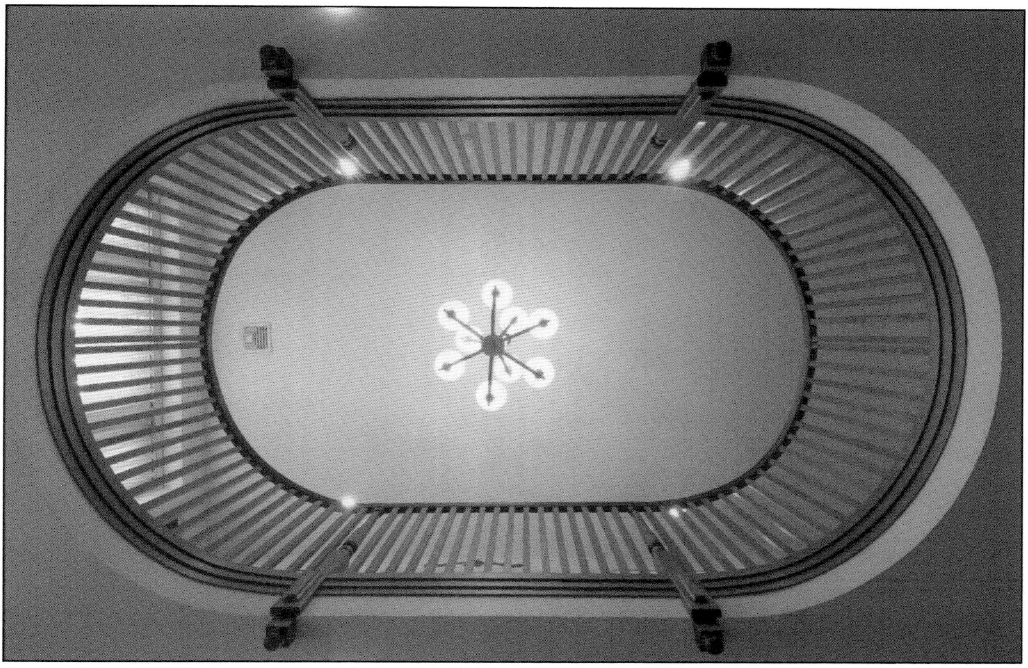

Stafford found a home on Woodbine Avenue that had been abandoned for three years and was in great disrepair. It was love at first sight. Most of the home had to be rebuilt. He removed all of the roof tiles, painstakingly numbering each tile, and then replaced them. An oval-shaped railing was installed on the second floor, creating a dramatic foyer and second-floor hall. (Both, courtesy of Rick Pullin.)

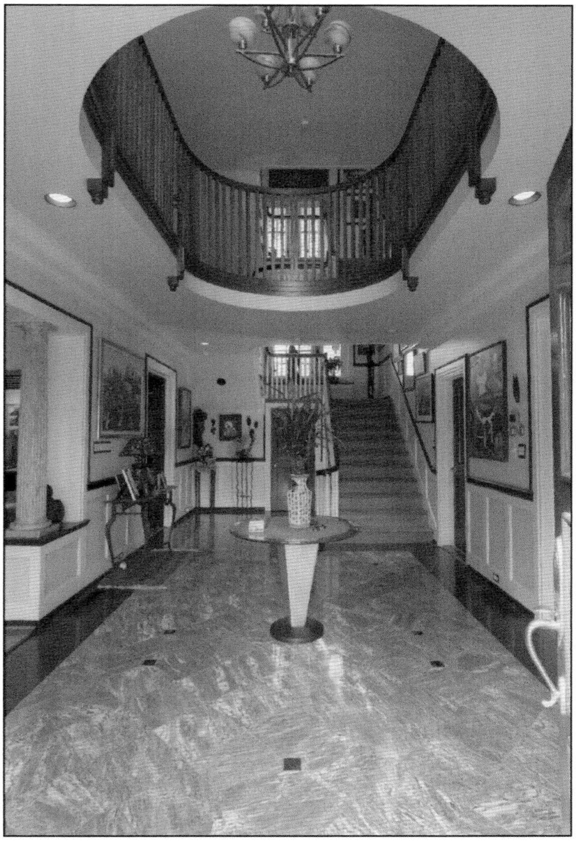

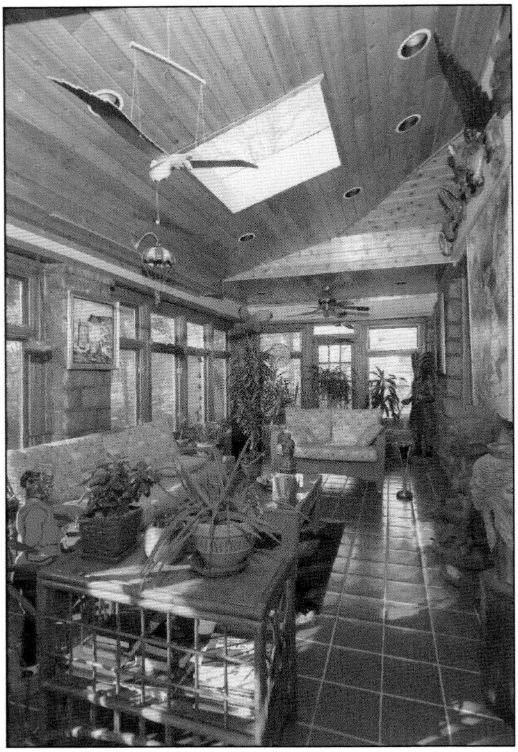

The rebuilt sunporch now includes a skylight, wood ceiling, and magnificent stained-glass doors leading into the living and billiards rooms, joined by a double-sided fireplace. (Both, courtesy of Rick Pullin.)

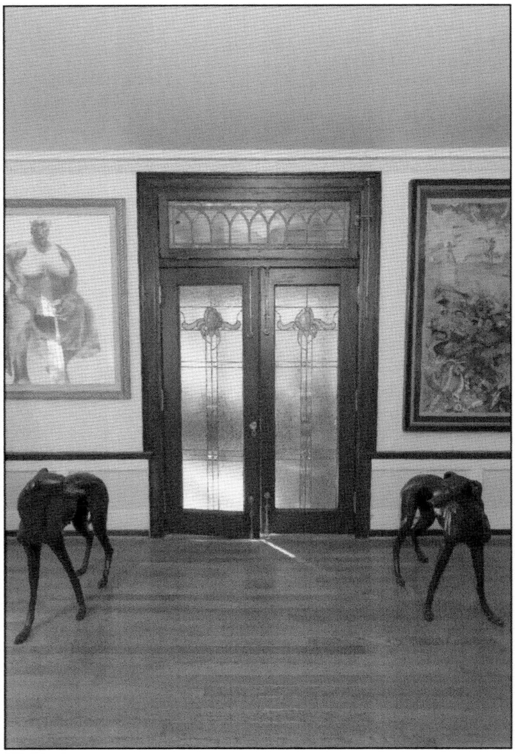

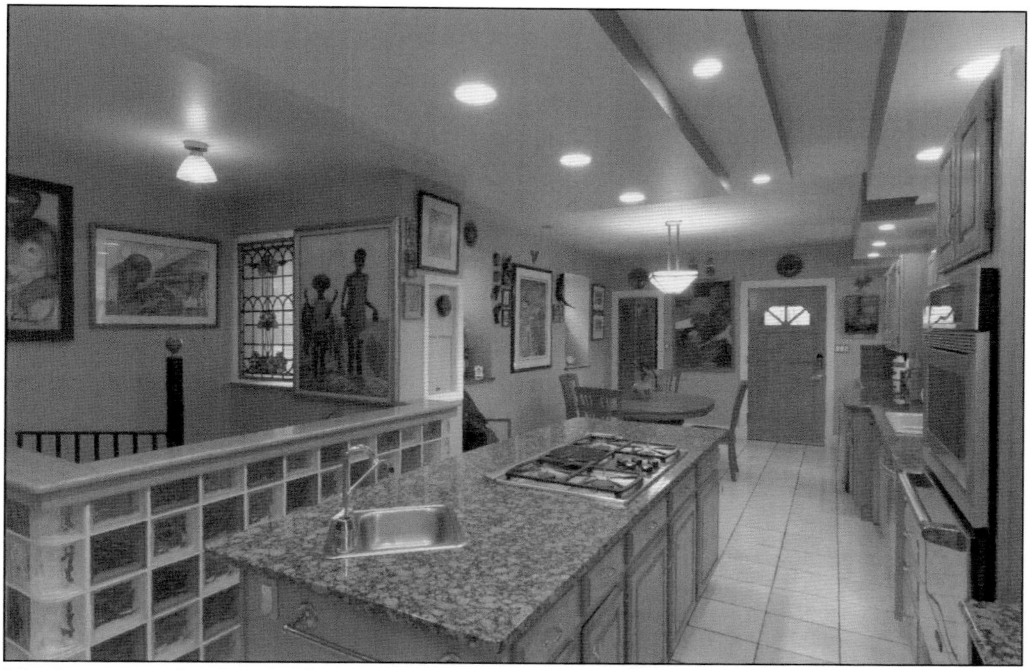

The large eat-in kitchen leads to an expansive tiered deck for outdoor entertaining. Spiral stairs lead to an area totally transformed from a dirt-floored dungeon to an entertainment space and office that run the length of the home. (Courtesy of Rick Pullin.)

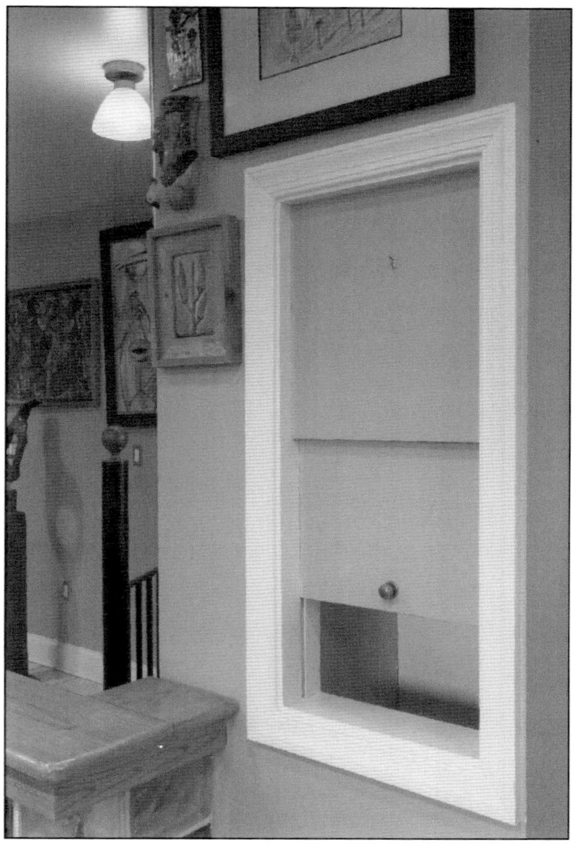

Whenever possible, Stafford maintained the original features of the house, such as this dumbwaiter, which goes from the kitchen to the third-floor servant's quarters. (Courtesy of Rick Pullin.)

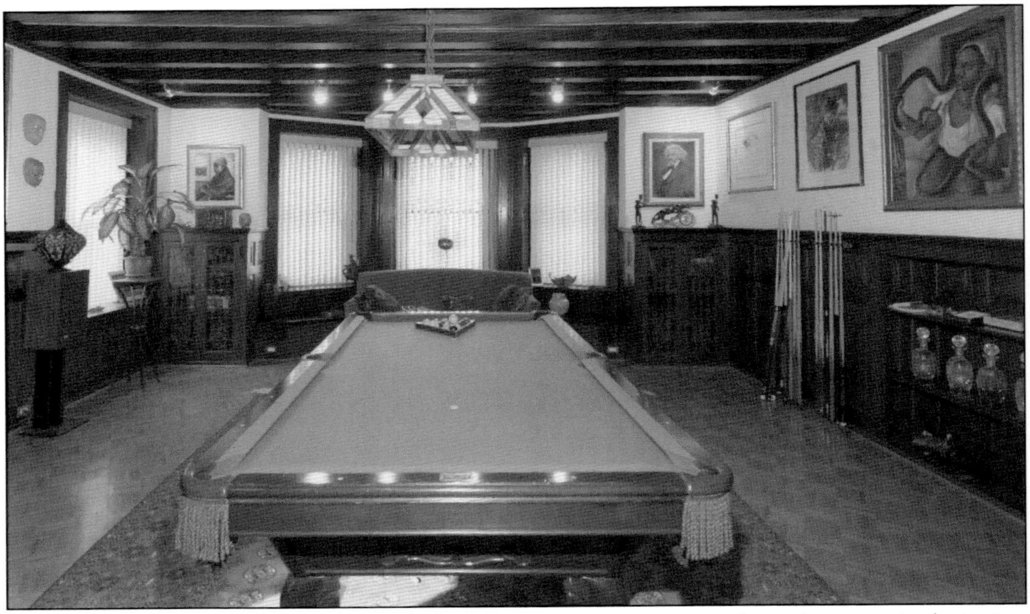

Much thought went into incorporating the homeowner's interests and requirements in designing the spaces throughout the house. The original house had many small rooms that Stafford combined to create a contemporary open floor plan. This grand billiard room with beamed ceiling, wainscoting, and many light sources provides for much entertainment and enjoyment. (Courtesy of Rick Pullin.)

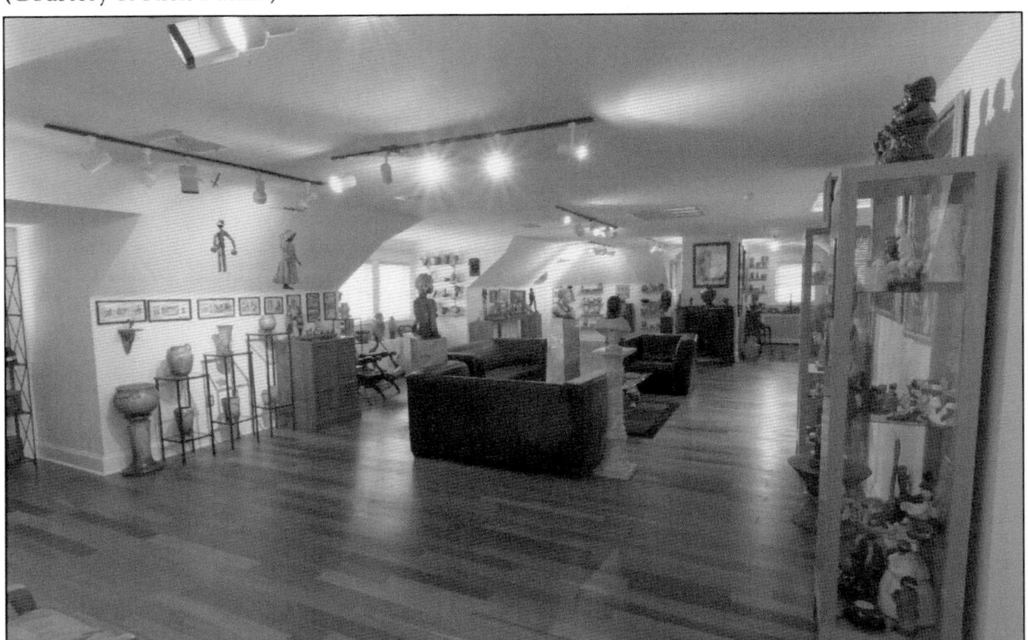

Stafford's love of art prompted him to build an art gallery on the third floor with a skylight over the stairwell to shine on his collection. Following nearly two years of working to restore the home, he was finally able to move in. (Courtesy of Rick Pullin.)

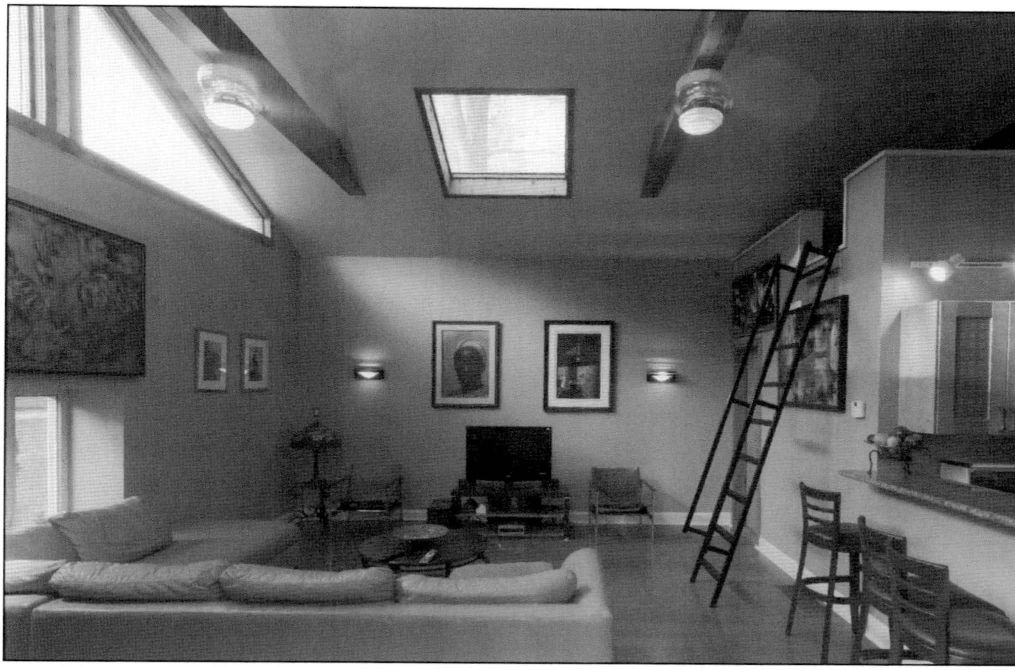

The carriage house, with a newly created second-floor living space, serves as a welcoming home for guests. It features a skylight, loft, and a spacious, open floor plan sure to keep family and friends coming back to visit. (Both, courtesy of Rick Pullin.)

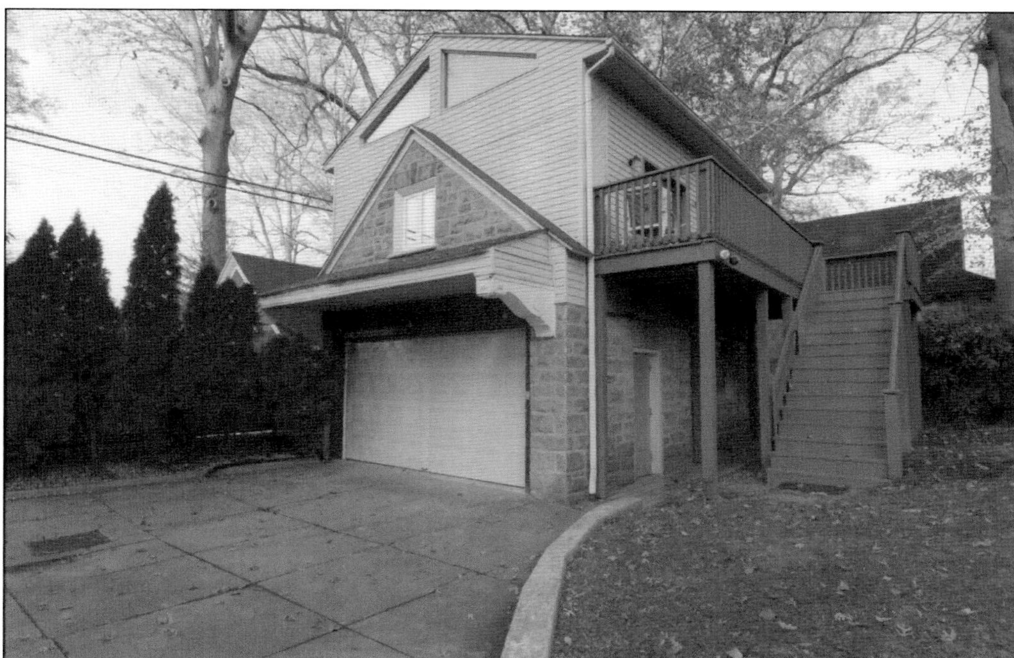

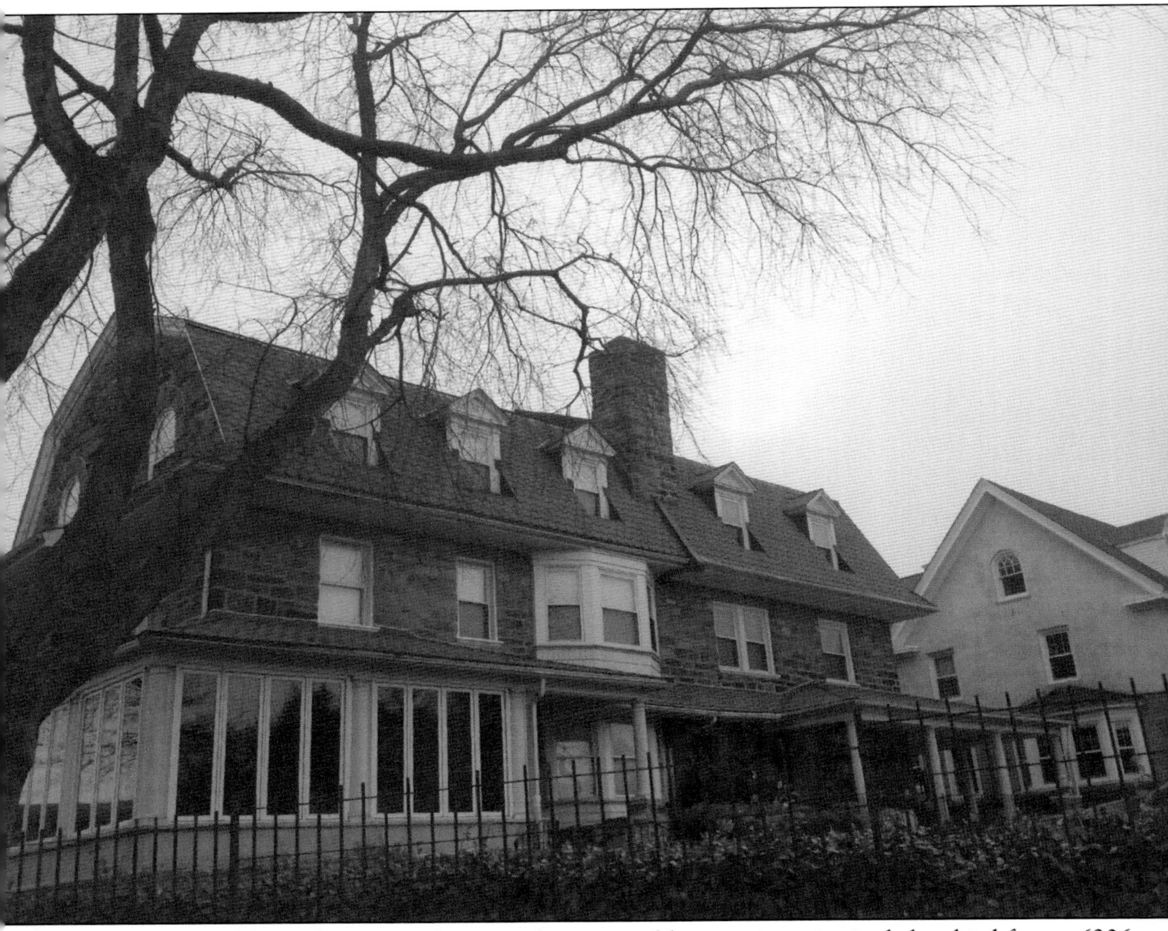

Abandoned for eight years, a kerosene heater used by transients ignited the third fire at 6306 Woodbine Avenue. A demolition threat from the fire marshal motivated the owner to sell to Tom Stafford, who wanted to restore this gateway to the community. Its many compelling features include a restored natural wine cellar. After this restoration, the owners of its twin sold their home to Stafford, who envisioned these homes becoming a social gathering place for the community. However, after renovating the home, he decided to sell. Stafford's trained eye directed him to another Overbrook Farms property at 2024R Upland Way. Occupying the large commercial building, adjacent to the railroad tracks, fulfilled his desire to work close to home. This property was later repurposed to become the Overbrook Station Lofts, an upscale and modern condominium complex. (Courtesy of Victoria Wilson.)

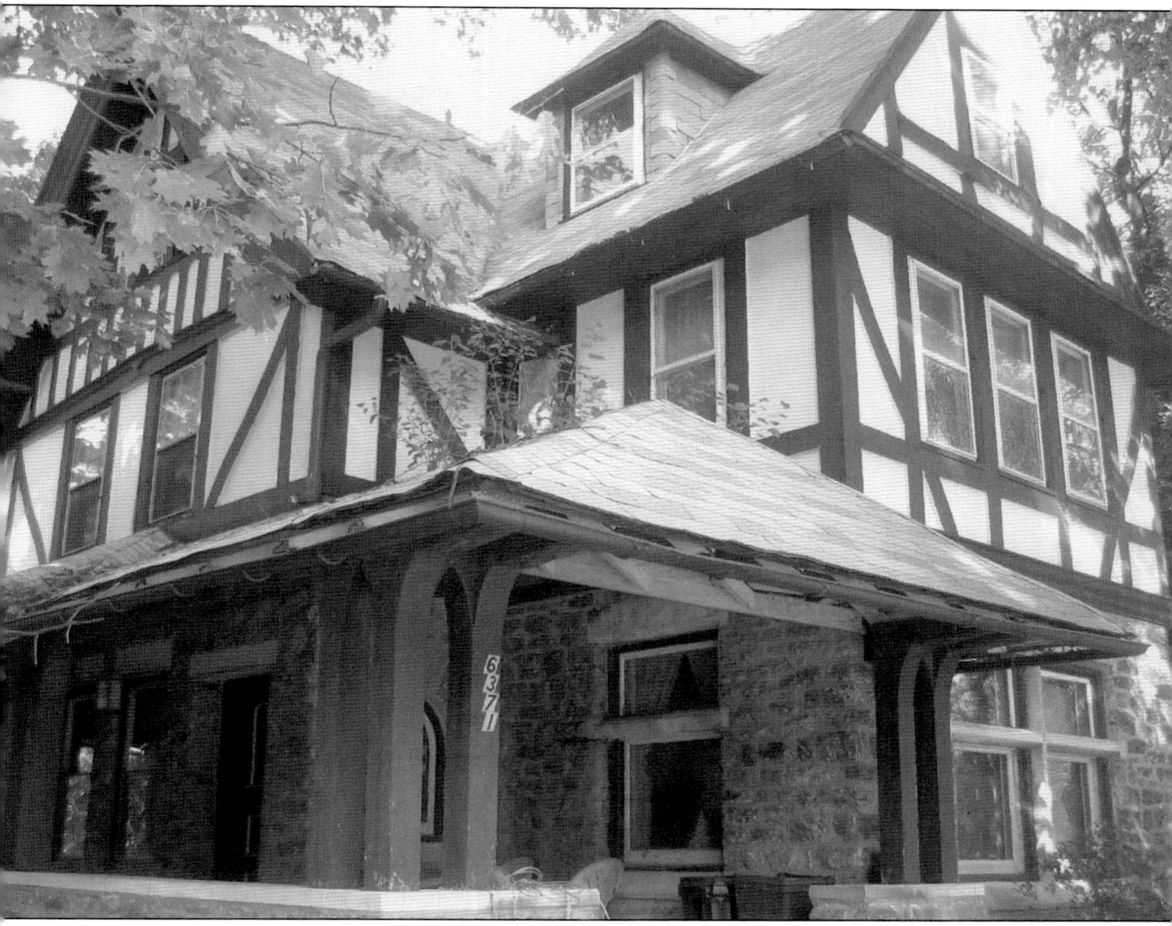

Truly a daunting undertaking, Mark Wallacavage and family saved an 1895 William L. Price twin from certain condemnation. Viewing its virtual distress signal, a tree growing through the roof, their answer was to snatch this long-abandoned and disfigured beauty from impending doom in 2008. Their commitment transformed the 3,800-square-foot Tudor to its former glory. (Courtesy of Mark Wallacavage.)

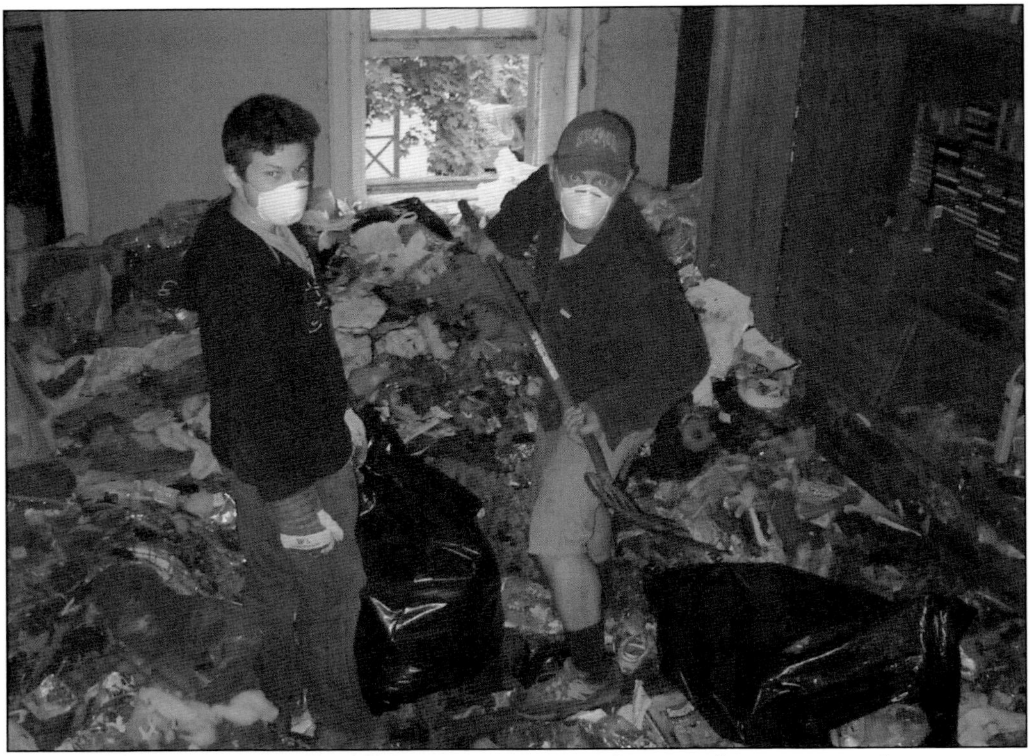

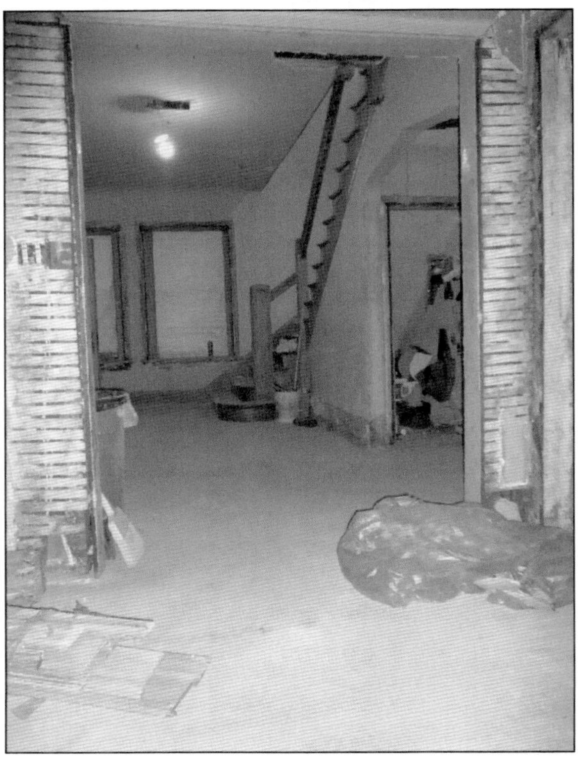

From condemnation to salvation required Wallacavage four years of rising at 4:00 a.m. to complete tasks before reporting to his nursing job, ridding the home of three frightening dumpsters worth of knee-deep excrement, employing 800 contractor bags to remove the accumulated hazards, and grappling with the economic consequences of an unscrupulous contractor who walked away with thousands of dollars and unmet tasks and deadlines. (Both, courtesy of Mark Wallacavage.)

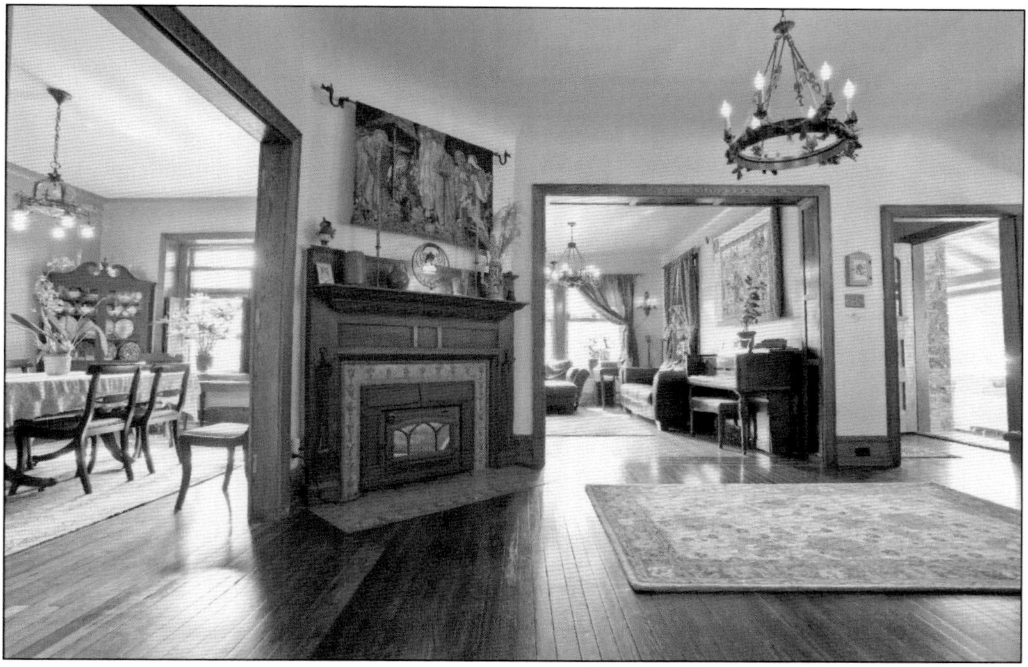

Mark Wallacavage credits a strong stomach earned through his nursing background for the fortitude it took to see the project through from beginning to end. He had help from friends, loans and materials from family, more friends, and good neighbors. *Craigslist*, auctions, estate and demolition sales, and Habitat ReStores provided materials to implement affordable, successful renovations. (Both, courtesy of Mark Wallacavage.)

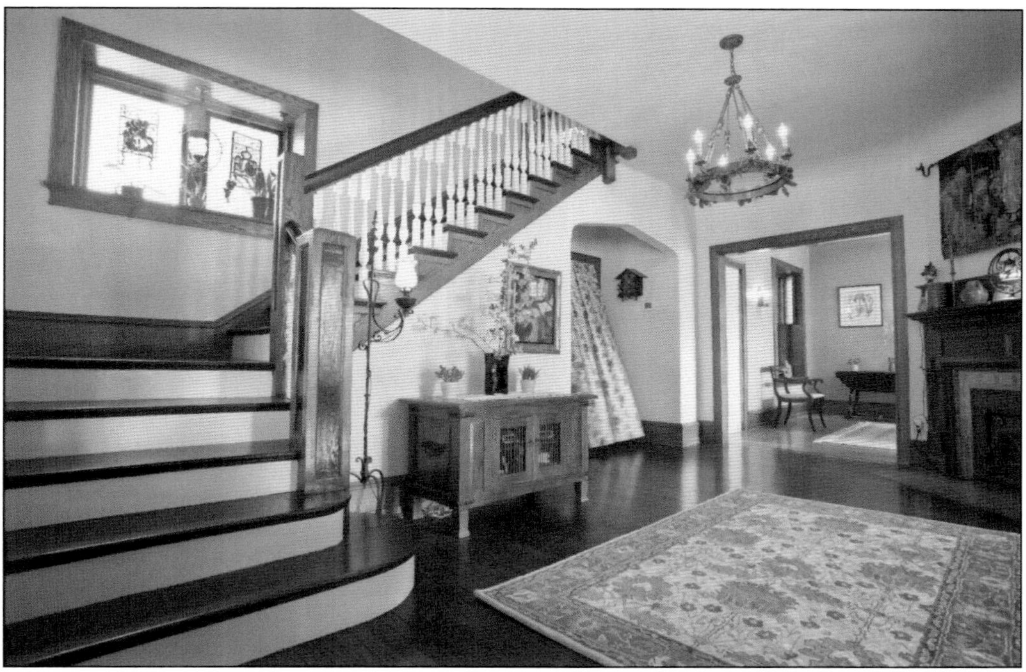

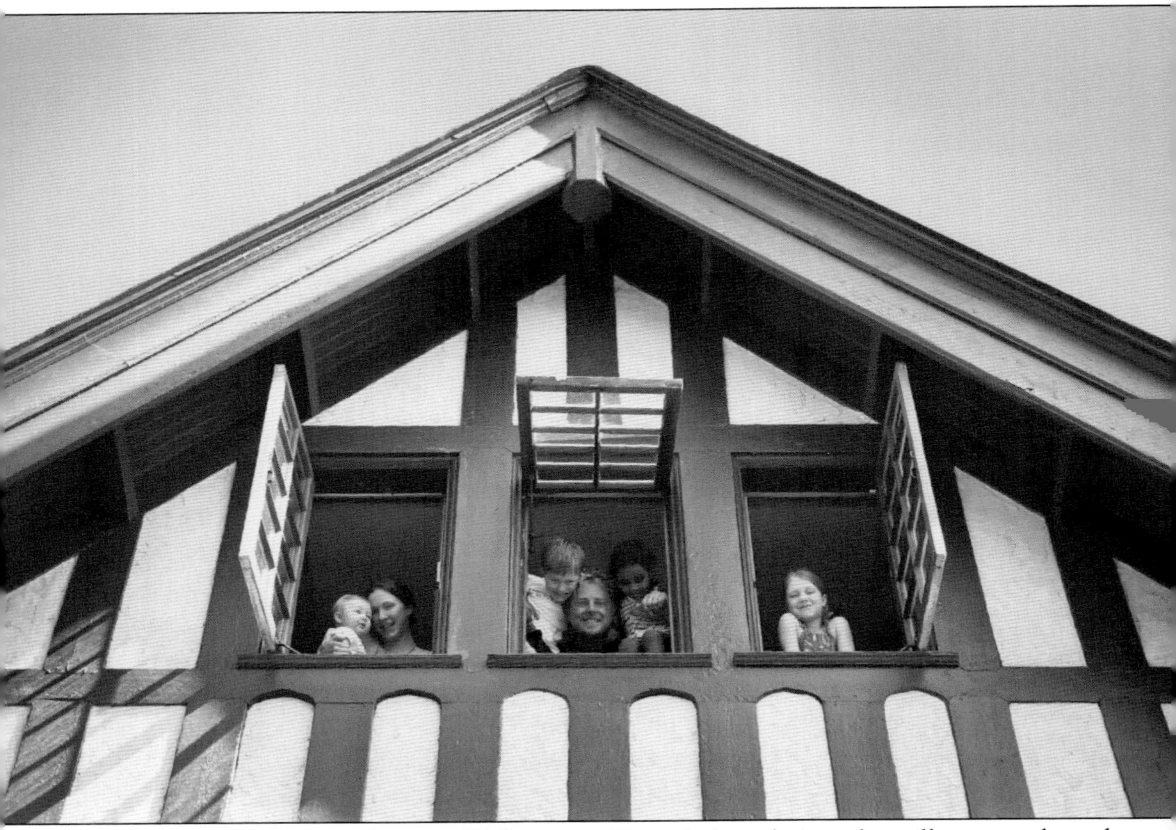

"Are we done yet? Hardly," says Wallacavage. Nevertheless, their to-date efforts won them the Best Whole House Remodel 2012 from *This Old House* magazine. As is true of many an Overbrook Farms house, it is a continuous labor of love. (Courtesy of Mark Wallacavage.)

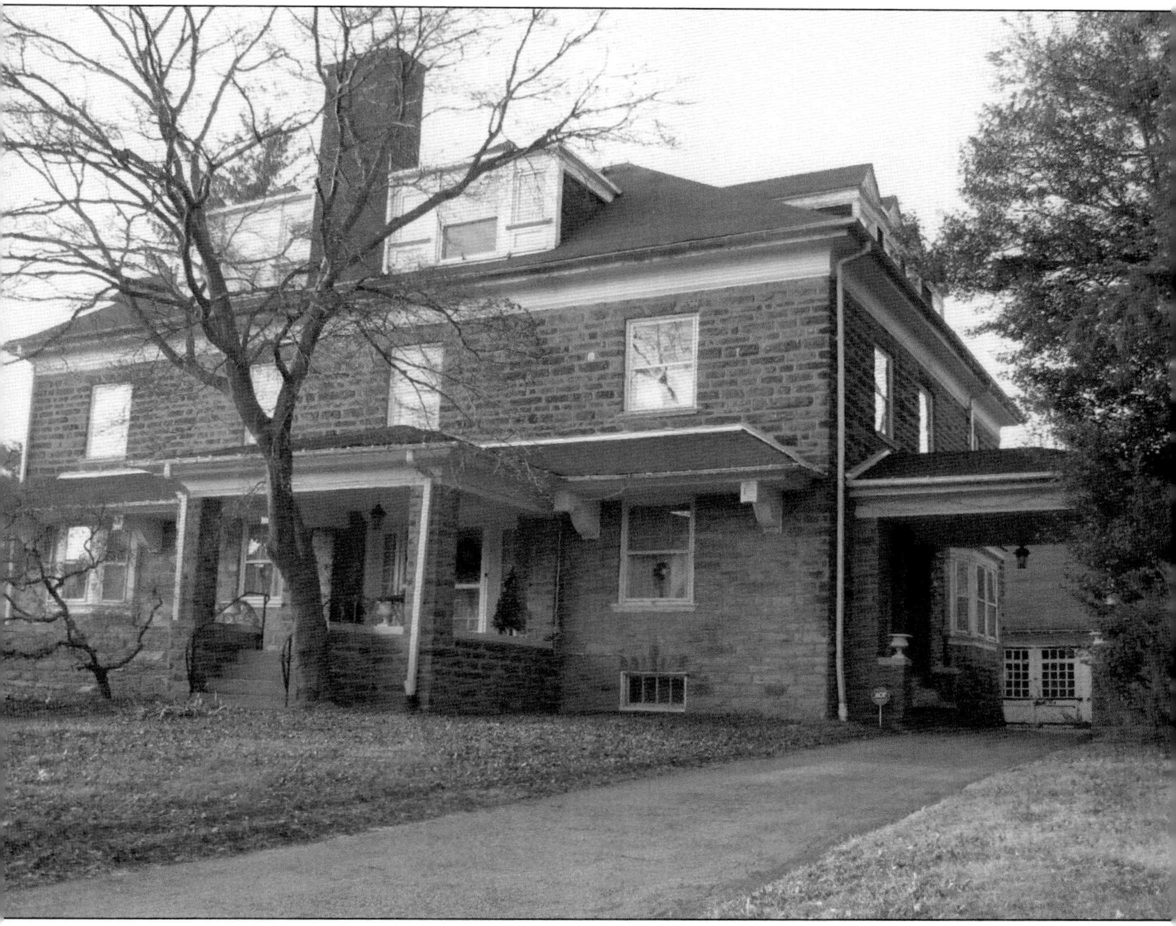

Originally built as twin houses between 1896 and 1897, the architectural team of Charles Barton Keen and Frank Mead designed 6357–6359 Woodbine Avenue as a modified Colonial Revival. Prominent businessman Frederick Geiger, founder of Geiger Instrument Co., seamlessly merged the twins beginning in 1914. It resulted in a 6,200-square-foot manse containing five third-floor bedrooms for live-in staff. A three-car carriage house features an apartment that once housed the resident horseman. A porte cochere along the right side of the house is one of only six extant examples in Overbrook Farms. Before the advent of private automobiles, this high-stepped carriage portal served as the house's main entrance from the library. (Courtesy of Kip Krieger.)

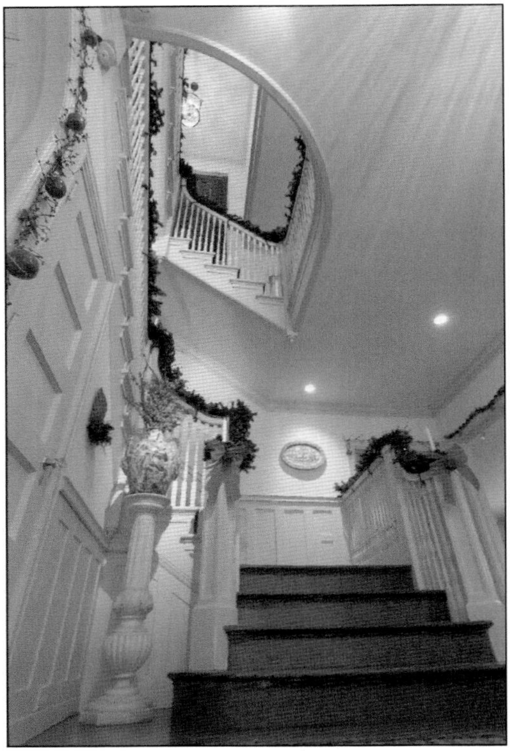

Many elements common to a gracious country house of the 1910s–1920s are in ample evidence here, including wainscoting, crown molding, oak flooring and broad beams, leaded and stained glass, multiple fireplaces, and built-in bookcases. The current owners painstakingly restored these details in a 2004 renovation. Most noteworthy is an open-string winding stair with 249 closely spaced turned balusters, four per tread. (Both, courtesy of Rick Pullin.)

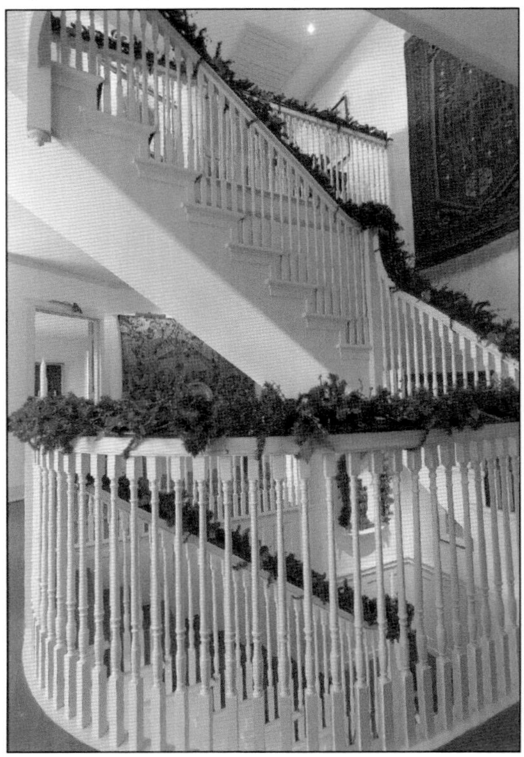

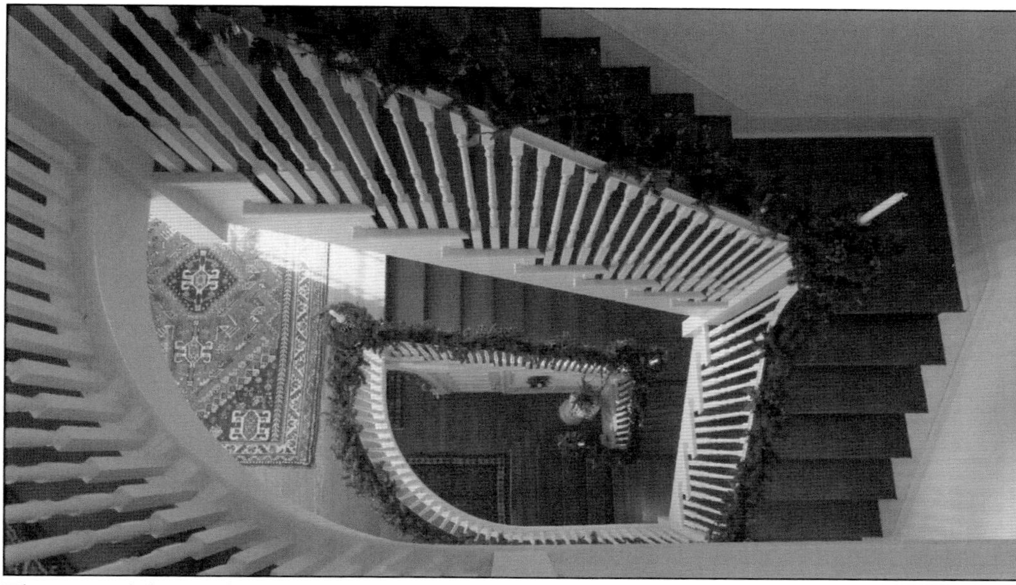

The view of the winding stair from its third-floor height is spectacular, highlighting the curves and angles of construction. While this dramatic stair showcases the public areas of the house, a much more Spartan servant/butler's back stair rises to the third floor as well so that staff may move about unseen. (Both, courtesy of Rick Pullin.)

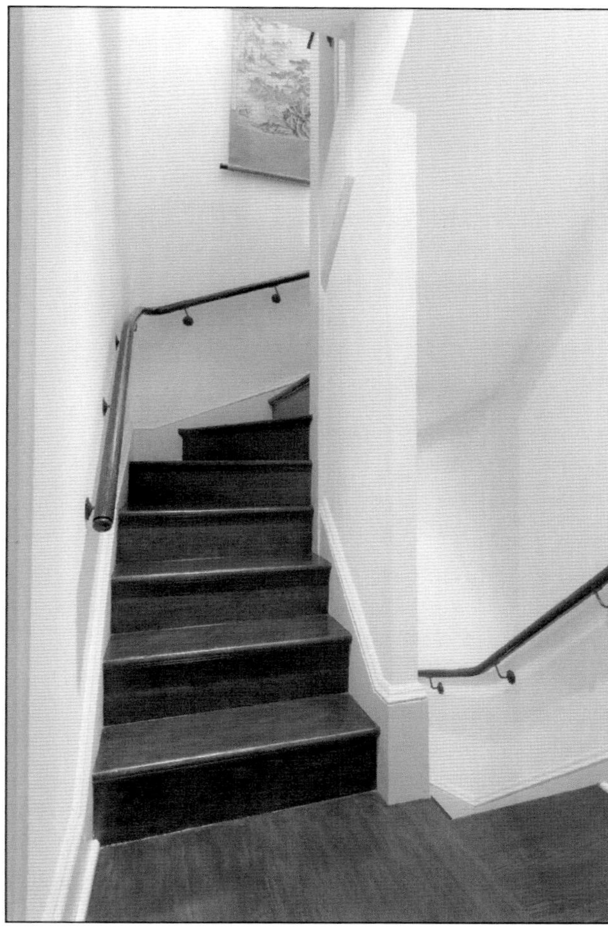

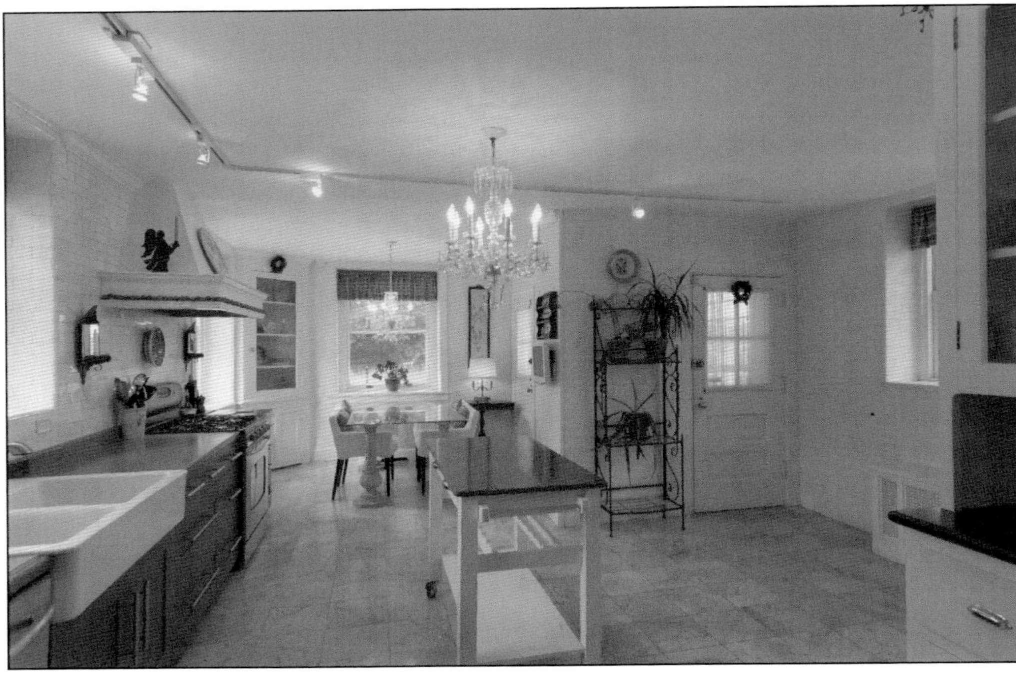

An updated kitchen and pantry blends traditional, efficient, and contemporary elements. The spacious kitchen has been brightened and fitted to modern demands. The space is complemented by a functional butler's pantry, featuring a mix of original built-in cabinetry and additional contemporary cabinets, counters, and appliances. (Both, courtesy of Rick Pullin.)

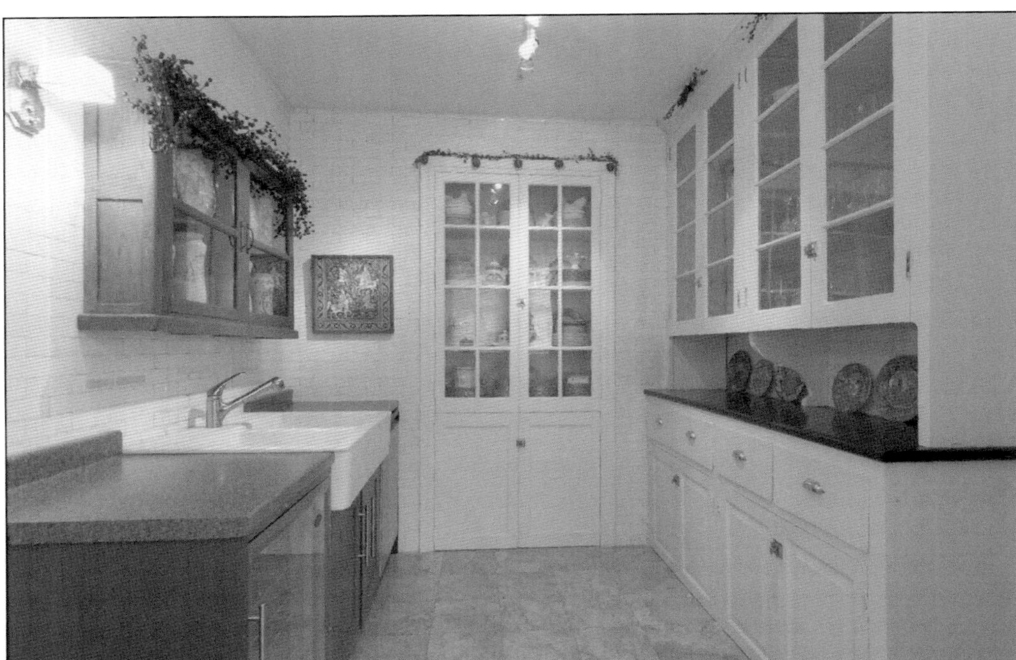

Located in the kitchen is a well-preserved servant's call box. Evident in the options offered by the box is a defined notion of how and where each room is located. (Courtesy of Rick Pullin.)

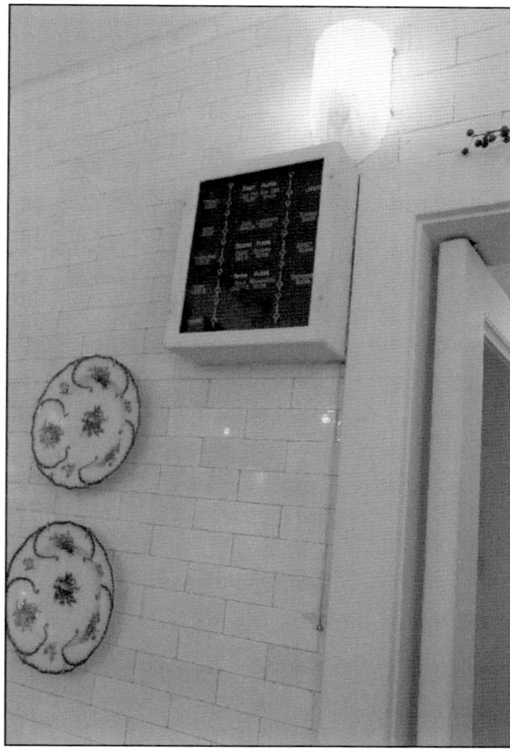

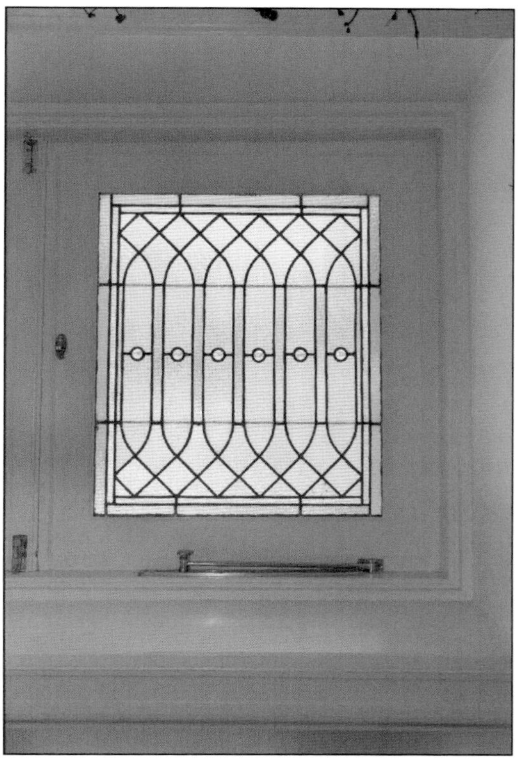

An Art Nouveau–inspired window breathes air and radiates beauty into the dining room of this home. (Courtesy of Rick Pullin.)

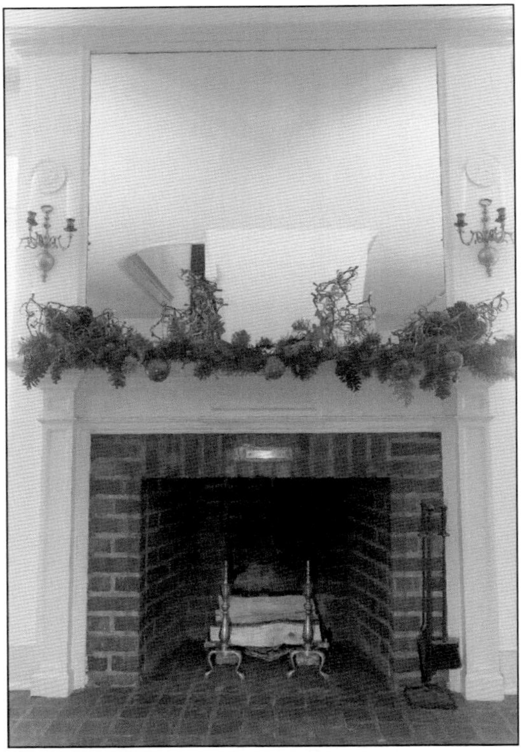

One of the house's most unique details is the presence of two souvenir bricks that feature engraved brass markers. Each was recovered from two houses important to the nation's history. Above the first-floor firebox is a brick from the McLean House in Appomattox, Virginia, where Civil War general Lee surrendered to Grant in 1865. (Courtesy of Rick Pullin.)

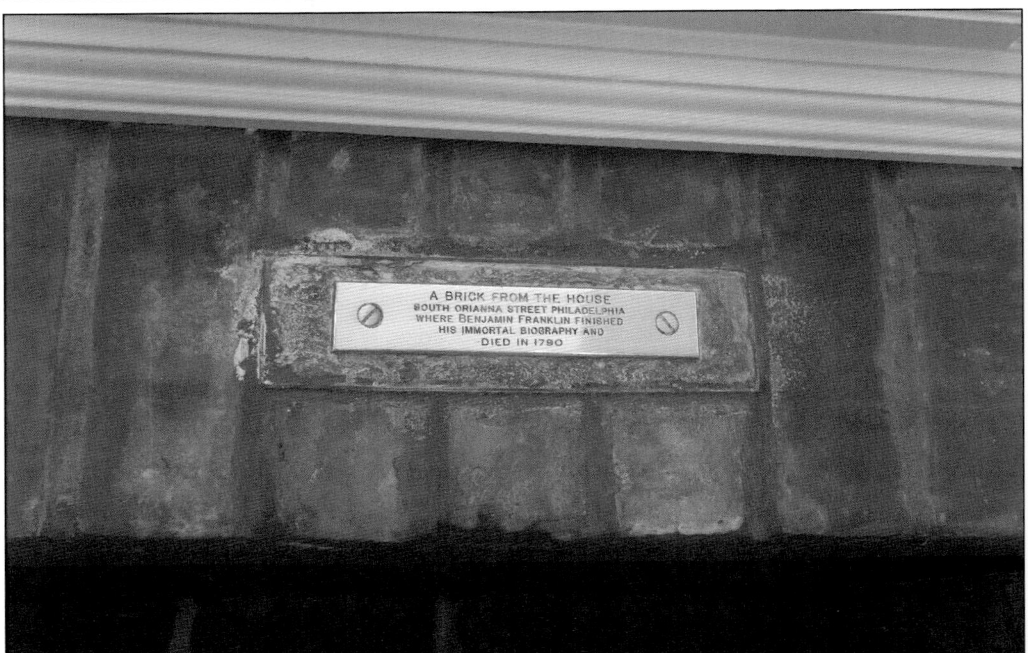

The second-floor hall firebox contains a brick from the Philadelphia house of Benjamin Franklin, razed, sadly, in the early 19th century. Today, this home's former profile is marked by an on-site steel skeleton structure outlining its original dimensions. (Courtesy of Rick Pullin.)

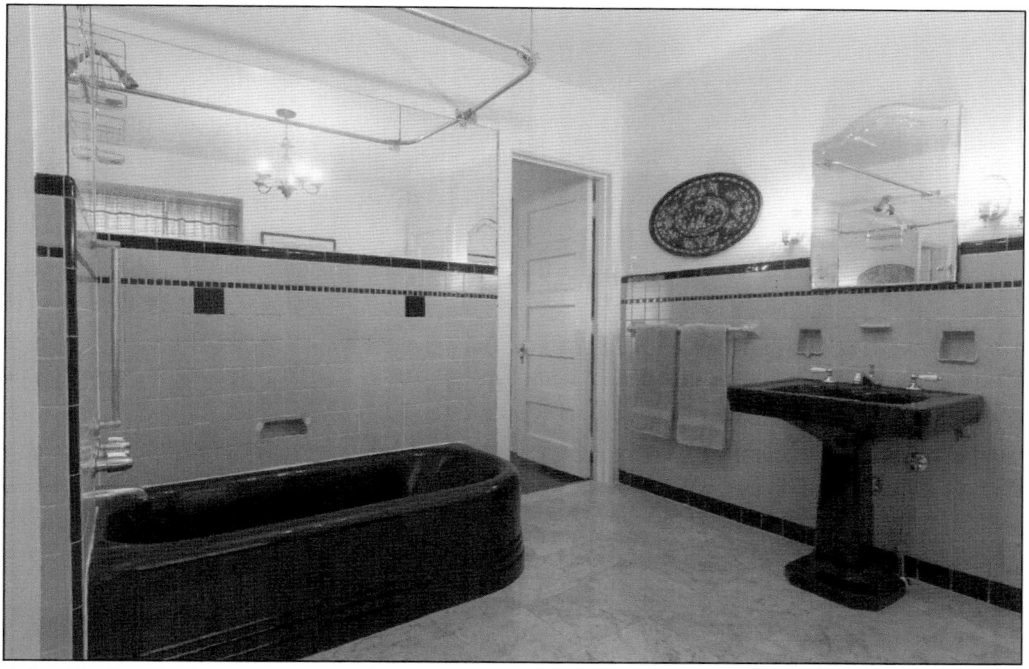

After Frederick Geiger's 1914 makeover, the renovations that most influenced the character of the house were undertaken by Carrie May Price in 1931. The prevailing Art Deco style is evident in several kitchen light fixtures and in bathrooms (a black and mauve tiled bath remains essentially intact). Features that may support an oral tradition that claimed the house once served as a Prohibition speakeasy (1920–1933) are the German silver sinks hidden in a closet of a former billiard room. (Courtesy of Rick Pullin.)

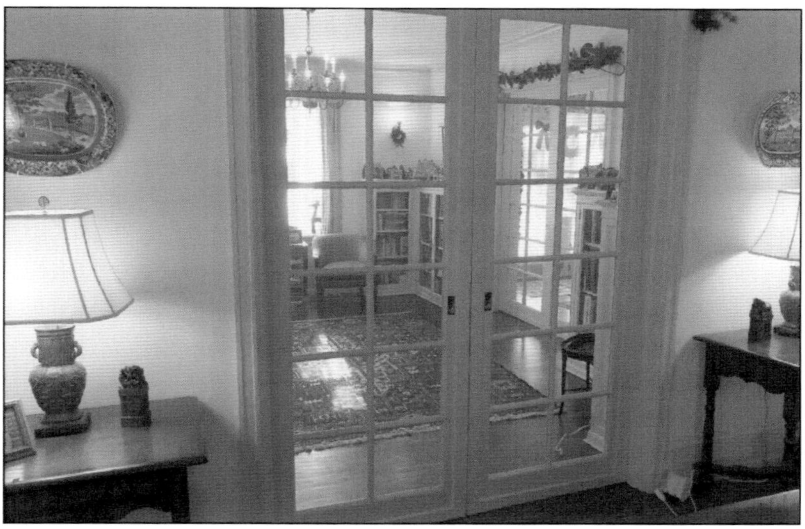

Four sets of pocket doors are found in this elegant house. Each set has 24 lights or windowpanes. This is uncommon, since most of the pocket doors throughout Overbrook Farms are wood paneled. (Courtesy of Rick Pullin.)

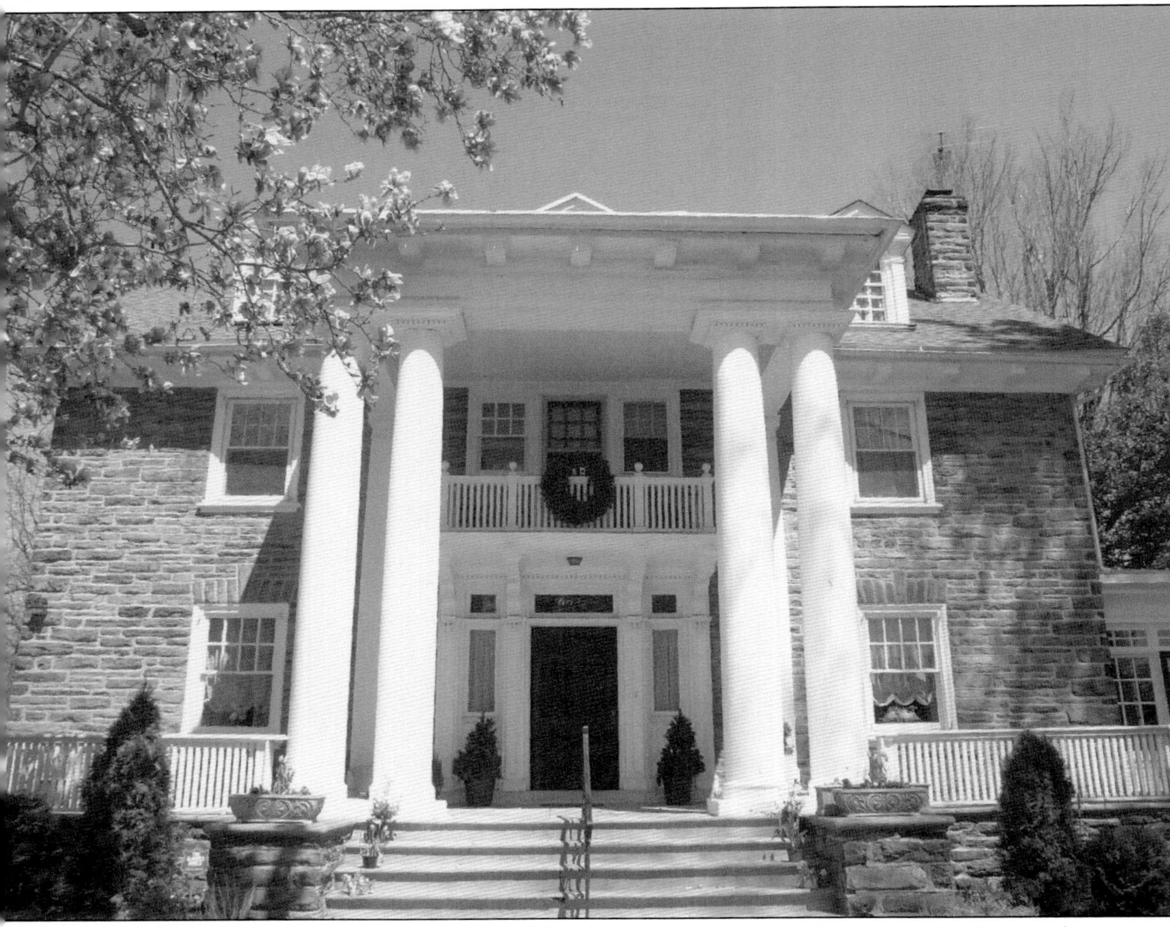

A grand-scale restoration was required of this 1909 Gothic Revival's four supporting Ionic columns, which were rotting. Rebuilt and restored to their former glory, the wood flourishes marking the top of the columns were painstakingly replaced one dentil at a time. (Courtesy of Victoria Wilson.)

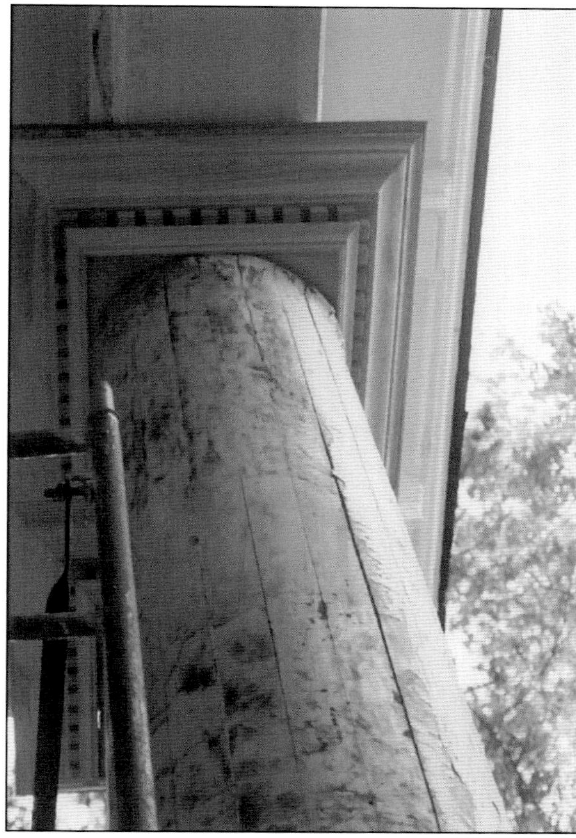

The columns, which took two years to finish, marked only one of innumerable roof-down and room-by-room renovations the owner implemented to restore and refresh her Drexel Road home. (Both, courtesy of Victoria Wilson.)

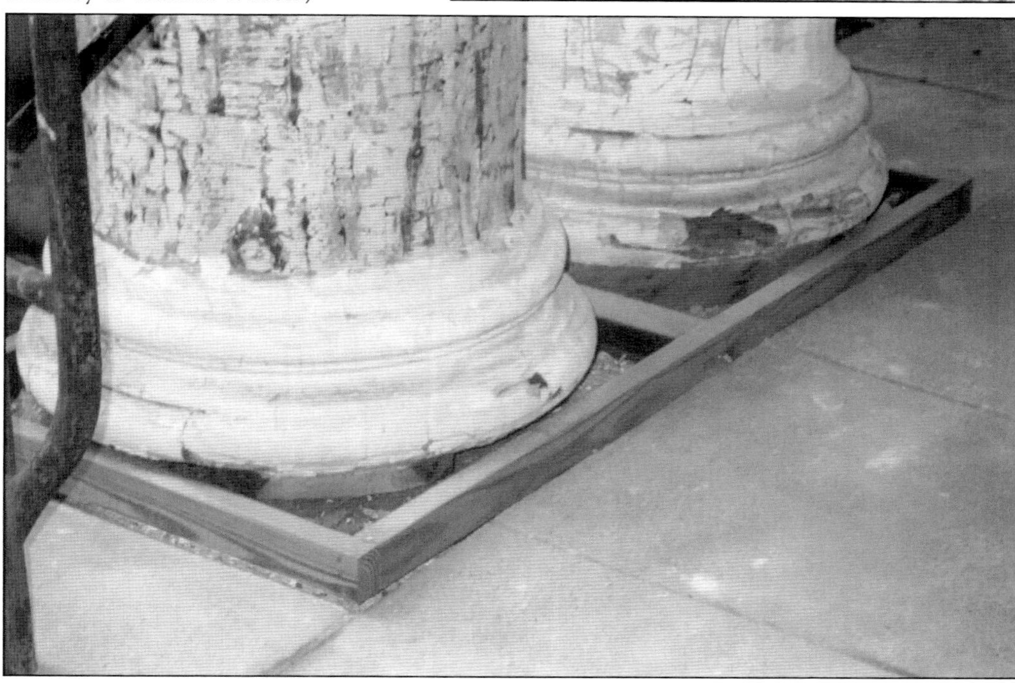

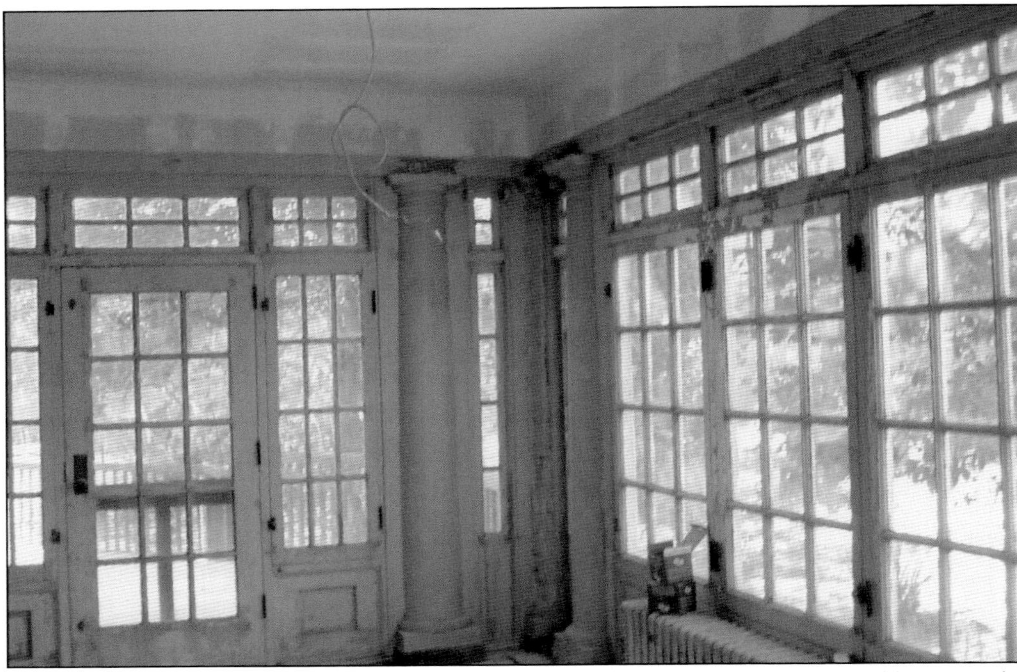

Deteriorated wood was replaced on the exterior and interior of this home, in addition to the installation of a new ceiling and flooring in the sunporch that enable one to enjoy this room most of the year. (Both, courtesy of Victoria Wilson.)

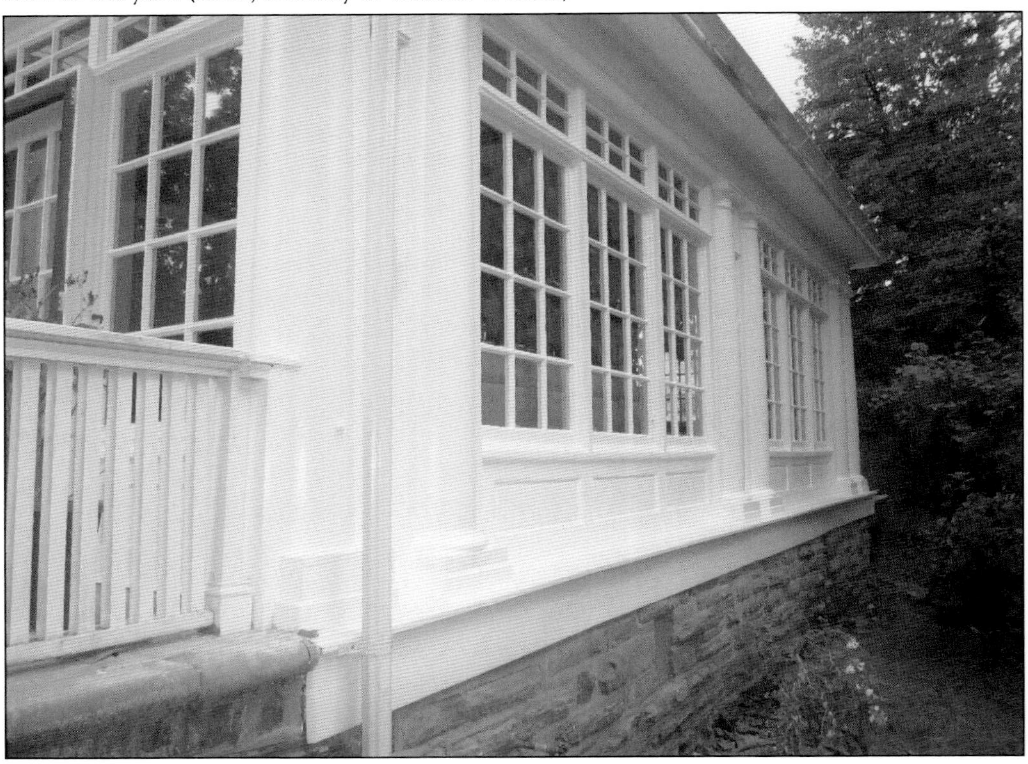

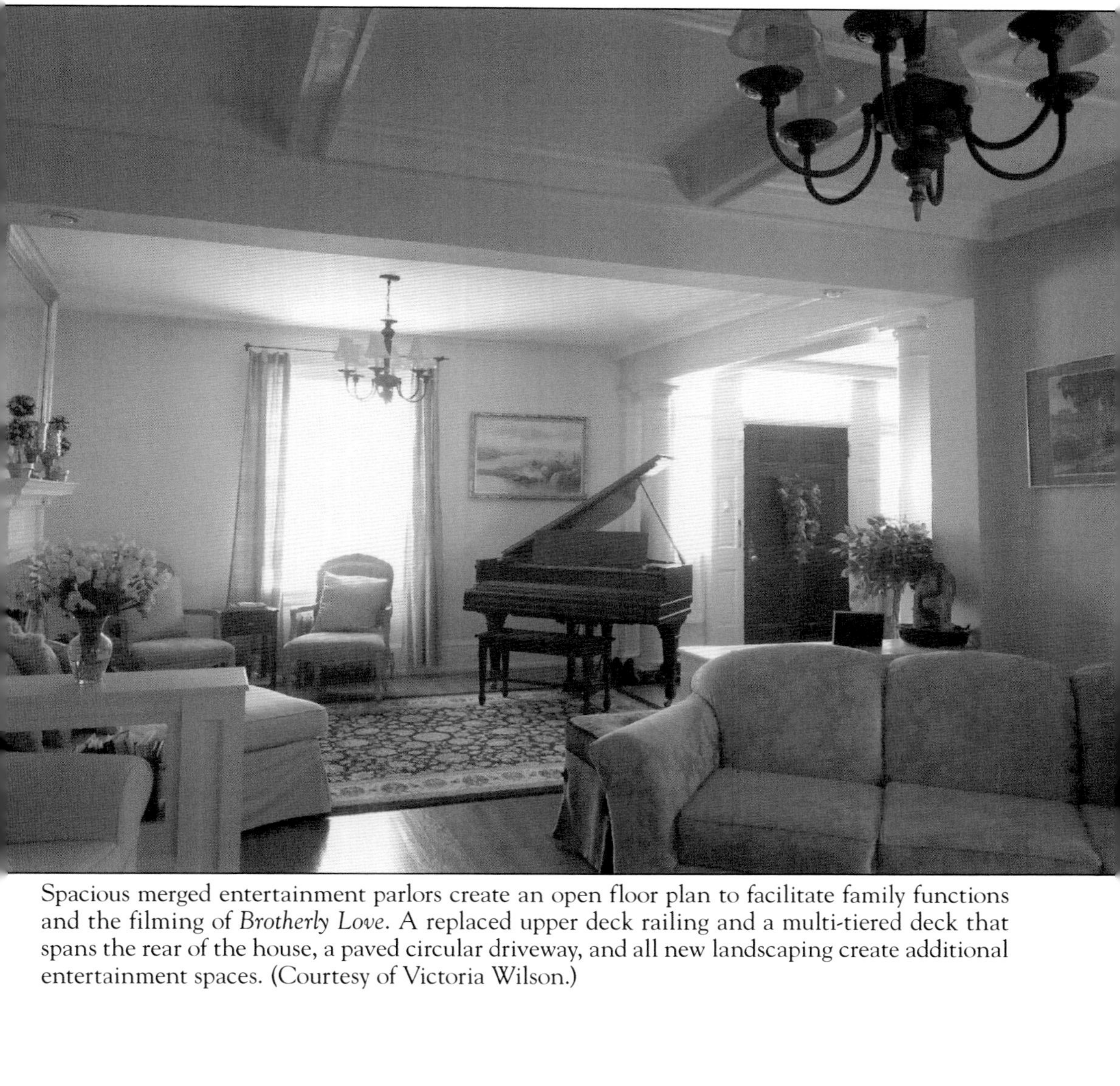

Spacious merged entertainment parlors create an open floor plan to facilitate family functions and the filming of *Brotherly Love*. A replaced upper deck railing and a multi-tiered deck that spans the rear of the house, a paved circular driveway, and all new landscaping create additional entertainment spaces. (Courtesy of Victoria Wilson.)

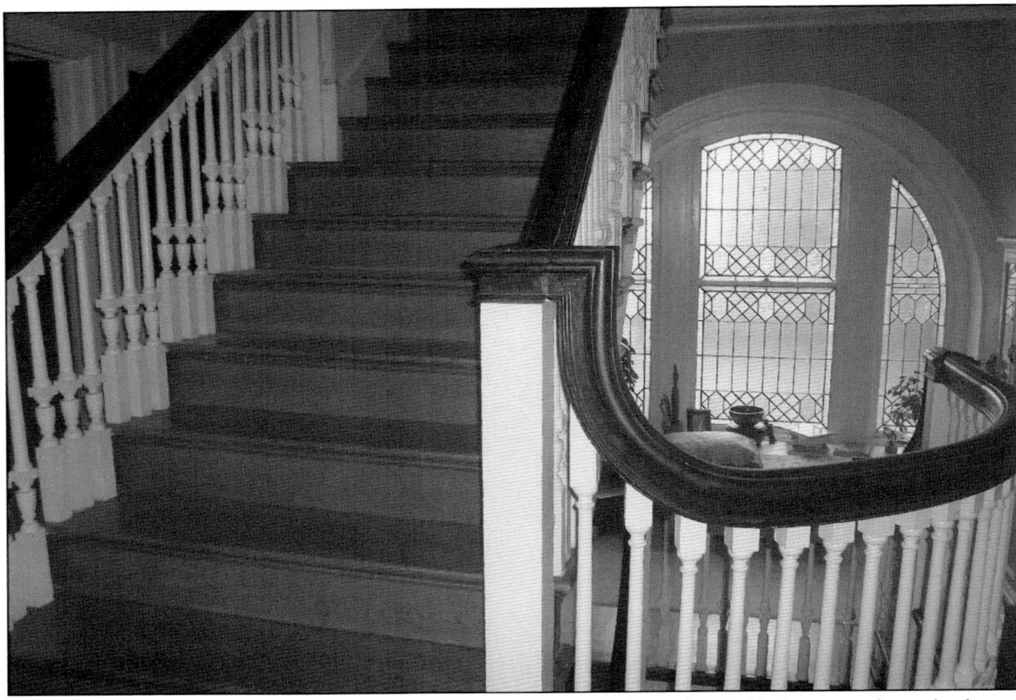

Filled with natural lighting from nearly 80 windows, including this Palladian window, the house was designed to reap the benefits from its many exposures to the sun. (Both, courtesy of Jabar Singh Wilson.)

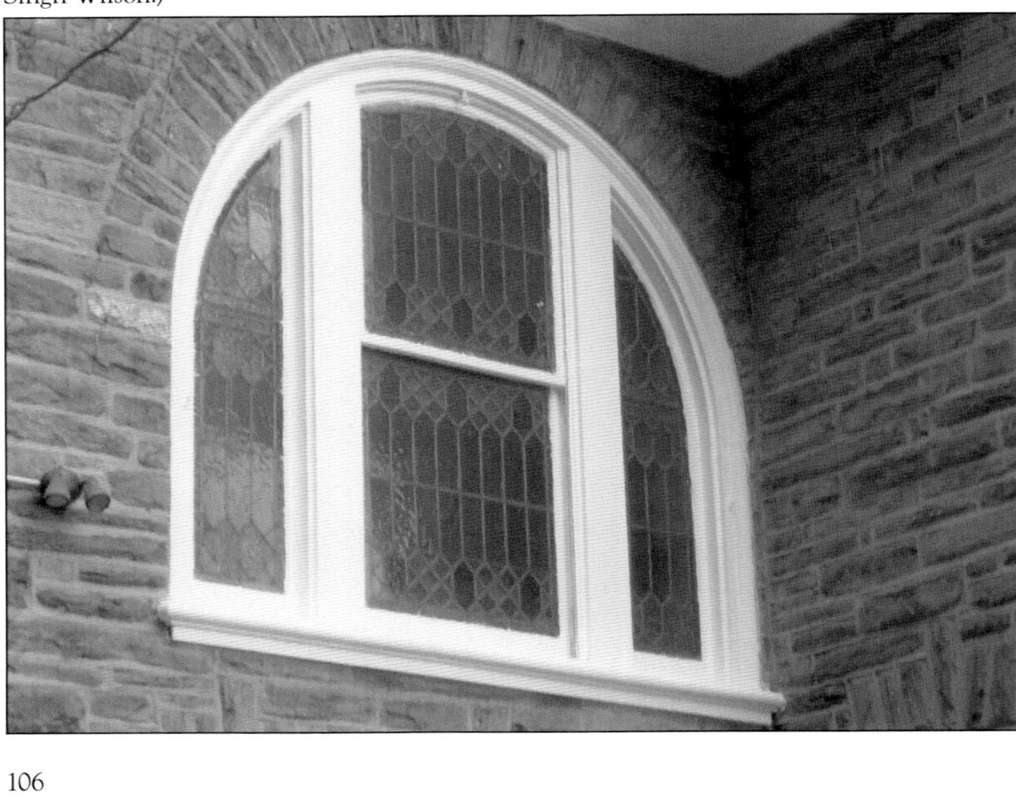

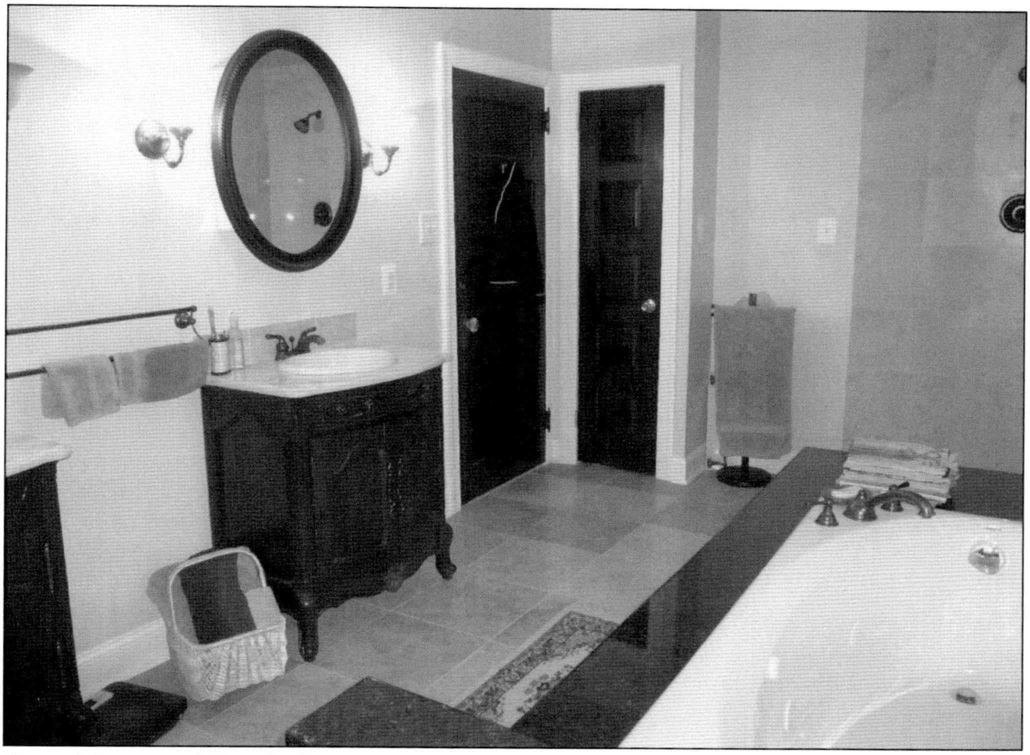

One of the second-floor bedrooms was transformed into a custom closet, and a smaller walk-in closet was removed to accommodate an enlarged master bathroom, thus creating a bedroom suite. While a third-floor bathroom renovation restored the original claw-foot tub, incorporated wainscoting, grass cloth, and upgraded fixtures mark improvements in the rest of the house. (Both, courtesy of Victoria Wilson.)

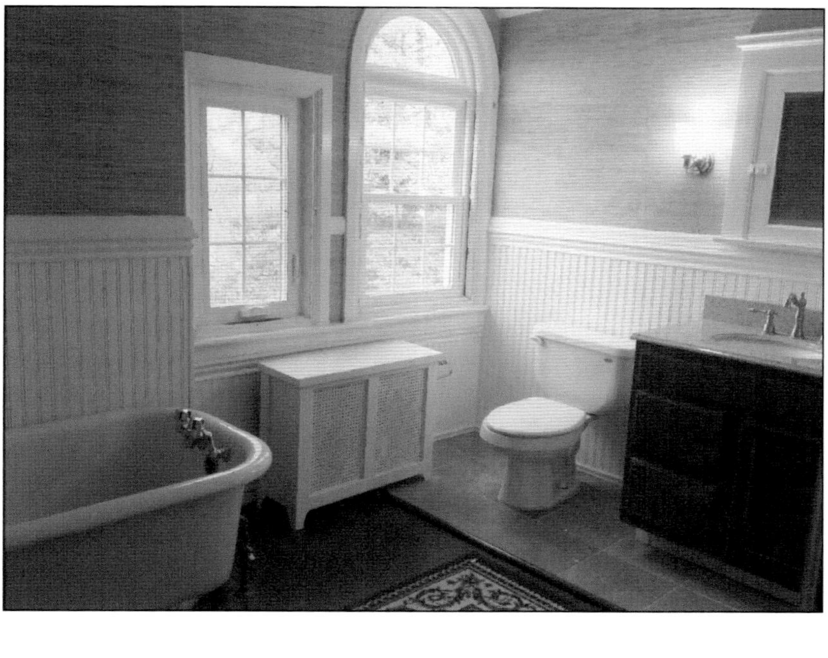

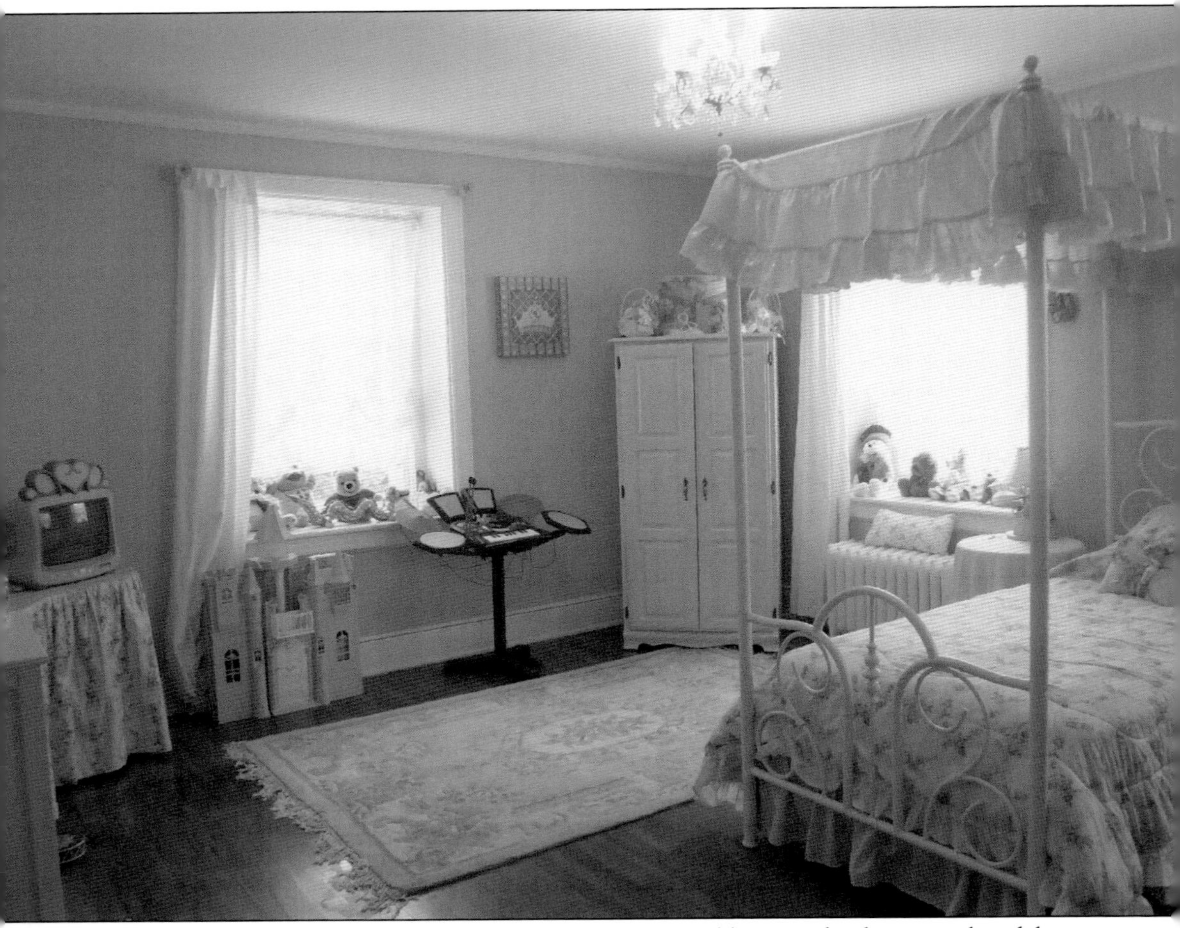

Stripping wallpaper, sanding original floors, repairing moldings, and re-hanging chandeliers were all part of the restoration project. Besides, that is just what a princess commands. (Courtesy of Victoria Wilson.)

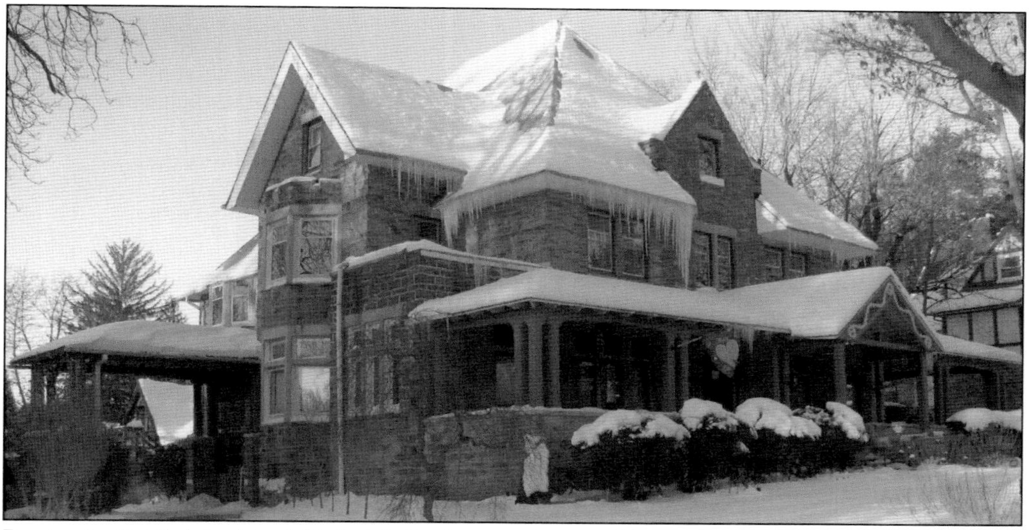

Benjamin P. Obdyke hired Philadelphia-born architect Chester Kirk in 1894. Kirk designed a one-of-a-kind Gothic Revival–style house on Drexel Road. The veranda is supported by posts and finished with a richly ornamented bargeboard that creates the end rafters of its gable roof. This lavish exterior treatment and the array of interior adornments evident throughout public rooms in the house reflect Kirk's training at the Pennsylvania Academy of the Fine Arts. The house is filled with magnificent custom woodwork, making it an attractive home for the current owner, a woodworker who has lovingly restored the home to its original grandeur. (Courtesy of Kip Krieger.)

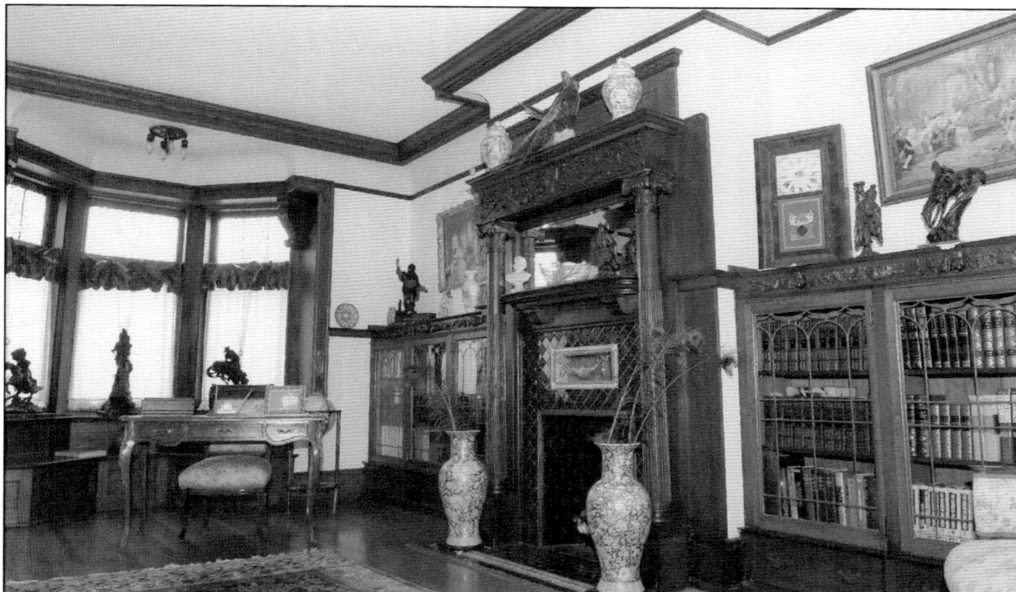

The center hall hosts a massive fireplace beneath an overmantel of carved limestone. The fireplace is topped and surrounded by Pompeiian brick laid in an intricate micro-tile design. Located left of the receiving hall is a library that features beveled leaded glass. Linen-fold carving over the doors features some form of ballflower design. Crown molding provides a decorative enhancement to the coved ceiling. (Courtesy of Larry Andreozzi.)

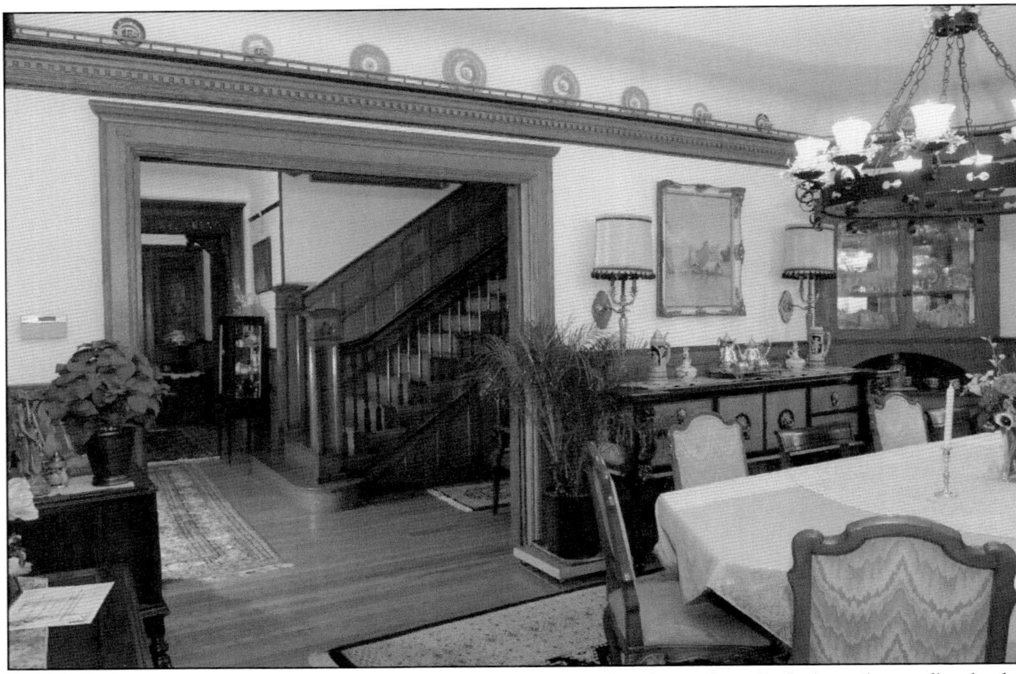

The dining room is fitted with simple corner cupboards whose beveled glass doors flank the triple bay window. The fireplace repeats linen-fold carvings and Ionic columns. A seven-piece assembled oak crown molding provides a decorative enhancement to the coved ceiling. (Courtesy of Larry Andreozzi.)

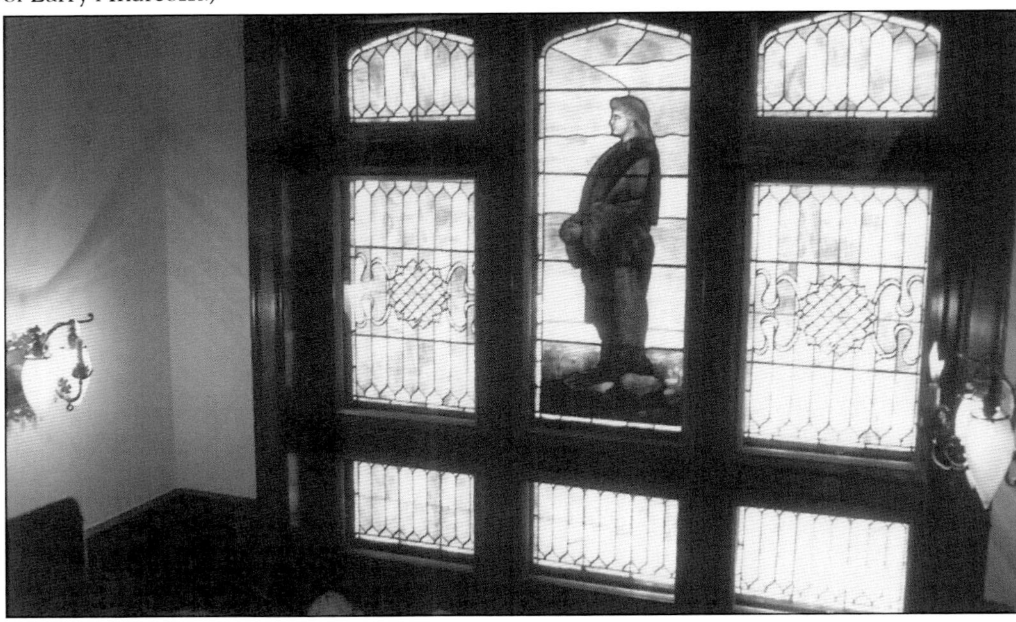

For many, the center hall's most striking feature is its grand stair with a subtly colored stained-glass window. The robed male figure in the central pane is of unknown origin. Lighting the stairs are the original wall fixtures, which are fitted for use with gas or electricity in the case that the electricity, new to that era, proved only a passing fad. (Courtesy of Larry Andreozzi.)

Eight

Custom Curiosities

It was an age of fascination with exotic places, curiosity about materials and aesthetics, the influence of artists, craftsmen, and philosophers, and a collective exhibitionism. The world's fair and travels abroad had brought the art and architecture of many nations to view, and a desire to display their cosmopolitan tastes made for a show of eclectic sensibilities.

Nowhere did all these impulses play out more strongly than in and about the home. Recently and historically, wealthy owners and striving professionals turned their homes into albums of accomplishment. While the architects whose work prevailed in Overbrook Farms shared aesthetics and influences, they strove to imprint their own special interpretation onto the properties they designed. Especially when custom commissions were involved, the architects let their imaginations soar, bringing their clients along on the flight.

The prevailing designs were heavily influenced by romantic revivals and eclecticism. Nature, philosophy, and ecclesiastical and archaeological discoveries all played their part in the design of residential architecture. And since Overbrook Farms was compellingly bordered by both nature and sacred places of worship, these influences are evidenced in the homes and flourishes apparent in the neighborhood.

Many of the details that graced these homes remain well-tended treasures and are apparent outside and inside the homes. Some notable items are here to view.

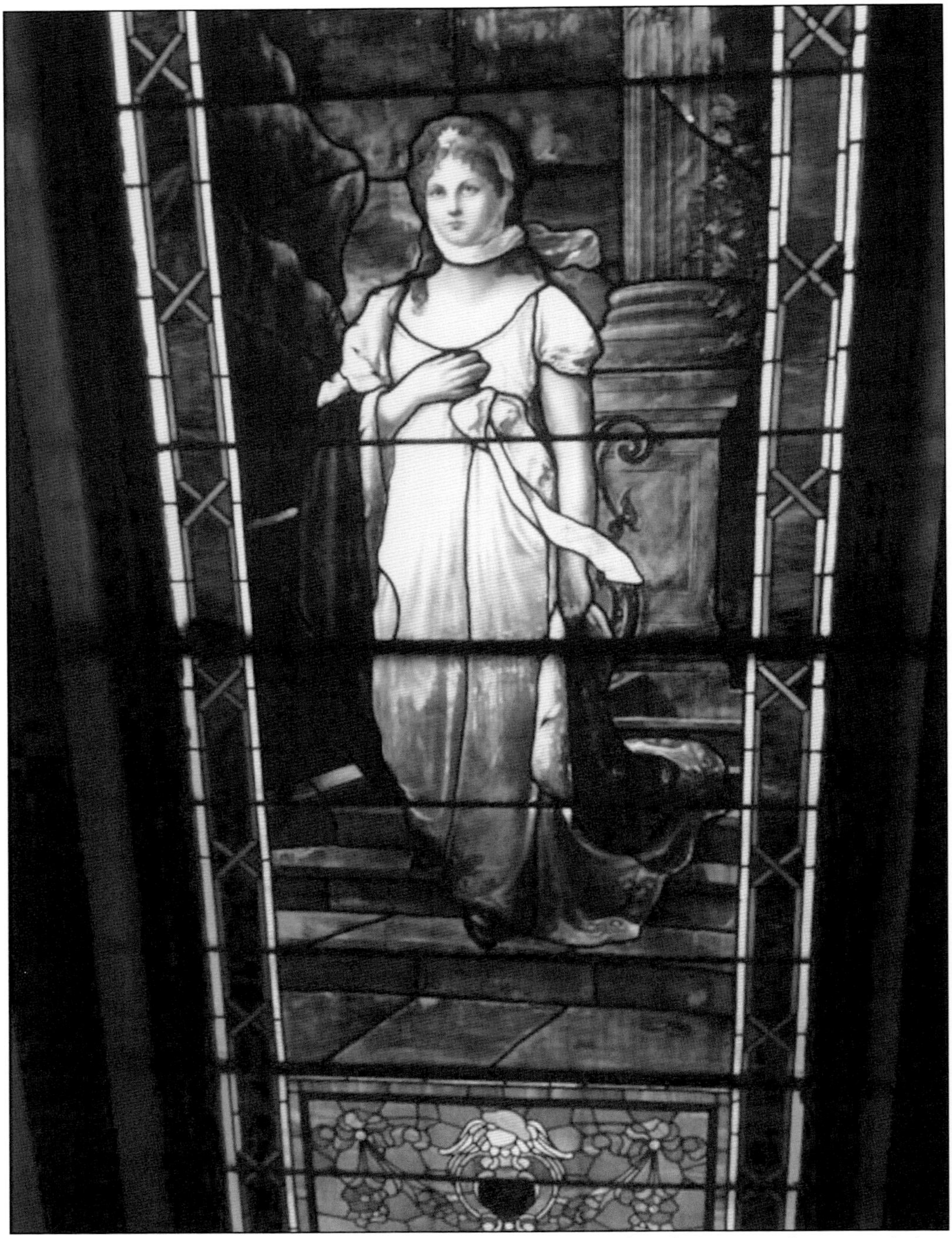

Soaring above a sweeping stairwell in the 5900 block of Overbrook Avenue, this stained glass was installed in 1903 by the home's original owners. Its 13-foot presence captures the portrait of celebrated and beloved Queen Louise of Prussia. First finished by Gustav Richter in Berlin in 1879, the portrait appeared some 60 years following the queen's death. The original painting is now in the Cologne Museum. (Courtesy of Adjoa Love-Dorsey.)

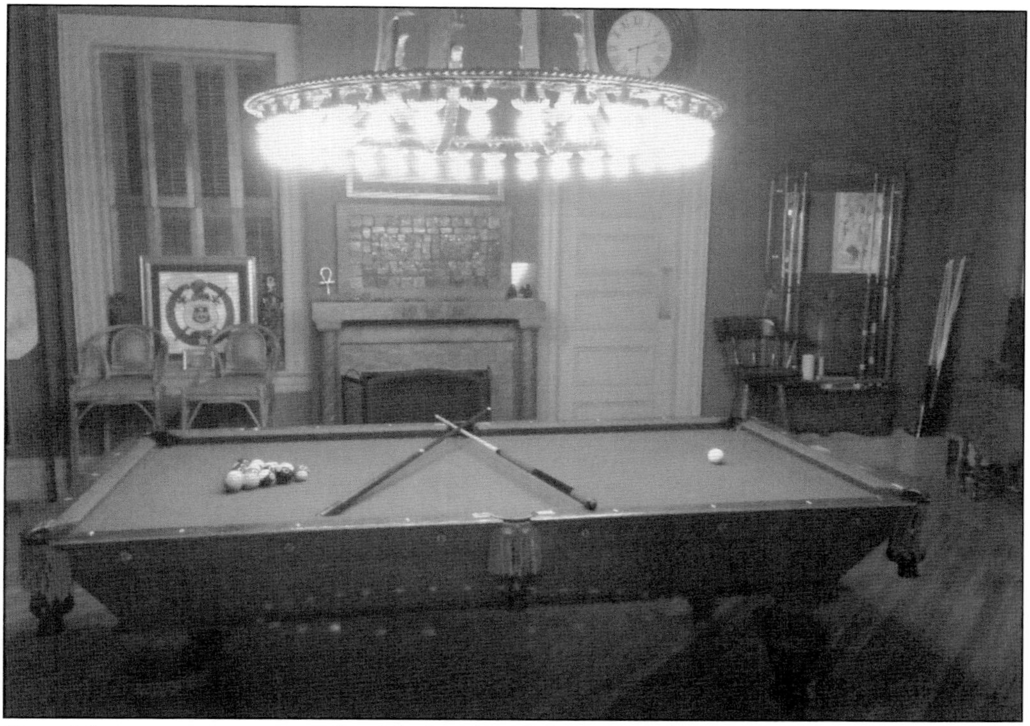

One of four quarter-sawn wood and Italian braided cast-iron fireplaces adorns the first floor of this home. The surround tiles were made by Moravian Pottery & Tileworks Mercer Museum, still in business in Doylestown, Pennsylvania. While in Europe, founder and builder Henry Chapman Mercer took pains to learn a Latinate-German phrase featured in the tile; "*Wo ever schaz ist da ist auch ever herz*," or "Where thy treasure is, there will thy heart be also." (Both, courtesy of Adjoa Love-Dorsey.)

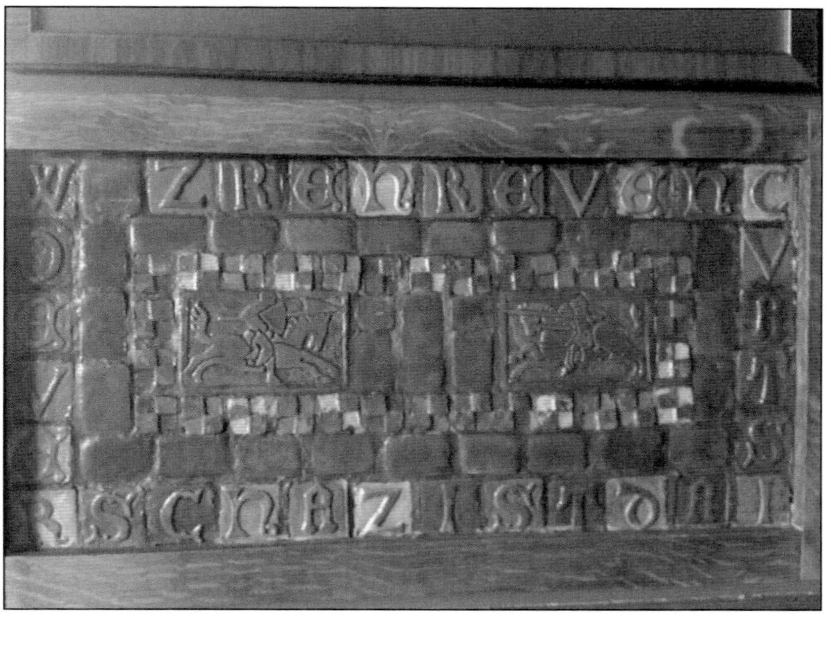

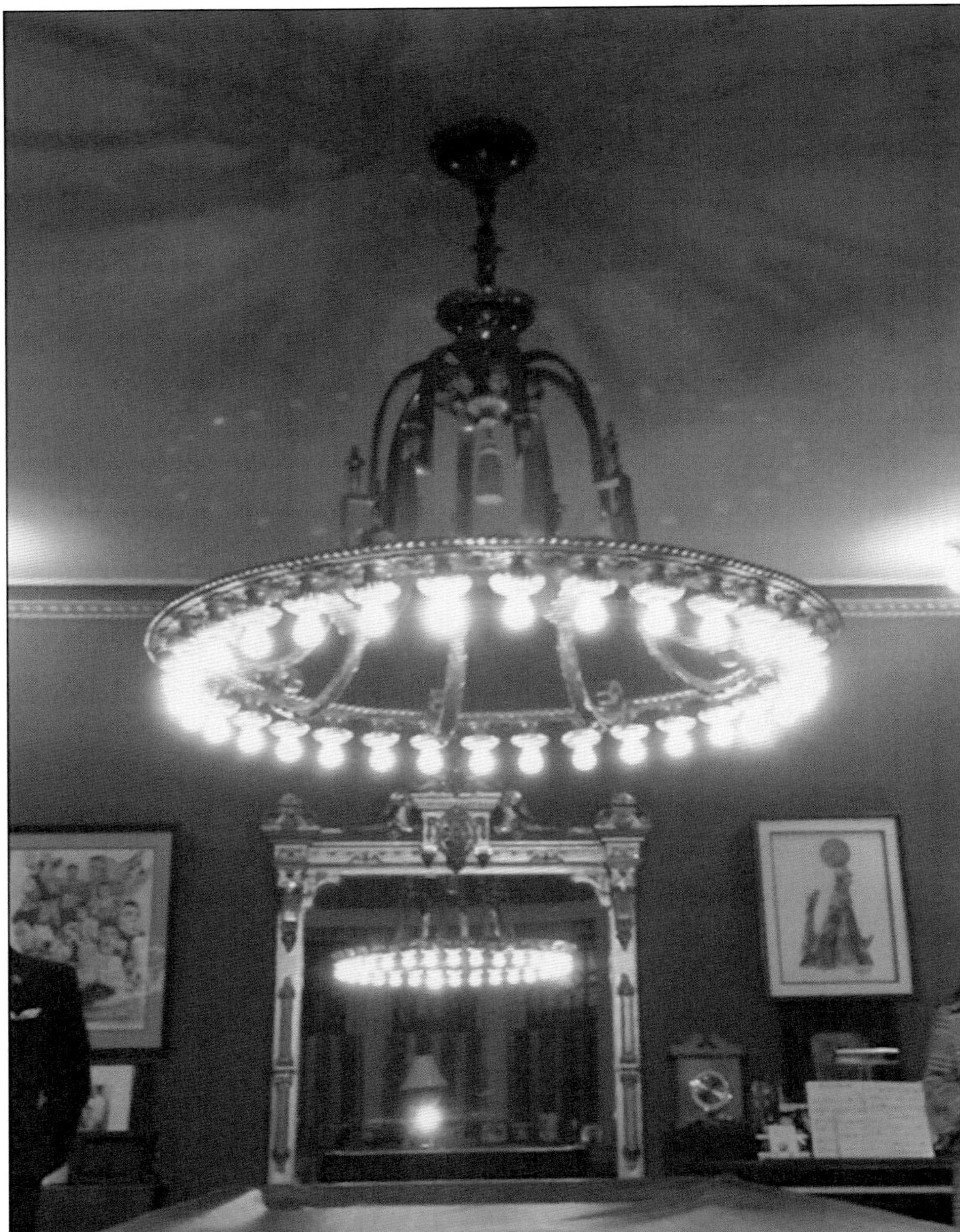

This tasseled, solid brass chandelier hung in the Center of the Farmers and Merchants Bank of Western Pennsylvania's main room until 1989. The chandelier and tassel were separate, and the owner rewired each to hang in the foyer and above the 150-year-old pool table, which is inlaid with ivory diamonds. The pair weighed approximately 600 pounds, and 45 lights ring the chandelier while 60 bulbs light the tassel. (Courtesy of Adjoa Love-Dorsey.)

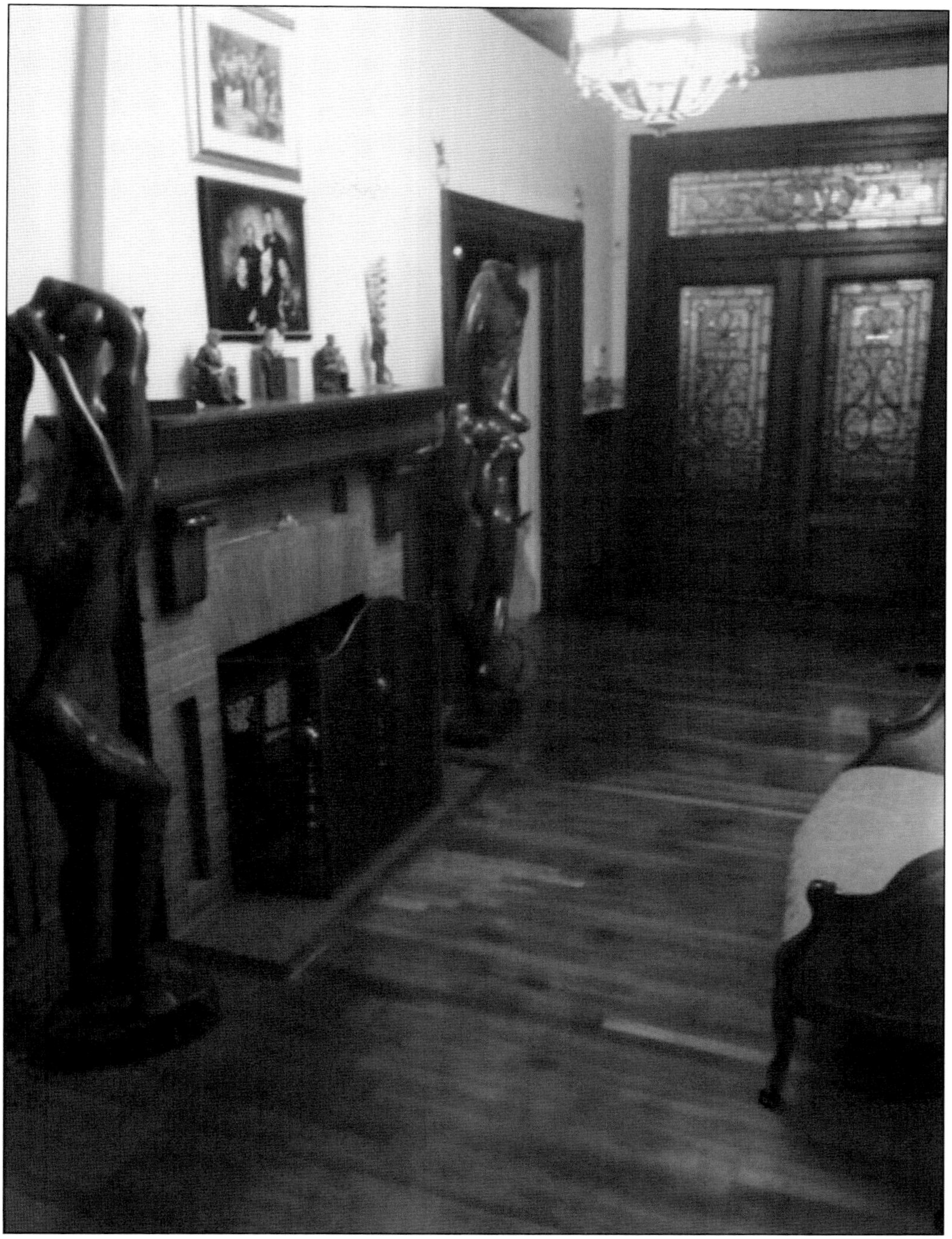

Characteristic of the period in which they were built, the foyers of many homes in Overbrook Farms served as warming rooms. This foyer, with its fireplace and mantle grotesques carved to represent people or animals, is a fine example. A closer look at the front door highlights the marvelous use of stained glass in a pattern that evokes a floral design while at the same time sharing the geometric patterns of other doors. (Courtesy of Adjoa Love-Dorsey.)

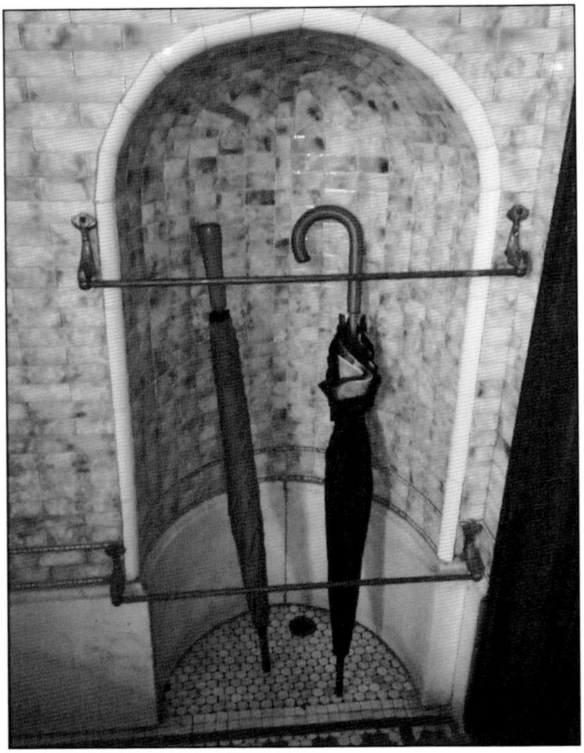

The vestibule contains a built-in umbrella rack made from marbled pink and green ceramic subway tile. Penny floor tile and custom wrought-iron umbrella hangers stow umbrellas that drain below the floor. (Courtesy of Adjoa Love-Dorsey.)

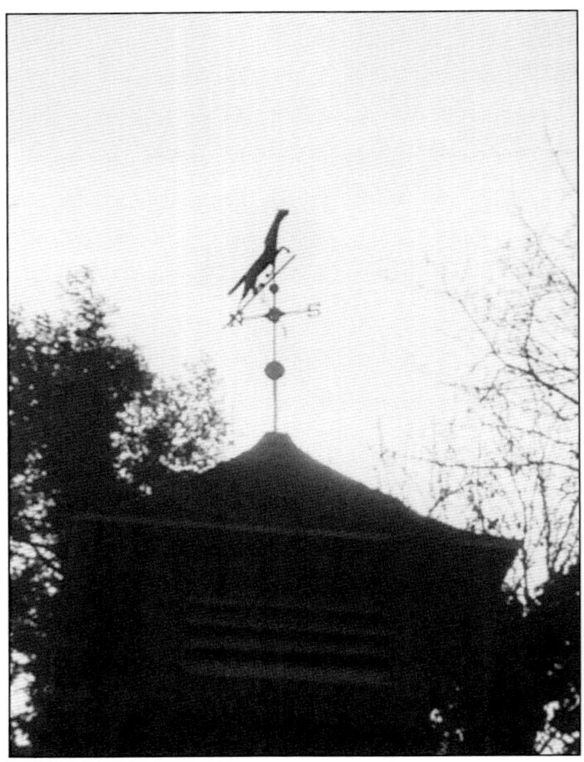

The original Black Hawk weather vane stands high above the carriage house and continues to function, providing the direction of prevailing winds for the current owners. (Courtesy of Adjoa Love-Dorsey.)

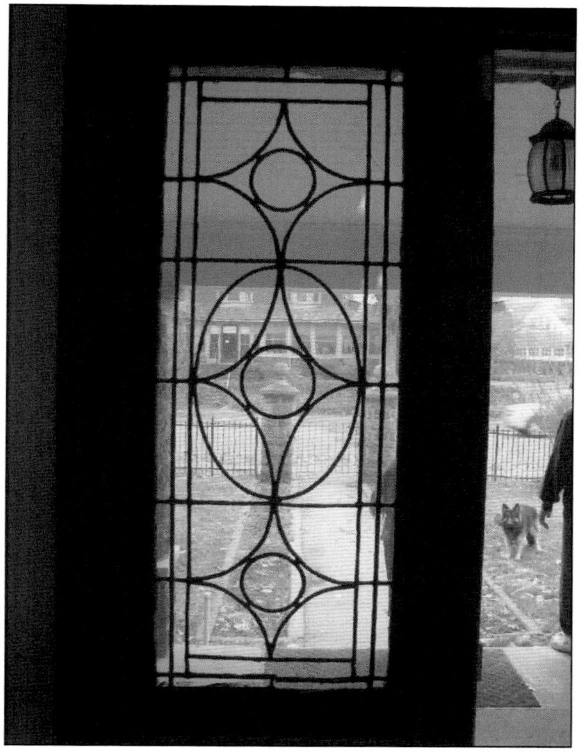

Beveled, leaded, and stained glass were prevalent in residential architecture from 1890 through the 1920s. The stylistic demands reflect various revivals, aesthetics, and geometric patterns. Although the geometric patterns on these two doors share some similarities, they prove to be very different in execution, as is true for architectural treatments found in homes throughout Overbrook Farms. (Both, courtesy of the OFC.)

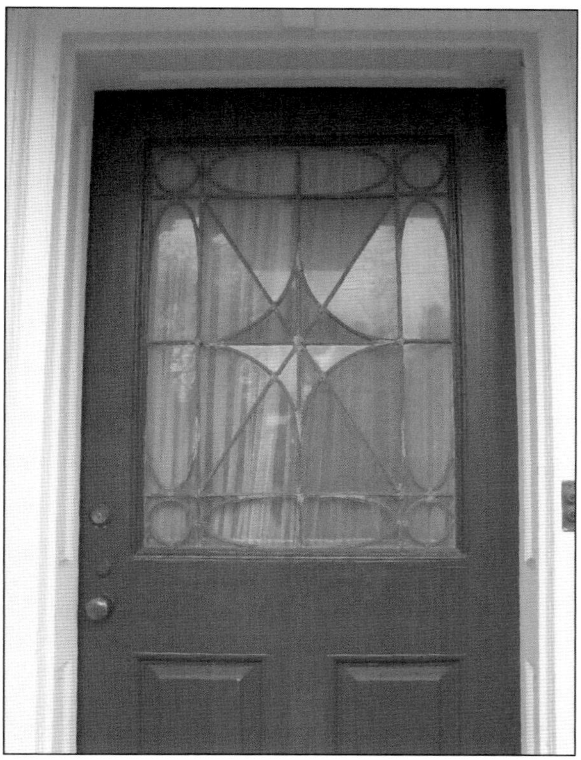

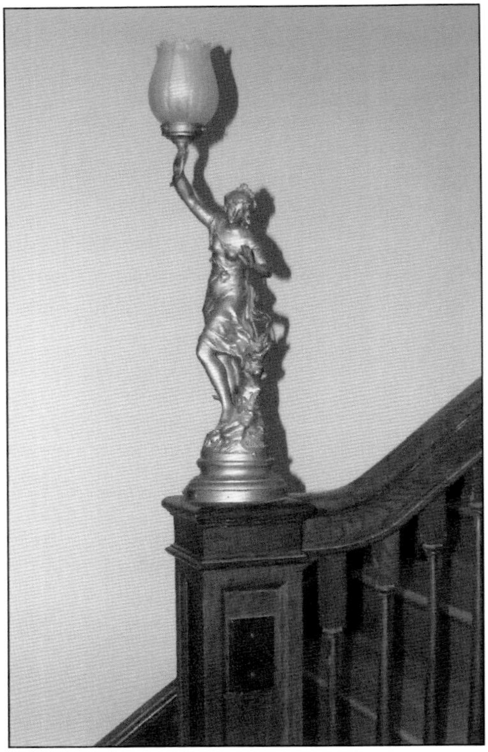

Newel post lights are freestanding upright fixtures popular in homes built from the mid-19th century until the 1920s. These fixtures helped to light stairways, especially those surrounded by dark paneling. One Overbrook Farms resident knows that the original blueprint of her home is stored in its newel post. This decorative fixture atop the home's newel post is made of Hubbell brass. (Courtesy of Adjoa Love-Dorsey.)

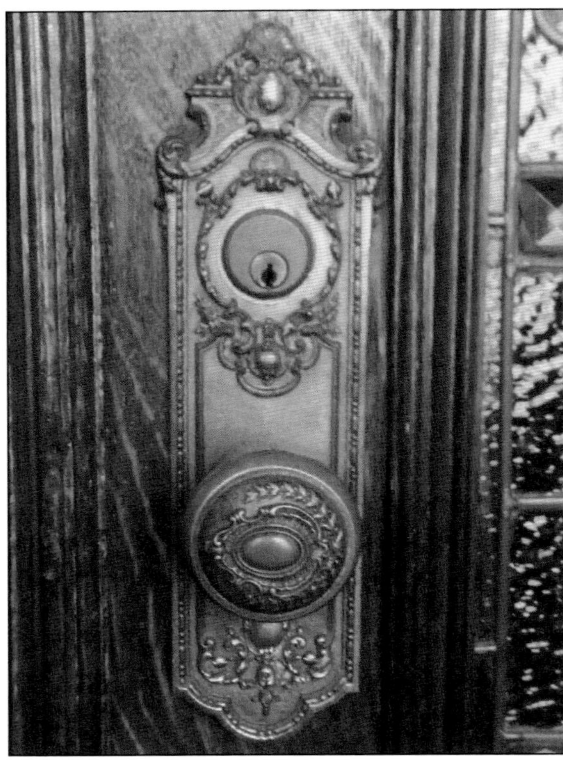

Homes with elaborate stained glass and intricate carvings often featured ornate hardware on the main entry doors. This brass doorknob and back plate has been functionally replaced by a modern lock, but it most likely sported a lock opened and closed with an oversized skeleton key when originally installed. (Courtesy of the OFC.)

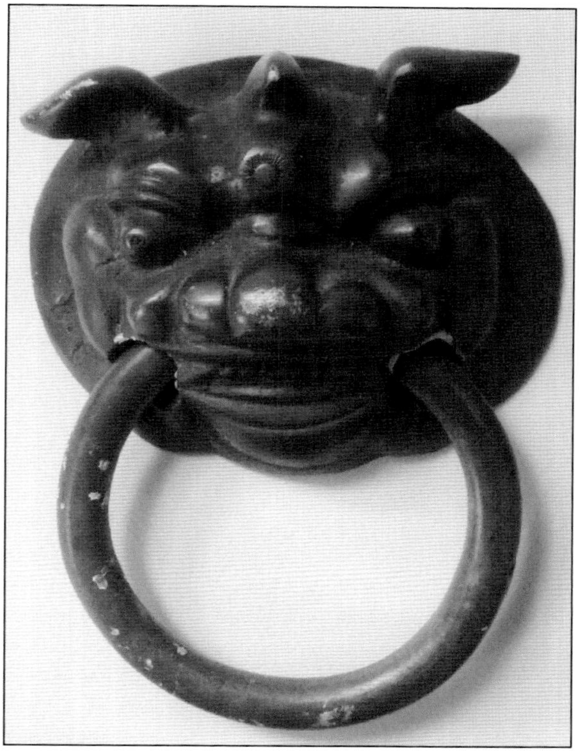

Carvings come in various shapes and sizes and may be located both indoors and on the exterior facade of a home. The two grotesques found here are in the interior. One sits above the carved archway of a door, where it has been painted to blend in with its surroundings. Another resides on a wall, where it was painted to contrast with its background. Both feature rings in the mouth of the figure. (Both, courtesy of the OFC.)

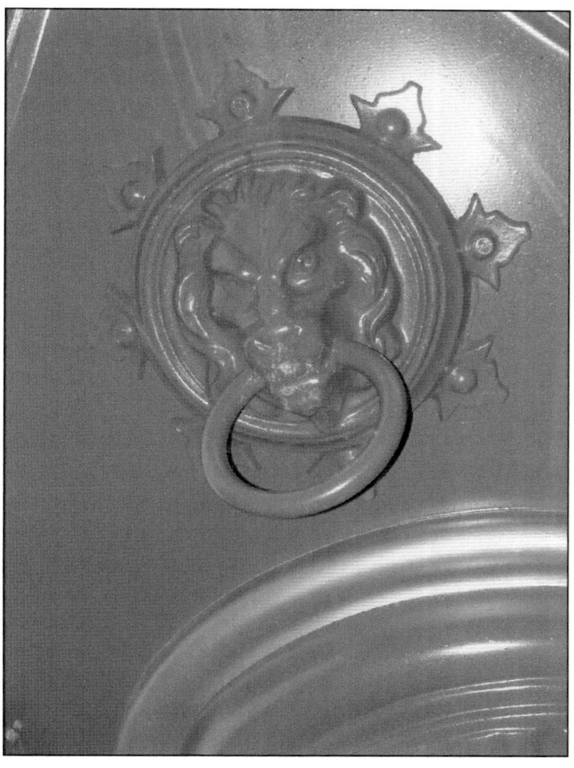

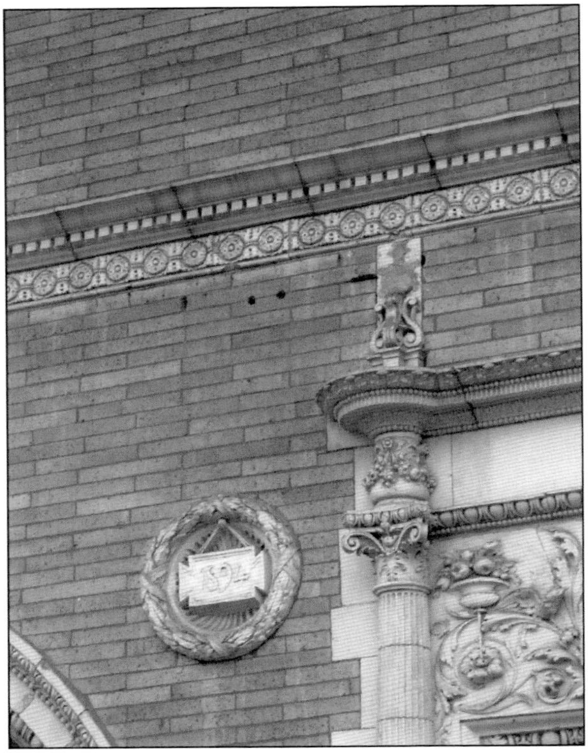

Not only do the styles of Overbrook Farms houses vary, but so also does their elaborate ornamentation. Reflecting the much-admired eclecticism of the times are tableaus with intricate carving reminiscent of those found on Greek and Roman ruins—carved laurel wreaths, molding, and cornices with dentils. (Courtesy of the OFC.)

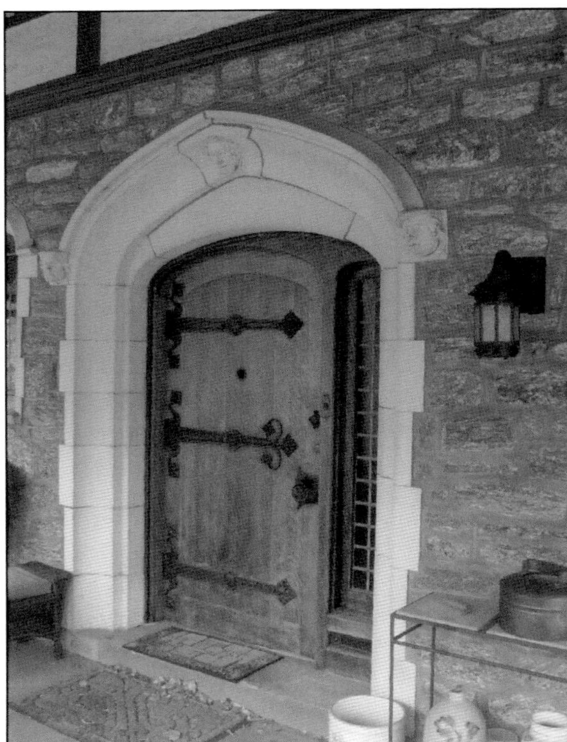

Designed by William Price in 1899, this Tudor Revival house, located on the 6300 block of Overbrook Avenue, saw a 1923 addition with a commanding front entry. A thick, wide wooden door with wrought-iron hinges is surrounded by a limestone arch with three welcoming grotesques. (Courtesy of the OFC.)

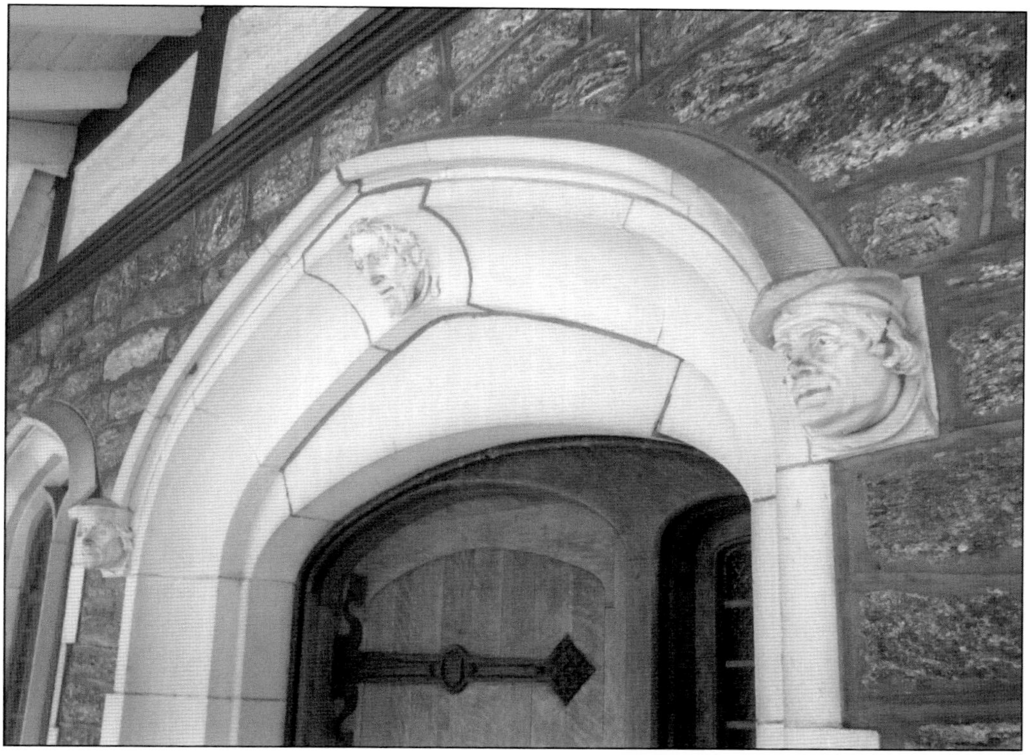

The intricacy of the limestone arch that surrounds the door of the William Price Tudor Revival in the 6300 block of Overbrook Avenue can be seen in these close-up views. The limestone blocks were shaped and carved to create the arch and provide texture to the surface. The careful carving of the grotesques exhibits the skill and whimsy of the sculptor. (Both, courtesy of the OFC.)

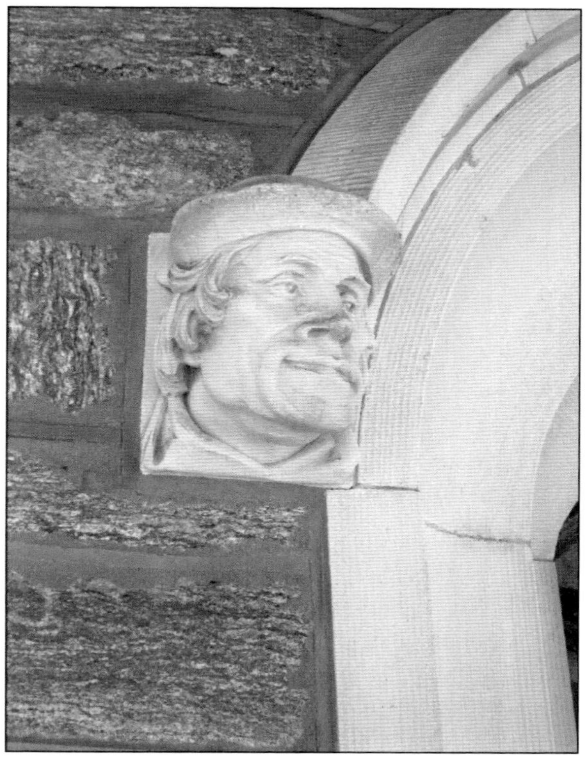

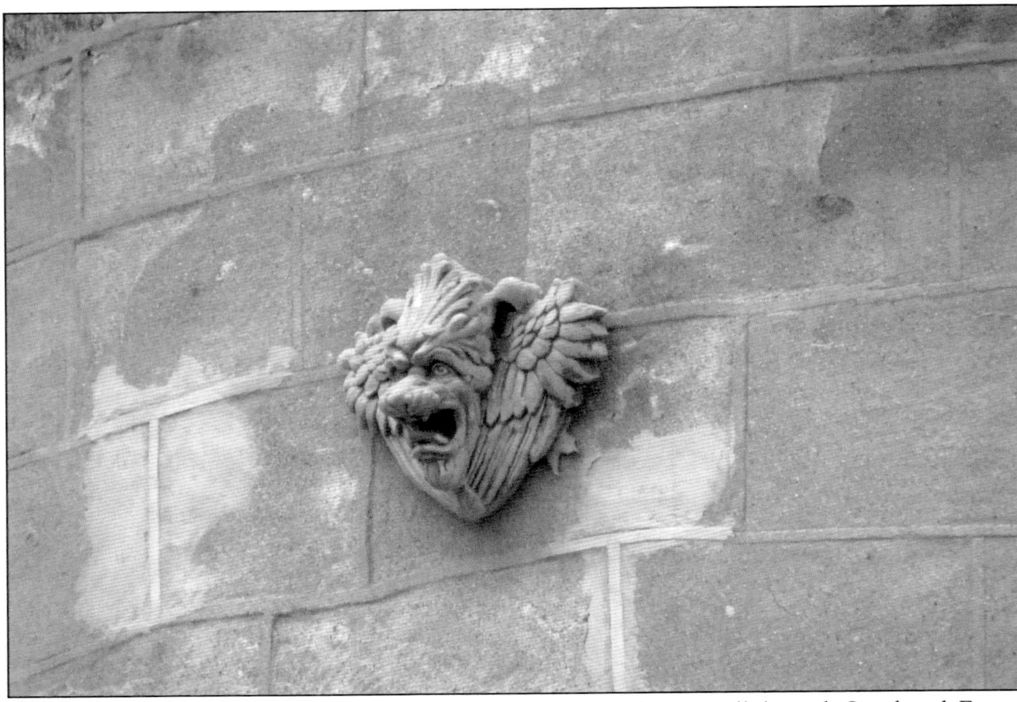

These two charming but very different grotesques were spotted on a stroll through Overbrook Farms. One will find more when wandering through the neighborhood. (Both, courtesy of the OFC.)

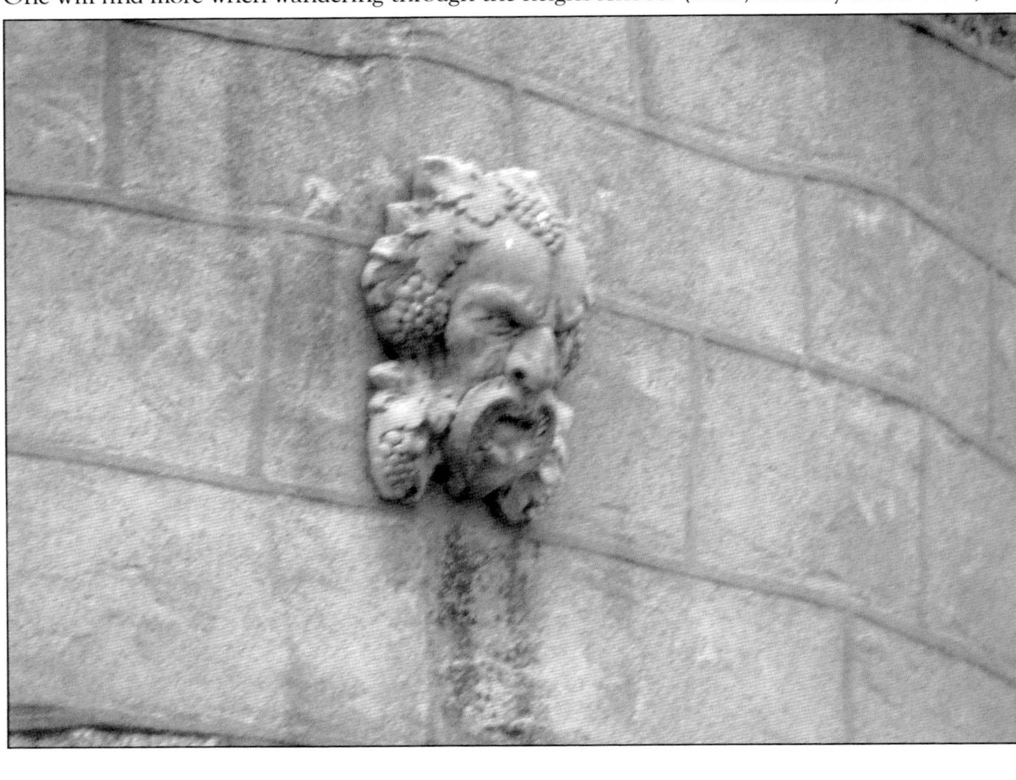

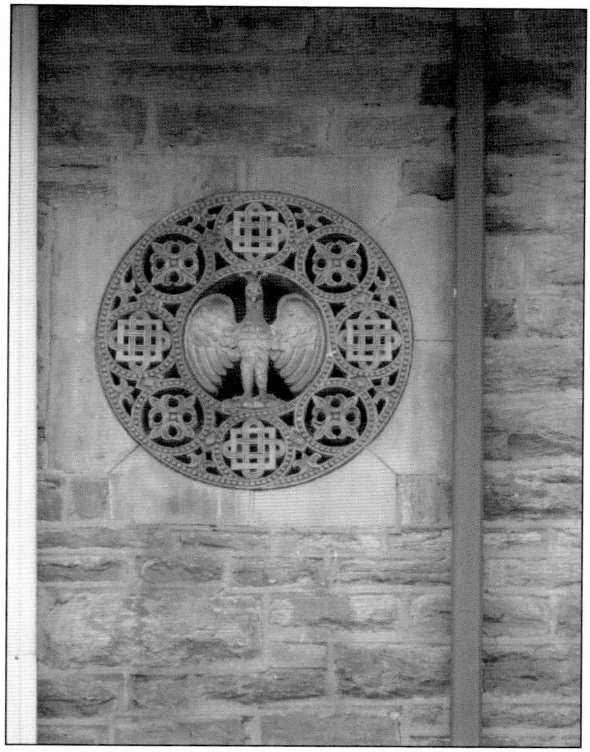

Not all of the grotesques found on the exteriors of Overbrook Farms homes are carvings of human heads. The two photographs here are excellent examples of the carvings of animals. These medallions each feature an eagle, but the execution of each is very different. (Both, courtesy of the OFC.)

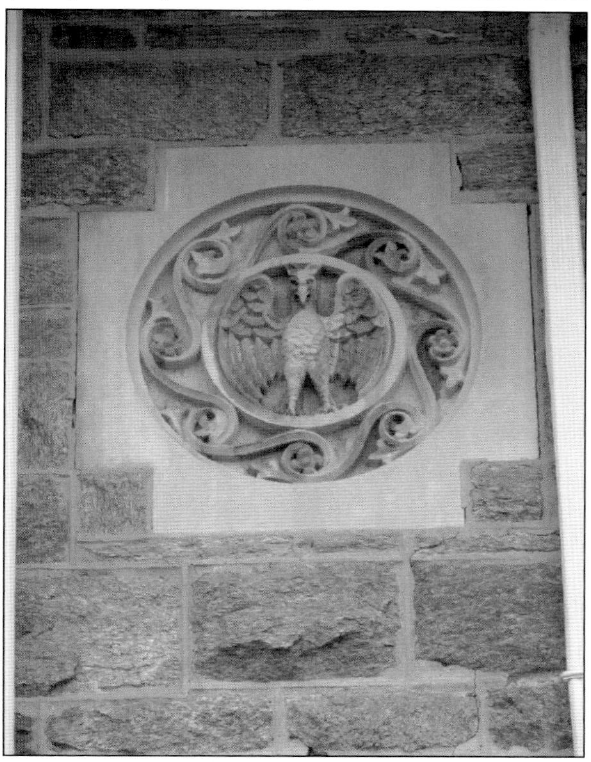

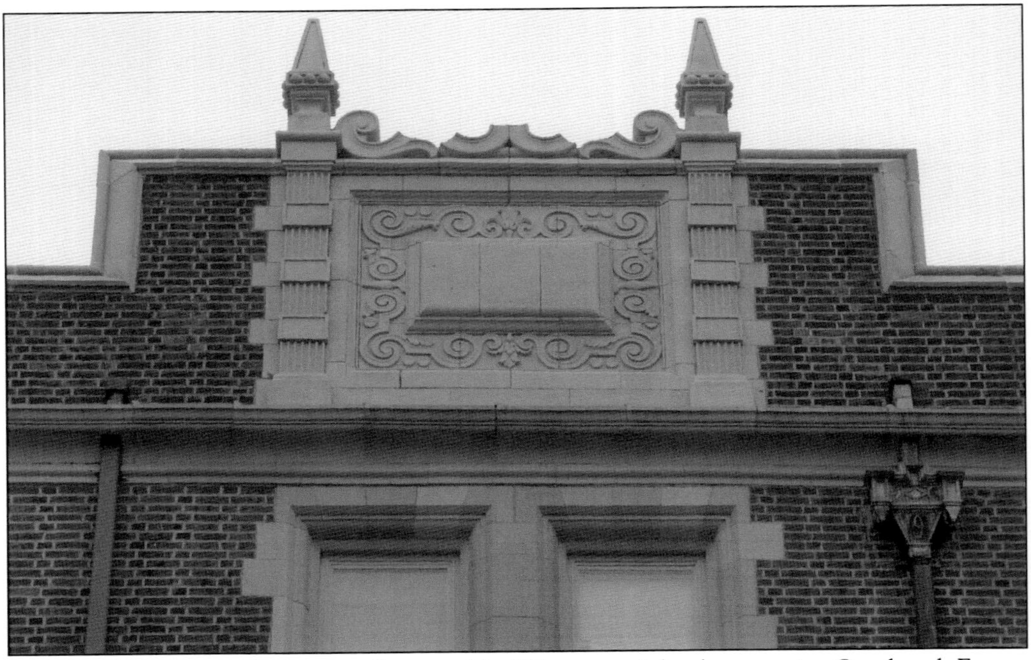

One should be sure to look at rooflines and building materials when touring Overbrook Farms. Here are two brick homes, yet they are very different in look and feel. One features a light-color brick, a slate roof, twin chimneys, and an intricate carved facade with curves and geometric shapes. The other home has a darker brick that highlights the light mortar used for pointing. Carved concrete creates a simple yet pleasing facade treatment. Though the two share many of the same shapes and carvings, the results reflect a totally different feel. (Both, courtesy of the OFC.)

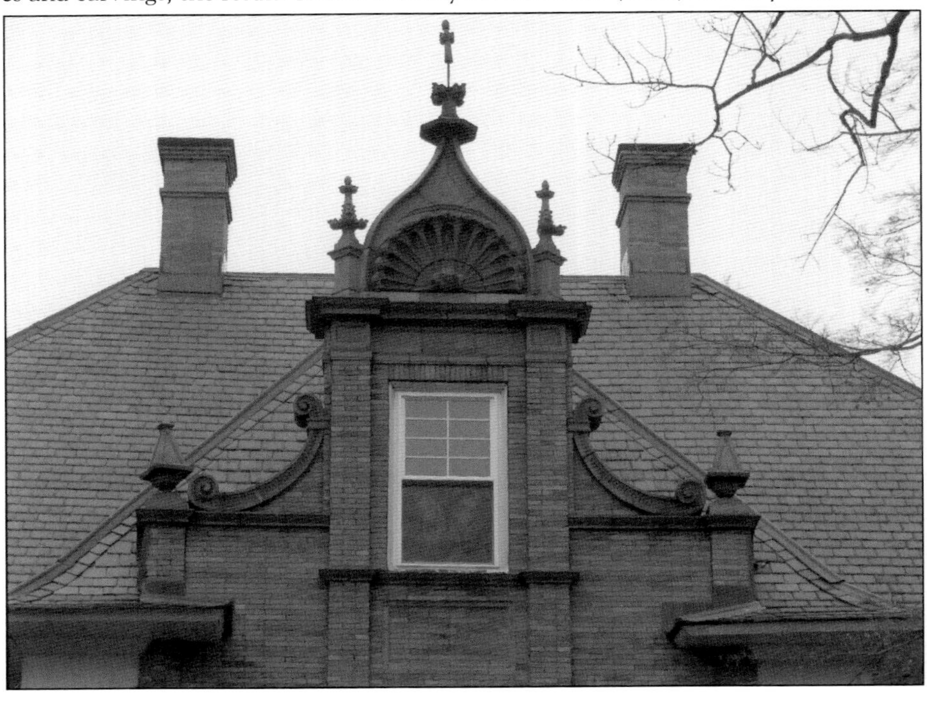

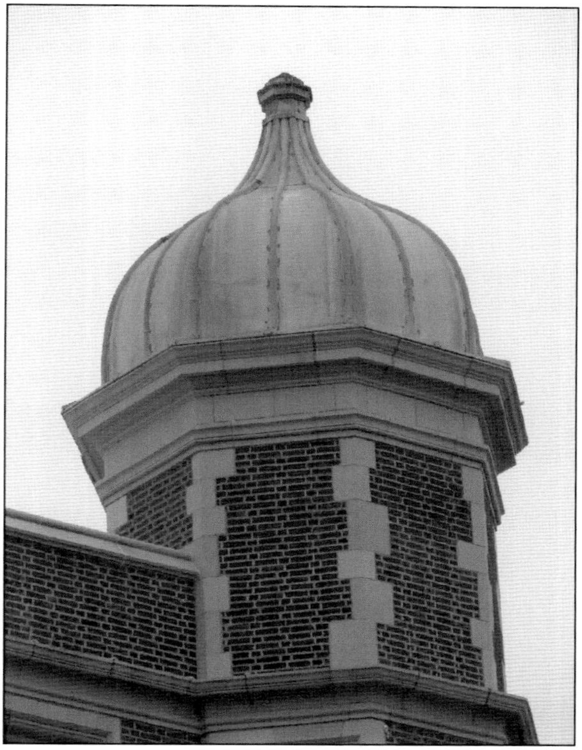

Many homes in Overbrook Farms have turrets at the roofline, or circular towers that may be anywhere from one to three stories high. Like the houses themselves, the building materials for these towers and turrets vary, as do the shapes of their roofs. The two shown here exemplify these contrasts. One is a multistory tower that has the heavy, rough-hewn look of Norman Revival, yet it features graceful arched windows and a smooth rounded dome with dentils underneath. The other is a brick and concrete roofline turret that is octagonal in shape and is topped with an onion-shaped dome. It is rewarding to look up when traveling through Overbrook Farms. (Both, courtesy of the OFC.)

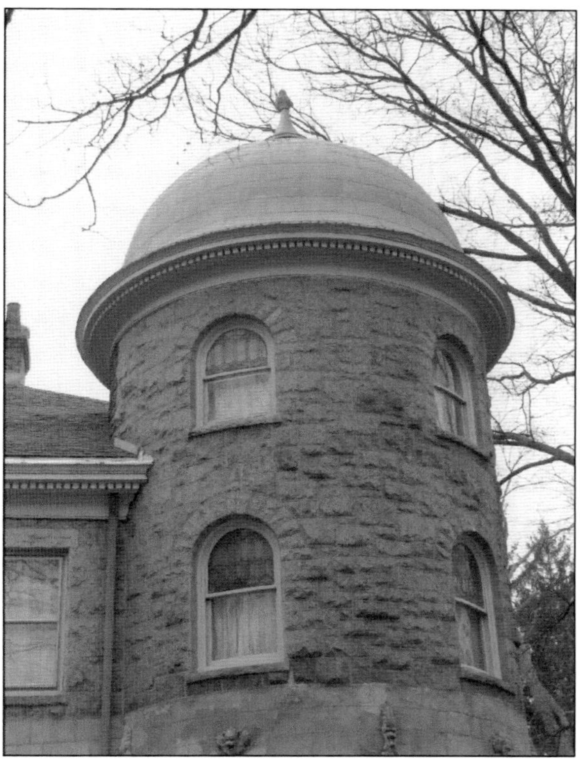

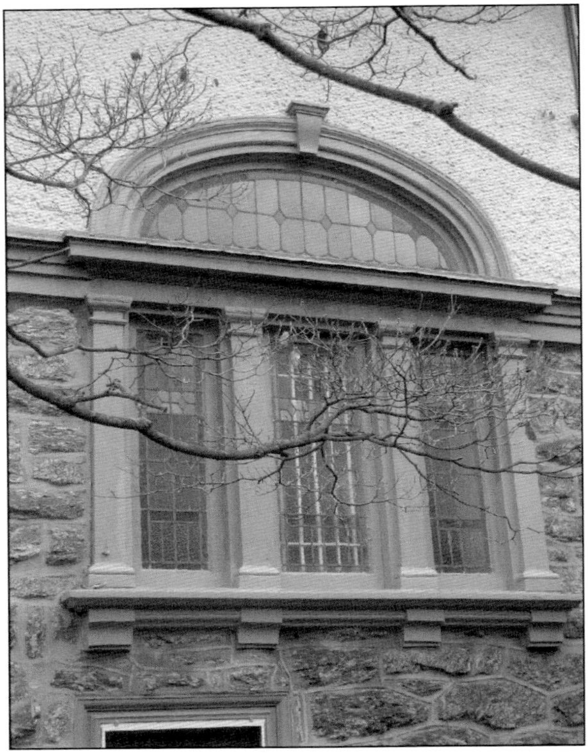

Windows come in all shapes and sizes. These two photographs prove that one needs to describe more than "a triple window topped by a fan or arched window above" when describing the array of windows peeking out from Overbrook Farms homes. One window here has a very classical look, with carved columns between three leaded stained-glass windows. A cornice separates these from the stained-glass fanlight above that features carved molding with a keystone. The other triple window has an open, airy feel. Its clear glass panes are topped by tracery in an open crosshatch or honeycomb pattern, echoed in the pointed-arch window atop. (Both, courtesy of the OFC.)

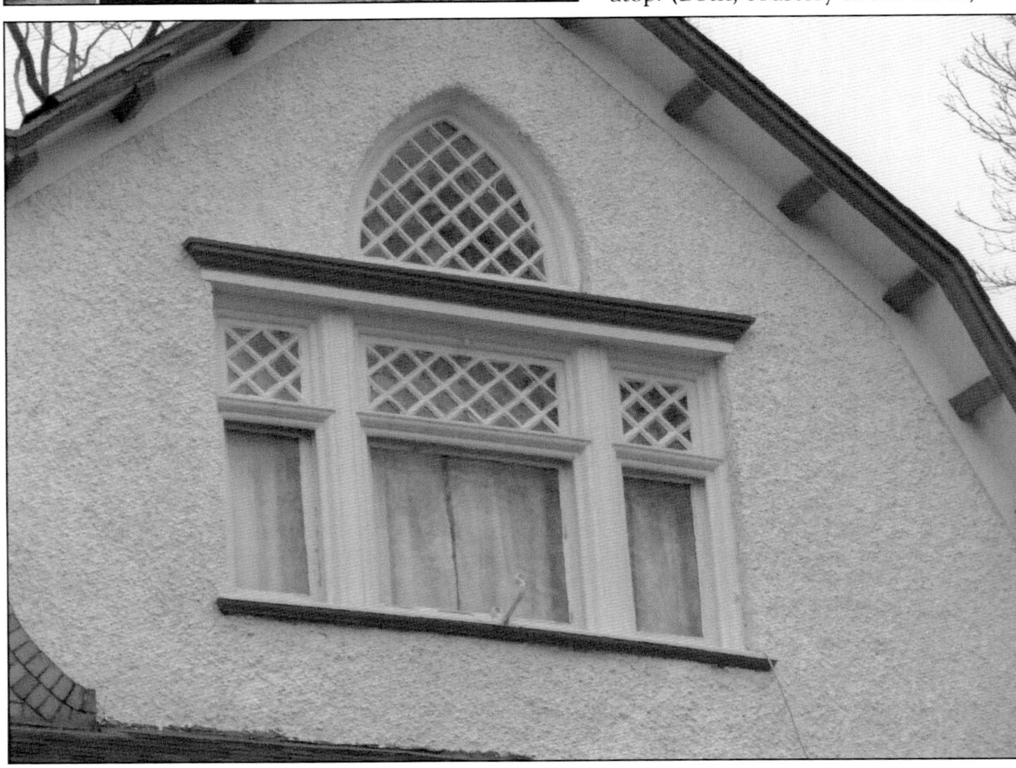

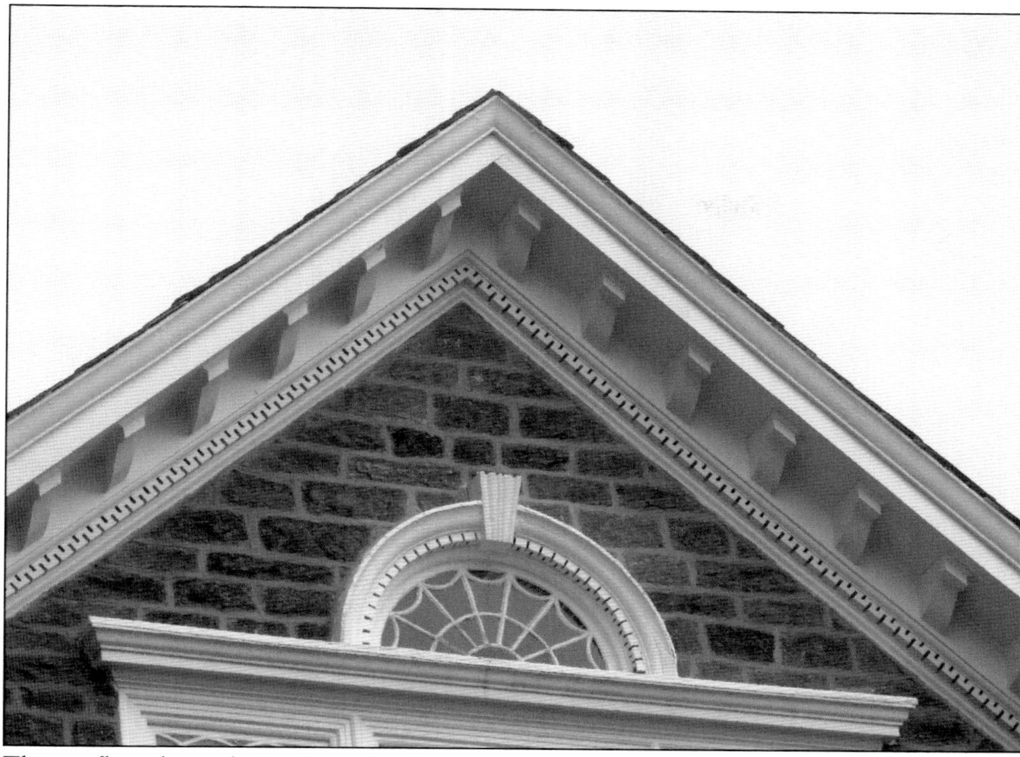

This roofline shows the intricate detail that can be found on some homes. Note the corbels—the brackets that project from the face of the wall to support the roof overhang and the dentils, or the small rectangular block that forms a molding beneath. Not only is the intricately carved molding of a large window visible, but it is also topped by a lovely fanlight, a semicircular window with radiating tracery. (Courtesy of the OFC.)

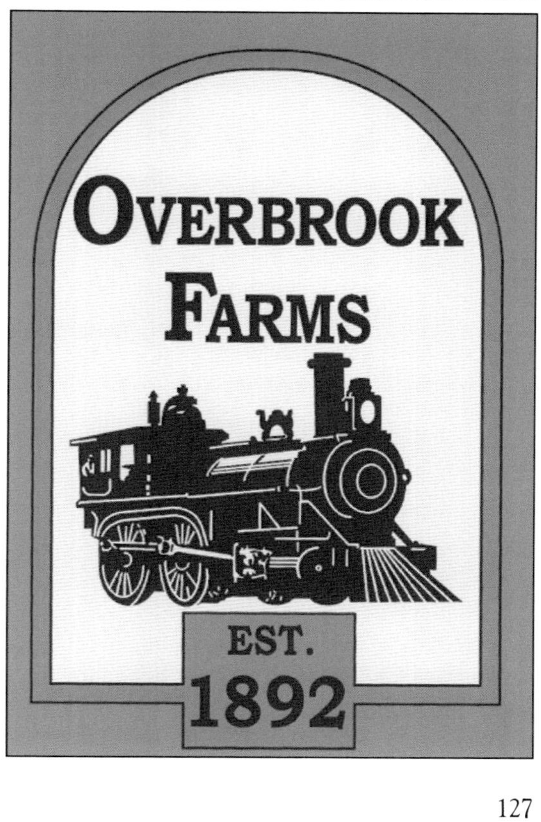

Those who have made Overbrook Farms their home found that the rails supported a dream that continues to capture more in its web as the passage of time and miles accumulate. Come to this firmly rooted place, and see what the years have kindly given. Simply, there is truly no place like home. (Courtesy of the OFC.)